The District Controller's View
THE SEVERN VA
KIDDERMINSTER - BEWDLEY - SH
WELLINGTON - BUILDWAS - MUC
HARTLEBURY - BEWDLEY - WOO

Engines from several depots worked over the Severn Valley but those from Kidderminster predominated with the 57xx Pannier Tanks being the most common. These very useful engines, which were produced over a period of more than twenty years until a total of 863 had been built, were allowed to take passenger trains of ten coaches - more than three times the normal load - to and from Shrewsbury and could work 27-wagon coal trains from Alveley to Stourport. Kidderminster was not a large shed and had an allocation of around fifteen engines, about half of which were 57xx 0-6-0T's. Most of the balance were 2-6-2 tanks used on the Shrewsbury and Birmingham services. 57xx No. 7700 of Gloucester stands on Kidderminster shed on the 10th November 1957. (A. Glover/A. Wycherley: KRM)

There was an irony in the fact that the railway which served the area in which the Industrial Revolution was nurtured remained one of the most rural of the Great Western Railway - and that was saying a great deal. Abraham Derby used the area to perfect the smelting of iron after which the revolution moved on to other parts of the Kingdom, leaving much of the Severn Valley untouched and unspoilt. Thus it was that the railways of the district tended to be pastoral rather than industrial in character.

The triangle bounded by Shrewsbury, Worcester and Birmingham was served by two through routes: The Severn Valley which ran North to South from Shrewsbury to Kidderminster and the Severn Junction which ran West to East from Craven Arms (latterly Much Wenlock) to Wellington on the Shrewsbury - Birmingham - Paddington main line. In addition there were the branches from Bewdley, on the Severn Valley, to Hartlebury and to Woofferton.

The Severn Valley and Severn Junction lines met at Buildwas, where each had its own part of the station; the Severn Valley using a set of up and down platforms in the traditional way while its neighbour had to manage with a single platform face set at a raised level.

In addition to the interesting gyrations that took place when two Severn Valley passenger services crossed at Buildwas, the station was notable for the coal trains which arrived for the adjacent power station (confusingly known as Ironbridge). These generally ran on an ad hoc basis from Oxley, Wolverhampton, via Madeley Junction and the Severn Junction although provision was made for special trains to run

> *Thanks for assistance with text and illustrations are due to N. Gough, Martin Smith, Richard and Pauline Annis, J. Hill, W. Becket, David Postle, Audie Baker, K. Laflin, P. Jordan and Peter Dobson.*

from Alveley or Shrewsbury over the Severn Valley. Neither route was especially suitable for the running of heavy coal trains - the Severn Valley was limited to forty-five wagons with restrictions on large engines - but a concession was made by which trains of power station coal via the Severn Junction could take up to sixty wagons with a 28xx 2-8-0.

An especial peculiarity of the Severn Valley was the use it made of GWR diesel railcars, a type of train which until 1960 was regarded as novel and interesting. For those who wished to experience a change from everyday steam, the Severn Valley offered considerable scope with about half its services being operated by Railcars. The proportion was even higher on the Bewdley - Woofferton branch where passenger steam was limited to the occasional Woofferton - Tenbury Wells auto and a 57xx-worked evening service between Kidderminster and Leominster. Even one of the - relatively speaking - long distance services between Kidderminster and Shrewsbury was worked by a railcar.

To the relief of the steam die-hard, the Severn Junction was wholly steam worked; the gradients having got the better of a railcar during trials.

With a catchment of less than ten thousand between Bewdley and Shrewsbury, prosperity depended not on passenger traffic but on freight and in this respect the focal point of the Severn Valley was Alveley Sidings; the railhead for Highley colliery, the output of which was taken by several trains a day to Stourport, Worcester and Kidderminster.

Whether watching movements from the picnic blanket, a carriage window or working on the line, it was a fascinating system - as indeed the section remaining (and happily preserved) still is.

WORKING TIMETABLE - PASSENGER & GOODS
SEVERN VALLEY (KIDDERMINSTER - SHREWSBURY) : 1955

Train From Class Shed Engine	05.20 Well Pass Well 460 57xx	ECS Kidd 51xx	05.05 Worcs ECS Worc 2 Dsl	05.30 Well Light Well 461 57xx	Pass Worc 1 Dsl	ECS Worc 1 Dsl	ECS Worc 1 Dsl	06.15 Stourp't K K106 43xx	06.05 Well EBV Well 463 57xx	05.45 B'ham Pass Tys 51xx	06.45 Worcs ECS Worc 3 Dsl	05.35 Well K Well 462 57xx	06.48 Well Pass Well 460 57xx	06.55 Worcs Pass W 451 51xx	06.15 B'ham Pass Tys 51xx	08.16 Well Pass Well 461 57xx	06.55 Worcs Pass W 451 51xx	08.16 Well Pass Well 461 57xx	08.10 H'bury Pass Worc 1 Dsl
KIDDERMINSTER		05.10			05.48				07.00					07.35					
Foley Park					05.52				07.04					07.39					
BEWDLEY					05.59			06.26	07.09					07.40	07.44		(07.40)		08.24
BEWDLEY		05/19	05/40		06.00			06.36			07/14			(07.53)	07.53				08.25
Northwood					06.04										07.57				
Arley		05.25	05/46		06.09			06/47							08.02				08.32
Kinlet																			
Highley			05.51		06.15			06/54							08.08				
ALVELEY					06.18	06.20	06.35	06.59							08.11				
Hampton Loade						06.23	06.38								08.13				
Eardington															08.19				
BRIDGNORTH															08.23				
BRIDGNORTH															08.30				
Linley															08.38				
Coalport															08.43				
Jackfield															08.46				
Iron Bridge															08.50				
BUILDWAS	05.51							06.50				07.16	07.23		08.50	08.54	(08.50)		
BUILDWAS				05/58									07.40		(08.56)	08.55	08.56		
Cressage													(Mxd			09.02			
Cound													ex			09.06			
Berrington													B'was)			09.12			
Sutton Bge Jcn																09/18			
SHREWSBURY																09.21			
Destination			Much W.									T. Wells	Much W.				Much W.		

SEVERN VALLEY (SHREWSBURY - KIDDERMINSTER) : 1955

Train From Class Shed Engine	Pass Kidd 51xx	Pass Well 460 57xx	Pass Worc 2 Dsl	Pass Worc 1 Dsl	06.50 Much W. Pass Well 461 57xx	Pass Worc 1 Dsl	Pass Tys 51xx	EBV Well 463 57xx	Pass Worc 1 Dsl	Pass Tys 51xx	07.57 T. Wells Pass Worc 3 Dsl	Pass Worc 1 Dsl	Light K 111 57xx	Pass Worc 1 Dsl	08.35 Much W Pass SY 100 51xx	Pass Well 460 57xx	10.15 Coton H K Well 462 57xx	K SY 150 43xx	K K106 43xx
SHREWSBURY															08.15			10/18	
Sutton Bge Jcn															08/18			10/22	
Berrington															08.26			10.32	
Cound															08.32				
Cressage															08.37				
BUILDWAS					06.59										08.43	08.44			
BUILDWAS		06.00			07.00			07.40							08.59	08.56	09.40		
Iron Bridge															09.03				
Jackfield															09.11				
Coalport															09.15				
Linley															09.21				
BRIDGNORTH															09.28				
BRIDGNORTH															09.35				
Eardington															09.40				
Hampton Loade				06.30		07.00									09.45				
ALVELEY				06.33		07.05													10.45
Highley			06.22			07.08									09.50				10.53
Kinlet																			
Arley	05.50		06.28			07.13					08.35				09.58				
Northwood	05.55		06.33			07.18					08.40				10.03				
BEWDLEY	05.58		06.36			07.21					08.43				10.06				
BEWDLEY	05.59		06.40				07.25		07.42	08.00	08.34	08.44		09.39	10.09				
Foley Park	06.04						07.30			08.05	08.39		09.30	09.44	10.14				
KIDDERMINSTER	06.08						07.35			08.09	08.43		09.35	09.48	10.18				
Destination	B'ham	Well	H'bury		Well		B'ham	K'ton	H'bury	B'ham		H'bury			St Jn	Well	H'wood		

LOCOMOTIVE ALLOCATION SUMMARY : KIDDERMINSTER (85D)											
Class	Oct-50	Oct-51	Oct-52	Oct-53	Oct-54	Oct-55	Oct-56	Oct-57	Oct-58	Oct-59	Oct-60
5MT: 56xx 0-6-2T (1927)						1	1	1	1	1	
4MT: 61xx 2-6-2T (1931)											2
4MT: 81xx 2-6-2T (1938)	1	1	1	1	1	1	1	1	1		
4MT: 51xx 2-6-2T (1928)	4	4	4	4	5	4	5	4	4	3	4
4MT: 45xx 2-6-2T (1927)	5	4	3	2	1	1	2	1	1	1	1
4MT: 43xx 2-6-0 (1911)	1	1	1	1			3	3	4	4	2
3MT: 2251 0-6-0 (1930)				1	1						
3MT 2-6-2T (1952)								1	1		
3F: 57xx 0-6-0T (1929)	5	5	4	6	7	5	4	3	2	4	4
2F: 16xx 0-6-0PT (1949)						1	1				
2F : 2021 0-6-0T (1897)	1	1	1	1							
1F : CMDP 0-6-0T	2	2	2	2							
Total	19	18	16	18	15	18	18	14	13	14	15

Complete details of the Kidderminster allocation are given elsewhere in the book

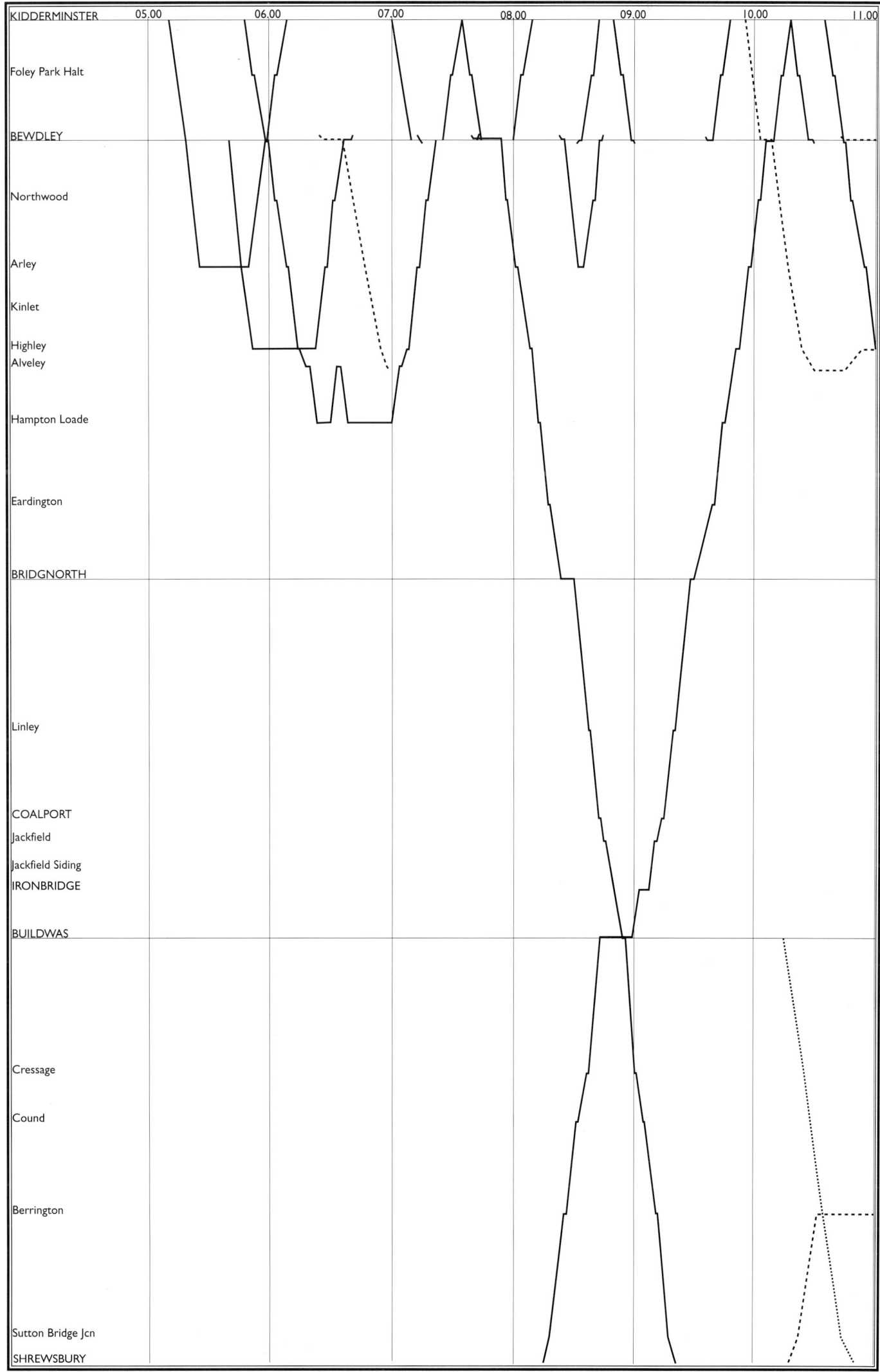

WORKING TIMETABLE – PASSENGER & GOODS

SEVERN VALLEY (KIDDERMINSTER – SHREWSBURY) : 1955

Train From		09.22 H'bury	08.47 Kem	Light	Eties			10.10 H'bury	10.10 H'bury	10.10 H'bury		11.17 Well	Light	Light Stour'pt	10.10 H'bury	12.40 S'port	Light H'bury	12.40 S'port
Class	Pass	K	Pass	G	K	Pass	Pass	K	K	K	K	Pass	G	G	K	K	G	K
Shed	Worc 2	K 111	Worc 1	Well 463	Well 463	K 110	Worc 3	Worc 1	K 108	K 108	K 108	K 109	Well 464	K 107	K 111	K 108	K 110	Walsall	K 110
Engine	Dsl	57xx	Dsl	57xx	57xx	57xx	Dsl	Dsl	57xx	57xx	57xx	57xx	57xx	57xx	57xx	57xx	57xx	4F 0-6-0	57xx
KIDDERMINSTER	08.50	09.05				09.55	10.18	10.35					11.30		12.10				
Foley Park	08.54	09.10					10.22	10.39											
BEWDLEY	08.59		09.36			10.03	10.27	10.44	10.45				11.40		12.20	12.40		12.50	12.56 (12.50)
BEWDLEY	09.00					10.08	10.29	10.45	11.05				11.50				(13.00)		13.00
Northwood								10.49											
Arley						10/17		10.55	11.16	11.26									13/10
Kinlet																			
Highley						10/23		11.00		11.35	11.45								13/17
ALVELEY						10.30					11.50				12.45				13.22
Hampton Loade								11.09								12/51			
Eardington								11.15											
BRIDGNORTH								11.19								13.09			
BRIDGNORTH								11.23											
Linley								11.31											
Coalport								11.38											
Jackfield								11.41											
Iron Bridge								11.44											
BUILDWAS				09.58				11.50					11.51						
BUILDWAS				10.15				11.57					11.56						
Cressage				10/25				12.06											
Cound								12.11											
Berrington				10/35				12.18											
Sutton Bge Jcn				10/41				12/29											
SHREWSBURY				10.58				12.32											
Destination		Woof'tn										Woof'tn	Much W						

SEVERN VALLEY (SHREWSBURY – KIDDERMINSTER) : 1955

Train From		10.05 Woof	10.15 Coton H	10.45 Alveley		11.15 Alveley	11.40 Much W			10.15 Coton H	10.15 Coton H	12.22 Woof'tn		13.00 Much W	Light	13.45 B'north		14.20 Alveley	
Class		Pass	K	K		K	Pass	K	Pass	K	K	Pass	K	Pass	G	K	K	K	Pass
Shed		Worc 2	SY 150	K 106	K 110	K 110	Well 461	K107/111	W 451	SY 150	SY 150	Worc 3	SY 150	Well 464	Walsall	K 108	K 108	K 110	K 110	Worc 1
Engine		Dsl	43xx	43xx	57xx	57xx	57xx	2 x 57xx	51xx	43xx	43xx	Dsl	43xx	57xx	4F 0-6-0	57xx	57xx	57xx	57xx	Dsl
SHREWSBURY									11.25										13.45
Sutton Bge Jcn									11/28										13/48
Berrington			11.03						11.35										13.56
Cound									11.41										14.02
Cressage			11.14						11.46	11.50									14.07
BUILDWAS							11.50		11.51	12.00				13.09					14.12
BUILDWAS							11.55		11.52	12.40			13.13						14.13
Iron Bridge									11.59		12.45		13.05						14.19
Jackfield									12.03										14.25
Coalport									12.06				13.13						14.28
Linley									12.12										14.35
BRIDGNORTH									12.19										14.42
BRIDGNORTH									12.23							13.45			(15.02)
Eardington									12.28										
Hampton Loade									12.33							13.58	14.10		
ALVELEY					11.15											14.15	14.20		
Highley				11.10	11.23	11.40			12.39								14.28	14.42	
Kinlet																			
Arley						11/47			12.45									14/50	
Northwood									12.50										
BEWDLEY		11.01		11.27					12.53			13.04							
BEWDLEY		11.03		11.37		11/57		12.50	12.55			13.05		13.14				15/00	
Foley Park		11.08																	
KIDDERMINSTER		11.12					13.00					13.13		13.24					
Destination				H'bury		S'port	Well		H'bury					Well				Worcs	

LOCOMOTIVE ALLOCATION SUMMARY : WELLINGTON (84H)											
Class	Oct-50	Oct-51	Oct-52	Oct-53	Oct-54	Oct-55	Oct-56	Oct-57	Oct-58	Oct-59	Oct-60
4MT : 51xx 2-6-2T (1928)	7	6	5	5	5	6	3	5	4	2	2
4F: 94XX 0-6-0T (1949)			1								
3MT(BR) 2-6-2T (1952)							3	3	3	4	
3MT : 44xx 2-6-2T (1904)	4	2									
3F : 57xx 0-6-0T (1929)	11	12	11	15	16	15	14	11	9	8	9
2MT (LMS) 2-6-2T (1946)										2	5
2F : 2021 0-6-0T (1897)	1	1	1	1							
2F : 16xx 0-6-0PT (1949)	1	1	1		1	1	1	1			
TOTAL	22	20	16	21	21	21	21	20	16	16	16

Complete details of the Wellington allocation are given towards the rear of the book)

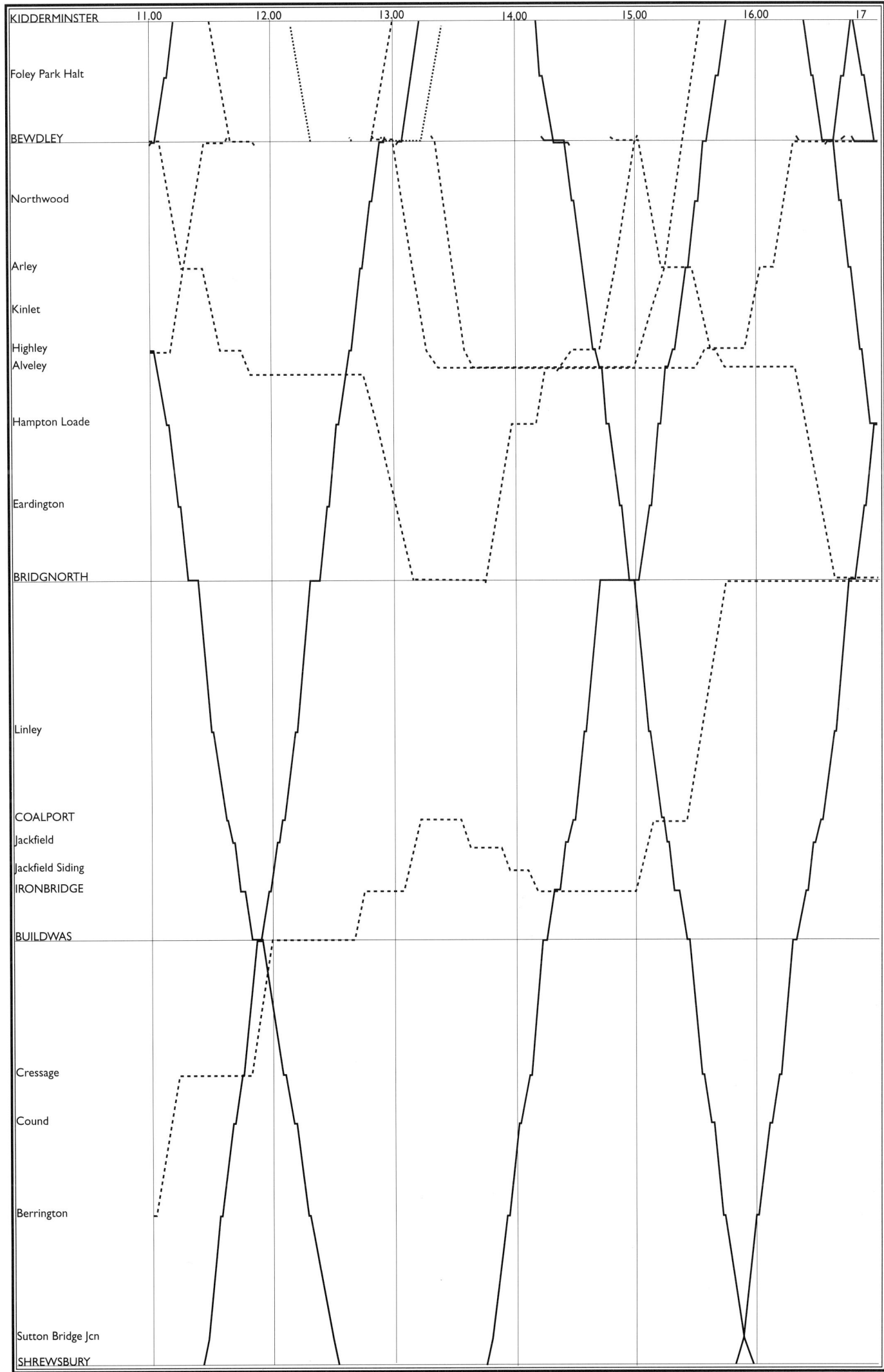

WORKING TIMETABLE - PASSENGER & GOODS

SEVERN VALLEY (KIDDERMINSTER - SHREWSBURY) : 1955

Train	12.30		13.05	13.33	13.40	13.33		14.00		14.15	14.15	15.10	16.05		16.07	14.15	15.10	16.30
From	H'bury		H'wood	Coalp't	H'hay	Coalp't		H'bury		H'bury	H'bury	Well	L. Jcn		H'bury	H'bury	M'ley Jn	Well
Class	K	K	K	K	K	K	K	B	B	K	K	Pass	Pass	K	Pass	K	Pass	Pass
Shed	K106	SY 150	Well 467	SY 150	Well 460	SY 150	Well 467	K 117	Worc 3	SBY 150A	SBY 150A	Well 461	Well 460	K 111	Worc 1	SBY 150A	Well 468	Well 464	SY 100
Engine	43xx	43xx	57xx	43xx	57xx	43xx	57xx	51xx	Dsl	43xx	43xx	57xx	57xx	57xx	Dsl	43xx	57xx	57xx	51xx
KIDDERMINSTER								14.10							16.00				16.23
Foley Park								14.14							16.05				16.28
BEWDLEY								14.15		14.19	14.50				16.21				16.22
BEWDLEY	13/20							14.24	14.26	15.02									16.38
Northwood								14.28											16.42
Arley	13/29							14.33			15.13	15.28							16.47
Kinlet																			
Highley	13/35							14.39				15/40							16.52
ALVELEY	13.40							14.43			15.45					16.20			
Hampton Loade								14.46								16/25			16.56
Eardington								14.52											17.08
BRIDGNORTH								14.56								16.39			17.13
BRIDGNORTH								14.59											17.16
Linley								15.07											17.24
Coalport			13.33					15.13											17.30
Jackfield			13.37		13.52			15.16											17.33
Iron Bridge					13.56		14.06	15.19											17.36
BUILDWAS			13.45		14.05		14.10	15.25				15.45	16.14			16.50			17.05	17.42
BUILDWAS							14.30	15.26				15.46	16.15					17.06	17.43
Cressage								15.34											17.51
Cound								15.38											17.58
Berrington								15.44											18.04
Sutton Bge Jcn								15/53											18/12
SHREWSBURY								15.58											18.15
Destination						Much W		Woof'tn				Much W.	Much W.			Much W.			

SEVERN VALLEY (SHREWSBURY - KIDDERMINSTER) : 1955

Train	10.15		13.45	15.00		10.15	13.45	13.45			13.45	15.47		13.45	16.40		17.30	
From	Coton H		Salop	Much W		Coton H	B'north	B'north			B'north	Woof'tn		B'north	Much W		Much W	
Class	K	K	Pass	Pass	Pass	K	K	K	K	K	K	Pass	Pass	K	Pass	K	Light	Pass
Shed	SY 150	K106	Worc 1	Well 467	Well 460	SY 150	K 108	K 108	Well 467	K 111	K 108	Worc 3	Worc 1	K 108	SY 101	Well 461	Well 468	Well 460	Worc 3
Engine	43xx	43xx	Dsl	57xx	57xx	43xx	57xx	57xx	57xx	57xx	57xx	Dsl	Dsl	57xx	51xx	57xx	57xx	57xx	Dsl
SHREWSBURY															15.50				
Sutton Bge Jcn															15/53				
Berrington															16.01				
Cound															16.07				
Cressage															16.12				
BUILDWAS				15.17											16.17	16.50		17.39	
BUILDWAS				15.25			16.01								16.18	16.55	17.06		
Iron Bridge			15.00												16.24				
Jackfield															16.29				
Coalport			15.08			15.25									16.32				
Linley															16.39				
BRIDGNORTH			(14.42)			15.45									16.46				
BRIDGNORTH			15.02												16.49				
Eardington			15.02												16.54				
Hampton Loade			15.12												16.58				
ALVELEY		15.00	15.16			15.30									17.04				
Highley		15/07	15.20			15.35	15.54								17.08				
Kinlet																			
Arley		15/14	15.26			16.02		16.08							17.14				
Northwood			15.31												17.19				
BEWDLEY			15.34				16.19	16.36							17.22				
BEWDLEY		15/23	15.36				16.38	16.42	17.10						17.24				18.00
Foley Park			15.41					16.15	16.43						17.29				18/05
KIDDERMINSTER		15.33	15.45				16.20	16.47				17.20			17.34				18.10
Destination				L'moor			H'wood					H'bury				Well		Well	

ALVELEY SIDINGS WORKING : 1955

Train	Arr	Engine	Shed/Diagram	Dep	Destination
06.15 Stourport (Empties)	06.59	43xx 2-6-0	Kidderminster 106		
09.55 Kidderminster (Empties)	10.30	57xx 0-6-0T	Kidderminster 110		
		43xx 2-6-0	Kidderminster 106	10.45	Hartlebury
		57xx 0-6-0T	Kidderminster 110	11.15	Stourport *
10.10 Hartlebury	11.50	57xx 0-6-0T	Kidderminster 108	12.45	Bridgnorth
12.40 Stourport (Empties) *	13.22	57xx 0-6-0T	Kidderminster 110		
13.10 Stourport (Empties)	13.40	43xx 2-6-0	Kidderminster 106		
13.45 Bridgnorth	14.15	57xx 0-6-0T	Kidderminster 108		(Fwd at 15.30)
		57xx 0-6-0T	Kidderminster 110	14.20	Worcester
		43xx 2-6-0	Kidderminster 106	15.00	Kidderminster
		57xx 0-6-0T	Kidderminster 108	15.30	Kidderminster
14.15 Hartlebury	15.45	43xx 2-6-0	Salop 150A	16.20	Shrewsbury (Coton Hill)

When required, the 11.15 Alveley - Stourport and 12.40 Stourport - Alveley could be diverted to Buildwas.

If the focal point of passenger traffic was Bewdley, the Severn Valley's freight equivalent was Alveley where the exchange sidings for Highley Colliery were located. As can be seen from the table of movements, Alveley was quite a busy location with seven arrivals and departures per day; some services being purely mineral - empties from Kidderminster or Stourport being exchanged for a train of coal - whilst others were mixed services that called to attach wagons of coal for local stations. A second outlet from Highley colliery ran to Highley station but use of this connection was generally limited to coal for landsale by local agents at Highley.

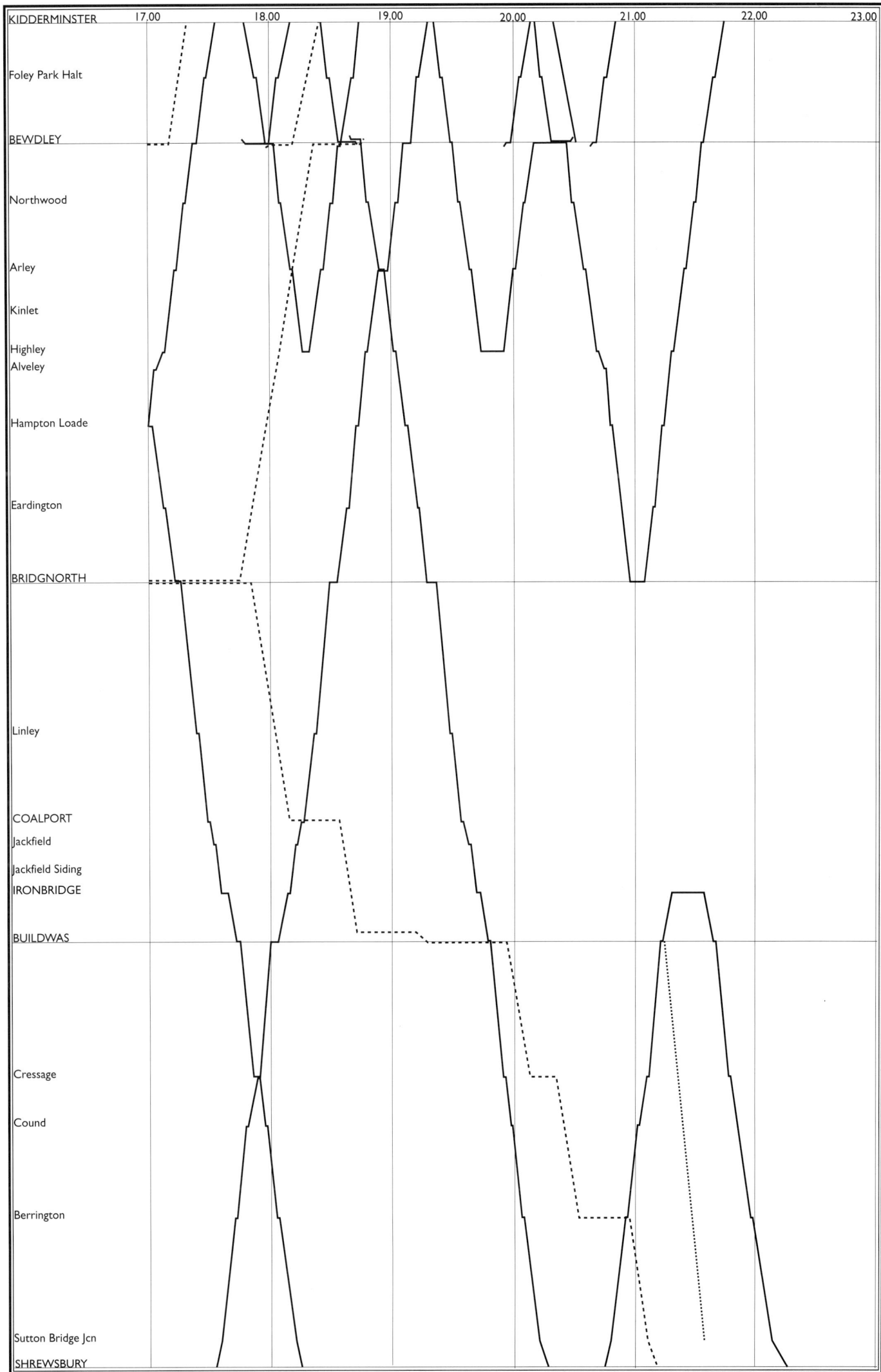

WORKING TIMETABLE - PASSENGER & GOODS

SEVERN VALLEY (KIDDERMINSTER - SHREWSBURY) : 1955

Train From		14.15 H'bury	17.30 H'bury	17.30 H'bury	17.50 Well		14.15 H'bury	18.25 H'bury	14.15 H'bury		14.15 H'bury	19.55 Well			14.15 H'bury	Light Much W	
Class	Pass	K	Pass	Pass	Pass	Pass	Pass	K	Pass	K	Pass	Pass	Pass	ECS	K	Light	Pass
Shed	K 110	SBY 150A	Worc 1	Worc 3	Worc 1	Well 461	Worc 3	SBY 150A	SY 101	SBY 150A	Worc 1	SBY 150A	Tys	Well 464	Worc 1	K 111	SBY 150A	Well 464	SY 101
Engine	57xx	43xx	Dsl	Dsl	Dsl	57xx	Dsl	43xx	51xx	43xx	Dsl	43xx	57xx	Dsl	57xx	43xx	57xx	51xx
KIDDERMINSTER	16.48			17.48			18.25				19.20		20.10			20.20		
Foley Park	16.52			17.53			18.29				19.24		20.14					
BEWDLEY	16.57		17.49	17.58			18.34		18.41		19.29		20.19			20.31		
BEWDLEY	16.59				18.02		18.43		18.45	19.30	19.30		20.26					
Northwood					18.06				18.49		19.34		20.30					
Arley					18.11				18.56		19.39		20.36					
Kinlet																		
Highley					18.16				19.02		19.44		20.42					
ALVELEY													20.46					
Hampton Loade									19.07				20.49					
Eardington									19.13									
BRIDGNORTH									19.17				20.58					
BRIDGNORTH		17.50							19.21									
Linley									19.29									
Coalport		18.09					19.11		19.35									
Jackfield									19.38									
Iron Bridge									19.41									21.35
BUILDWAS					18.18		19.17		19.47	(19.17)			20.30					21.39
BUILDWAS					18.20		(19.56)		19.48	19.56			20.31				21.15	21.40
Cressage									19.55	20.07			20.20					21.48
Cound									19.59									
Berrington									20.05				20.32			20.57		21.59
Sutton Bge Jcn									20/12							21/06	21/35	22/07
SHREWSBURY									20.17							21/11		22.17
Destination		L'ster				Much W.	Woof'tn						Much W.			Coton H.	Well'tn	

SEVERN VALLEY (SHREWSBURY - KIDDERMINSTER) : 1955

Train From	15.25 Woof'tn	10.15 Coton H		17.45 Much W		17.45 Much W		17.33	19.05 Much W	18.30 Salop			19.50 Woof'tn	21.00 Much W	
Class	K	K	Pass	Pass	Pass	Pass	K	Pass	Pass	Pass	Pass	Pass	Pass	Light	Pass
Shed	K 109	SY 150	Worc 1	Well 464	K 117	Well 464	Well 460	K 117	Well 461	K 110	Worc 1	Tys	Worc 3	Worc 1	Well 464	SY 101
Engine	57xx	43xx	Dsl	57xx	51xx	57xx	57xx	51xx	57xx	57xx	Dsl	51xx	Dsl	Dsl	57xx	51xx
SHREWSBURY				17.33												20.45
Sutton Bge Jcn				17/37												20/48
Berrington				17.43												20.56
Cound				17.49												21.02
Cressage				17.54												21.07
BUILDWAS				17.54	17.59	(17.54)			19.14						21.10	21.13
BUILDWAS			(18.02)	18.00	18.02	18.15			19.15						(21.15)	21.14
Iron Bridge					18.09											21.19
Jackfield					18.13											
Coalport					18.16											
Linley					18.22											
BRIDGNORTH					18.29											
BRIDGNORTH		17.45			18.33										21.05	
Eardington					18.38										21.10	
Hampton Loade		17.58			18.43										21.15	
ALVELEY															21.20	
Highley		18/05	18.20		18.48					19.55						
Kinlet																
Arley		18/11	18.26		18.53			18.58			20.01				21.26	
Northwood			18.31					19.03			20.06				21.31	
BEWDLEY	18.01	18.21	18.34					19.06		19.57	20.10			20.39	21.34	
BEWDLEY	18.11	18.45	18.35					19.09		19.59		20.28	20.41	21.35	
Foley Park			18.40					19.14		20.04			20.46	21.40	
KIDDERMINSTER	18.22		18.44					19.18		20.08			20.50	21.45	
Destination		H'bury			Well		Well		Well			Worcs				

Stourport, on the Hartlebury - Bewdley section, had a relatively heavy freight service, much of which consisted of trip workings to and from Hartlebury which was the main point of exchange with the Worcester - Oxford (OWW) main line. In this connection, it is interesting to recall that the little-known Hartlebury was of much greater traffic significance than its neighbour, Kidderminster. The latter dealt with only twenty-five main line goods workings a day whilst Hartlebury Yard saw as many as forty-five.

There were several rail-served factories at Stourport but the most important was the power station which was fed largely by coal from Alveley residual supplies being tripped from Hartlebury.

STOURPORT YARD WORKING : 1955

Train	Arr	Engine	Shed/Diagram	Dep	Destination
Light ex Kidderminster loco	05.45	57xx 0-6-0T	Kidderminster 105		Pilot
Light ex Kidderminster loco	05.45	43xx 2-6-0	Kidderminster 106		
		43xx 2-6-0	Kidderminster 106	06.15	Alveley
07.10 Hartlebury	07.20	57xx 0-6-0T	Kidderminster 107		
		57xx 0-6-0T	Kidderminster 105	07.45	Light to Hartlebury
08.22 Hartlebury	08.37	57xx 0-6-0T	Kidderminster 105		
		57xx 0-6-0T	Kidderminster 105	09.00	EBV Hartlebury
		57xx 0-6-0T	Kidderminster 107	10.20	Hartlebury
10.10 Hartlebury	10.20	57xx 0-6-0T	Kidderminster 108	10.35	Bridgnorth
10.40 Hartlebury	10.55	57xx 0-6-0T	Kidderminster 105		
10.45 Alveley	11.49	43xx 2-6-0	Kidderminster 106		(Fwd at 12.00)
		57xx 0-6-0T	Kidderminster 105	11.50	Hartlebury
		43xx 2-6-0	Kidderminster 106	12.00	Hartlebury
11.15 Alveley	12.10	57xx 0-6-0T	Kidderminster 110		
		57xx 0-6-0T	Kidderminster 110	12.20	Light to Hartlebury
Light ex Hartlebury	12.35	57xx 0-6-0T	Kidderminster 110		
		57xx 0-6-0T	Kidderminster 110	12.40	Alveley
12.30 Light ex Hartlebury	12.40	43xx 2-6-0	Kidderminster 106		
		43xx 2-6-0	Kidderminster 106	13.10	Alveley
14.15 Hartlebury	14.25	43xx 2-6-0	Salop 150A	14.40	Shrewsbury (Coton Hill)
14.20 Alveley	15.12	57xx 0-6-0T	Kidderminster 110		(Fwd at 15.25)
15.00 Hartlebury	15.15	57xx 0-6-0T	Kidderminster 105		
		57xx 0-6-0T	Kidderminster 110	15.25	Worcester
		57xx 0-6-0T	Kidderminster 105	18.45	Hartlebury
Pilot		57xx 0-6-0T	Kidderminster 104	18.57	Light to Hartlebury
10.15 Shrewsbury	18.57	43xx 2-6-0	Salop 150	19.06	Hartlebury
19.30 Hartlebury	19.45	57xx 0-6-0T	Kidderminster 107		
		57xx 0-6-0T	Kidderminster 107	21.05	Light to Hartlebury

56xx 0-6-2T 6696, newly moved from Croes Newydd (Wrexham) to Worcester arrives in Kidderminster Yard on 30th October 1960 with a train of coal for Foley Park sugar beet factory. (Brian Moone: KRM)

Although an LMS engine paid a daily visit to Bewdley in order to turn after working in from Wichnor Junction, the sight of such foreigners was rare enough to get many a camera shutter clicking. Rarer still was the sight of an 8F 2-8-0 on a passenger working - sanctioned only in emergencies - which was almost certainly due to the failure of the booked Walsall engine resulting in the hurried substitution of 48313 of Bescot. The train is an excursion from Walsall to Stourport via Bewdley. (B. Moone: KRM)

LOCOMOTIVE ALLOCATIONS & TRANSFERS : KIDDERMINSTER (85D)

Engine	Class	Aug-50	Sep-50	Oct-50	Nov-50	Dec-50	Jan-51	Feb-51	Mar-51	Apr-51	May-51	Jun-51	Jul-51
8101	4MT : 81xx 2-6-2T (1938)												
4100	4MT : 51xx 2-6-2T (1928)												
4153	4MT : 51xx 2-6-2T (1928)												
4175	4MT : 51xx 2-6-2T (1928)												
5110	4MT : 51xx 2-6-2T (1928)												
4578	4MT : 45xx 2-6-2T (1927)												
4584	4MT : 45xx 2-6-2T (1927)												To M'llech	X
4586	4MT : 45xx 2-6-2T (1927)										To Glouc	X	X
4594	4MT : 45xx 2-6-2T (1927)												
4596	4MT : 45xx 2-6-2T (1927)	X	X	X	X	X	X	X	X	X	Ex Worcs		
4599	4MT : 45xx 2-6-2T (1927)											To Worcs	X
5518	4MT : 45xx 2-6-2T (1927)	X	X	X	X	X	X	X	X	X	Ex Glouc		
6382	4MT : 43xx 2-6-0 (1911)												
3601	3F : 57xx 0-6-0T (1933)												
4625	3F : 57xx 0-6-0T (1933)												
7700	3F : 57xx 0-6-0T (1929)												
8718	3F : 57xx 0-6-0T (1929)												
8727	3F : 57xx 0-6-0T (1929)												
2051	2F : 2021 0-6-0T (1897)												W/D
28	1F : CMDP 0-6-0T												
29	1F : CMDP 0-6-0T												

LOCOMOTIVE ALLOCATIONS & TRANSFERS : KIDDERMINSTER (85D)

Engine	Class	Aug-51	Sep-51	Oct-51	Nov-51	Dec-51	Jan-52	Feb-52	Mar-52	Apr-52	May-52	Jun-52	Jul-52
8101	4MT : 81xx 2-6-2T (1938)												
4100	4MT : 51xx 2-6-2T (1928)												
4153	4MT : 51xx 2-6-2T (1928)												
4175	4MT : 51xx 2-6-2T (1928)												
5110	4MT : 51xx 2-6-2T (1928)												
4578	4MT : 45xx 2-6-2T (1927)												
4594	4MT : 45xx 2-6-2T (1927)							To Worcs	X	X	X	X	X
4596	4MT : 45xx 2-6-2T (1927)												
5518	4MT : 45xx 2-6-2T (1927)												
6382	4MT : 43xx 2-6-0 (1911)												
3601	3F : 57xx 0-6-0T (1933)												
4625	3F : 57xx 0-6-0T (1933)								To Worcs	X	X	X	X
7700	3F : 57xx 0-6-0T (1933)												
8718	3F : 57xx 0-6-0T (1933)												
8727	3F : 57xx 0-6-0T (1933)												
2101	2F: 2021 0-6-0T (1897)	X	Ex Worcs										
28	1F : CMDP 0-6-0T												
29	1F : CMDP 0-6-0T												

LOCOMOTIVE ALLOCATIONS & TRANSFERS : KIDDERMINSTER (85D)

Engine	Class	Aug-52	Sep-52	Oct-52	Nov-52	Dec-52	Jan-53	Feb-53	Mar-53	Apr-53	May-53	Jun-53	Jul-53
8101	4MT : 81xx 2-6-2T (1938)												
4100	4MT : 51xx 2-6-2T (1928)												
4153	4MT : 51xx 2-6-2T (1928)												
4175	4MT : 51xx 2-6-2T (1928)												
5110	4MT : 51xx 2-6-2T (1928)												
4578	4MT : 45xx 2-6-2T (1927)												
4596	4MT : 45xx 2-6-2T (1927)												
5518	4MT : 45xx 2-6-2T (1927)												
6382	4MT : 43xx 2-6-0 (1911)												
7301	4MT : 43xx 2-6-0 (1911)	X	X	X	X	X	X	X	X	X	X	Ex Worcs	
2207	3MT: 2251 0-6-0 (1930)	X	X	X	X	X	X	X	X	X	Ex Worcs		
3601	3F : 57xx 0-6-0T (1933)												
4641	3F : 57xx 0-6-0T (1933)	X	X	X	X	X	X	X	Ex Hereford				
7700	3F : 57xx 0-6-0T (1933)												
8718	3F : 57xx 0-6-0T (1933)												
8727	3F : 57xx 0-6-0T (1933)												
8731	3F : 57xx 0-6-0T (1933)	X	X	X	X	X	X	X	X	X	Ex Worcs		
2101	2F: 2021 0-6-0T (1897)											To Worcs	X
2144	2F: 2021 0-6-0T (1897)	X	X	X	X	X	X	X	X	X	X	Ex Worcs	
28	1F : CMDP 0-6-0T												
29	1F : CMDP 0-6-0T												

LOCOMOTIVE ALLOCATIONS & TRANSFERS : KIDDERMINSTER (85D)

Engine	Class	Aug-53	Sep-53	Oct-53	Nov-53	Dec-53	Jan-54	Feb-54	Mar-54	Apr-54	May-54	Jun-54	Jul-54
8101	4MT : 81xx 2-6-2T (1938)												
4100	4MT : 51xx 2-6-2T (1928)												
4153	4MT : 51xx 2-6-2T (1928)												
4175	4MT : 51xx 2-6-2T (1928)												
5110	4MT : 51xx 2-6-2T (1928)												
4578	4MT : 45xx 2-6-2T (1927)		To Barry	X	X	X	X	X	X	X	X	X	X
4596	4MT : 45xx 2-6-2T (1927)												
5518	4MT : 45xx 2-6-2T (1927)												
6382	4MT : 43xx 2-6-0 (1911)		To Worcs	X	X	X	X	X	X	X	X	X	X
7301	4MT : 43xx 2-6-0 (1911)						To Hereford	X	X	X	X	X	X
2207	3MT: 2251 0-6-0 (1930)												
3601	3F : 57xx 0-6-0T (1933)												
4614	3F : 57xx 0-6-0T (1933)	X	X	X	X	Ex Worcs							
4641	3F : 57xx 0-6-0T (1933)												
7700	3F : 57xx 0-6-0T (1933)												
8718	3F : 57xx 0-6-0T (1933)												
8727	3F : 57xx 0-6-0T (1933)												
8731	3F : 57xx 0-6-0T (1933)												
2144	2F: 2021 0-6-0T (1897)									To Worcs	X	X	X
28	1F : CMDP 0-6-0T				W/D	X	X	X	X	X	X	X	X
29	1F : CMDP 0-6-0T						W/D	X	X	X	X	X	X

LOCOMOTIVE ALLOCATIONS & TRANSFERS : KIDDERMINSTER (85D)

Engine	Class	Aug-54	Sep-54	Oct-54	Nov-54	Dec-54	Jan-55	Feb-55	Mar-55	Apr-55	May-55	Jun-55	Jul-55
6679	5MT : 56xx 0-6-2T (1927)	X	X	X	X	X	X	Ex Tondu					
8101	4MT : 81xx 2-6-2T (1938)												
4100	4MT : 51xx 2-6-2T (1928)												
4114	4MT : 51xx 2-6-2T (1928)	X	Ex Worcs						To S.T. Jcn	X	X	X	X
4153	4MT : 51xx 2-6-2T (1928)												
4175	4MT : 51xx 2-6-2T (1928)												
5110	4MT : 51xx 2-6-2T (1928)												
4596	4MT : 45xx 2-6-2T (1927)												
5518	4MT : 45xx 2-6-2T (1927)		To Glouc	X	X	X	X	X	X	X	X	X	X
5394	4MT : 43xx 2-6-0 (1911)	X	X	X	X	X	Ex Glouc						
2207	3MT: 2251 0-6-0 (1930)												
3601	3F : 57xx 0-6-0T (1933)												
4614	3F : 57xx 0-6-0T (1933)												
4641	3F : 57xx 0-6-0T (1933)												
7700	3F : 57xx 0-6-0T (1933)												
8718	3F : 57xx 0-6-0T (1933)												
8727	3F : 57xx 0-6-0T (1933)												
8731	3F : 57xx 0-6-0T (1933)												
1661	2F: 16xx 0-6-0PT (1949)	X	X	X	X	X	X	X	NEW				

LOCOMOTIVE ALLOCATIONS & TRANSFERS : KIDDERMINSTER (85D)

Engine	Class	Aug-55	Sep-55	Oct-55	Nov-55	Dec-55	Jan-56	Feb-56	Mar-56	Apr-56	May-56	Jun-56	Jul-56
6679	5MT : 56xx 0-6-2T (1927)												
6690	5MT : 56xx 0-6-2T (1927)	X	X	X	X	X	X	X	X	Ex Glouc		To Glouc	X
8101	4MT : 81xx 2-6-2T (1938)												
4100	4MT : 51xx 2-6-2T (1928)												
4114	4MT : 51xx 2-6-2T (1928)	X	X	X	X	X	X	Ex S. T. Jcn				To Penzance	Ex Penzance
4153	4MT : 51xx 2-6-2T (1928)												
4175	4MT : 51xx 2-6-2T (1928)												
5110	4MT : 51xx 2-6-2T (1928)												
4596	4MT : 45xx 2-6-2T (1927)												
5394	4MT : 43xx 2-6-0 (1911)												
6326	4MT : 43xx 2-6-0 (1911)	X	X	X	X	X	X	X	Ex Glouc				
6334	4MT : 43xx 2-6-0 (1911)	X	Ex Worcs									To Worcs	
6382	4MT : 43xx 2-6-0 (1911)	X	Ex Worcs										
2207	3MT: 2251 0-6-0 (1930)									To Gloucs	X	X	X
82008	3MT 2-6-2T (1952)	Ex Barry											
3601	3F : 57xx 0-6-0T (1933)												
4614	3F : 57xx 0-6-0T (1933)			To Worcs	X	X	Ex Worcs						To Worcs
4641	3F : 57xx 0-6-0T (1933)												
7700	3F : 57xx 0-6-0T (1933)											To Glouc	X
8718	3F : 57xx 0-6-0T (1933)												
8727	3F : 57xx 0-6-0T (1933)												
8731	3F : 57xx 0-6-0T (1933)		To Glouc	X	X	X	X	X	X	X	X	X	X
1661	2F: 16xx 0-6-0PT (1949)												

LOCOMOTIVE ALLOCATIONS & TRANSFERS : KIDDERMINSTER (85D)

Engine	Class	Aug-56	Sep-56	Oct-56	Nov-56	Dec-56	Jan-57	Feb-57	Mar-57	Apr-57	May-57	Jun-57	Jul-57
6679	5MT : 56xx 0-6-2T (1927)												
8101	4MT : 81xx 2-6-2T (1938)												
4100	4MT : 51xx 2-6-2T (1928)											To Gloucs	X
4114	4MT : 51xx 2-6-2T (1928)												
4139	4MT : 51xx 2-6-2T (1928)	X	X	X	X	X	X	X	Ex Bristol (BR)			To Gloucs	X
4153	4MT : 51xx 2-6-2T (1928)												
4175	4MT : 51xx 2-6-2T (1928)												
5110	4MT : 51xx 2-6-2T (1928)												
4596	4MT : 45xx 2-6-2T (1927)									To Worcs	X	X	X
5518	4MT : 45xx 2-6-2T (1927)	Ex Glouc											
5394	4MT : 43xx 2-6-0 (1911)												
6314	4MT : 43xx 2-6-0 (1911)	X	X	X	X	X	X	X	Ex Hereford				
6326	4MT : 43xx 2-6-0 (1911)								To Hereford	X	X	X	X
6340	4MT : 43xx 2-6-0 (1911)	X	X	X	X	X	X	X	X	Ex Worcs		To S'bge	X
6382	4MT : 43xx 2-6-0 (1911)												
82008	3MT 2-6-2T (1952)												
3601	3F : 57xx 0-6-0T (1933)												
4641	3F : 57xx 0-6-0T (1933)												
8718	3F : 57xx 0-6-0T (1933)												
8727	3F : 57xx 0-6-0T (1933)											To Gloucs	X
1661	2F: 16xx 0-6-0PT (1949)												

LOCOMOTIVE ALLOCATIONS & TRANSFERS : KIDDERMINSTER (85D)

Engine	Class	Aug-57	Sep-57	Oct-57	Nov-57	Dec-57	Jan-58	Feb-58	Mar-58	Apr-58	May-58	Jun-58	Jul-58
6669	5MT : 56xx 0-6-2T (1927)	X	X	X	X	X	X	X	X	X	X	Ex Glouc	To Glouc
6679	5MT : 56xx 0-6-2T (1927)												
8101	4MT : 81xx 2-6-2T (1938)												
4114	4MT : 51xx 2-6-2T (1928)												
4153	4MT : 51xx 2-6-2T (1928)												
4175	4MT : 51xx 2-6-2T (1928)								To Glouc	X	Ex Glouc		
5110	4MT : 51xx 2-6-2T (1928)												
5518	4MT : 45xx 2-6-2T (1927)												
5355	4MT : 43xx 2-6-0 (1911)	X	Ex Salop										
5394	4MT : 43xx 2-6-0 (1911)												
6314	4MT : 43xx 2-6-0 (1911)												
6382	4MT : 43xx 2-6-0 (1911)												
82008	3MT 2-6-2T (1952)	To Worcs	X	X	Ex Worcs	To Worcs	X	X	X	X	X	X	X
3601	3F : 57xx 0-6-0T (1933)												
4625	3F : 57xx 0-6-0T (1933)	X	X	X	X	X	X	X	X	X	X	Ex Worcs	To Worcs
4641	3F : 57xx 0-6-0T (1933)									To Reading	X	X	X
7777	3F : 57xx 0-6-0T (1933)	X	X	X	X	X	X	X	X	X	X	Ex Worcs	
8718	3F : 57xx 0-6-0T (1933)												
1661	2F : 16xx 0-6-0PT (1949)			To Worcs	X	X	X	X	X	X	X	X	X

LOCOMOTIVE ALLOCATIONS & TRANSFERS : KIDDERMINSTER (85D)

Engine	Class	Aug-58	Sep-58	Oct-58	Nov-58	Dec-58	Jan-59	Feb-59	Mar-59	Apr-59	May-59	Jun-59	Jul-59
6679	5MT : 56xx 0-6-2T (1927)												
8101	4MT : 81xx 2-6-2T (1938)												
4109	4MT : 51xx 2-6-2T (1928)	X	X	X	Ex N. Abbot				To Worc	X	X	X	X
4114	4MT : 51xx 2-6-2T (1928)												
4153	4MT : 51xx 2-6-2T (1928)												
4175	4MT : 51xx 2-6-2T (1928)												
5110	4MT : 51xx 2-6-2T (1928)												
5518	4MT : 45xx 2-6-2T (1927)												
5333	4MT : 43xx 2-6-0 (1911)	X	X	X	X	X	X	Ex Hereford					
5355	4MT : 43xx 2-6-0 (1911)										W/D	X	X	X
5394	4MT : 43xx 2-6-0 (1911)							W/D	X	X	X	X	X
5396	4MT : 43xx 2-6-0 (1911)	X	X	X	Ex Worcs	To Worcs	X	X	X	X	X	X	X
5396	4MT : 43xx 2-6-0 (1911)	X	X	X	X	X	X	X	Ex Worc		To Worc	X	X
6314	4MT : 43xx 2-6-0 (1911)												
6367	4MT : 43xx 2-6-0 (1911)	Ex Tyseley	To Worcs	X	X	X	X	X	X	X	X	X	X
6382	4MT : 43xx 2-6-0 (1911)		To Truro	Ex Truro									
6388	4MT : 43xx 2-6-0 (1911)	X	X	X	X	X	X	X	X	X	X	Ex Didcot	
82030	3MT 2-6-2T (1952)	X	X	X	X	X	X	X	X	X	X	Ex Worc	To Worc
3601	3F : 57xx 0-6-0T (1933)												
4629	3F : 57xx 0-6-0T (1933)	X	X	X	X	X	X	X	X	X	Ex Worc		
7777	3F : 57xx 0-6-0T (1933)			To Worcs	X	X	X	X	X	X	X	X	X
8701	3F : 57xx 0-6-0T (1933)	X	X	X	X	X	X	Ex Hereforc	To Glouc	X	X	X	X
8718	3F : 57xx 0-6-0T (1933)												
1417	1P : 14xx 0-4-2T (1932)	X	X	X	Ex B'head		To Swindon	X	X	X	X	X	X
1457	1P : 14xx 0-4-2T (1932)	X	X	X	Ex Croes N.		To M'llech	X	X	X	X	X	X

LOCOMOTIVE ALLOCATIONS & TRANSFERS : KIDDERMINSTER (85D)

Engine	Class	Aug-59	Sep-59	Oct-59	Nov-59	Dec-59	Jan-60	Feb-60	Mar-60	Apr-60	May-60	Jun-60	Jul-60
6679	5MT : 56xx 0-6-2T (1927)												
6128	4MT : 61xx 2-6-2T (1931)	X	X	X	X	X	X	X	X	X	X	X	Ex Southall
6144	4MT : 61xx 2-6-2T (1931)	X	X	X	X	X	X	X	X	X	X	X	Ex Southall
8101	4MT : 81xx 2-6-2T (1938)												
4114	4MT : 51xx 2-6-2T (1928)												
4153	4MT : 51xx 2-6-2T (1928)												
4175	4MT : 51xx 2-6-2T (1928)												
5110	4MT : 51xx 2-6-2T (1928)			To Salop	X	X	X	X	X	X	X	X	X
5518	4MT : 45xx 2-6-2T (1927)												
5333	4MT : 43xx 2-6-0 (1911)										W/D	X	X
6314	4MT : 43xx 2-6-0 (1911)												
6368	4MT : 43xx 2-6-0 (1911)	X	X	X	X	X	X	X	X	X	X	Ex Glouc	To Worc
6382	4MT : 43xx 2-6-0 (1911)												To Worc
6388	4MT : 43xx 2-6-0 (1911)												
3601	3F : 57xx 0-6-0T (1933)												
4629	3F : 57xx 0-6-0T (1933)												
5791	3F : 57xx 0-6-0T (1933)	X	X	Ex Salop									
8718	3F : 57xx 0-6-0T (1933)												

WORCESTER, BEWDLEY, BRIDGNORTH, BUILDWAS, and SHREWSBURY.

Miles	Down.	Week Days.																		Sundays		
		mrn	mrn	mrn	mrn	mrn	mrn	aft	aft	aft	aft	aft	aft	aft	aft	aft	aft	aft	aft			
	Worcester (Shrub H) dep.	..		7 5		9 42		12B11	1245	2 5	3 7	3B26	4 43	5B16	7 17	7B35	..	8 0	9A25	..	..	..
2½	Fernhill Heath	..	Mondays only.	7 11	Saturdays only.	9 48		..	1251	2 11	..	..	4 49	..	..	..	..	8 7	..	..	..	..
5½	Droitwich Spa	..		7 17		9 54	Saturdays only.	12A22	1257	2 17	3 18	3A36	4 56	5A26	7 28	7A45	..	8 15	9A35	..	..	..
9	Cutnall Green	..		..		10 1		..	1 4	2 25	..	..	5 4	..	..	..		8 24	..	..	..	..
11¼	Hartlebury arr.	..		7 26		10 6		m	1 9	2 30	3 28	..	5 10	..	7 38	..		8 30	....	..	..	..
	Hartlebury dep.	..		7 29		10N10		12 7	1 35	2N35	3N40	4 25	5 30	..	7N45	..		8 35	9A46	..	..	..
14¼	Stourport-on-Severn ¶	..		7 36		10N18		12 38	1 45	2N45	3N49	4 33	5 39	..	7N54	..	Saturdays only.	8 50	..	..	..	..
16¾	**Bewdley 135, 138** arr.	..		7 43		10N25		12 45	1 54	2N52	3N56	4 41	5 47	..	8N1	..		8 56	..	..	..	..
—	**120** Birmingham (S.H) dep	m		6 20		9 45	1045	11 40	1 0	1E25	1J25	3 48	5 0		7 10			8 20	9 45	..	..	..
—	**138** Kidderminster "	5 40	6 10	7 39		10 45	12 4	12 40	1 50	3E8	2V23	4 40	5 46		8 2			9 13	1045	..	..	..
—	**Bewdley** dep.	5 50	6 28	7 52	..	10 55	1214	12 56	2 3	3E20	3 57	4 54	6 0		8 18			9 23	1054	..	..	..
20¾	Arley	5 57	6 34	7 59	..	11 2	1221	1 3	2 10	3E27	4 4	5 2	6 7		8 26			9 34	11 1	..	..	..
22¾	Highley	6 3	6 40	8 5	1015	11 9	1227	1 10	2 18	3E33	4 10	5 10	6 14		8 33			9 41	11 7	..	..	..
25	Hampton Loade	..	6 45	8 11	1020	11 14	..		2 23	..	4 16	5 15	6 19		8 40			9 46	..	..	..	..
27¼	Eardington	..	..	8 17	1026	11 19	..	Saturdays only.	2 29	..	4 22	5 22	6 24		..			..	..	..	..	..
29½	**Bridgnorth** arr.	..	6 52	8 21	1031	11 24	..		2 33	..	4 27	5 26	6 29		8 48		m	9 54	..	..	..	..
	Bridgnorth dep.	..	..	8 25	..	11 28	..		2 41	..	m	5 32	6 42		m		8 52		..	..	..	..
33¾	Linley	..	..	8 33	..	11 35	..		2 49	..	..	5 40	6 50		..		8 59	Saturdays only.	..	..	..	..
36¼	Coalport **H 487**	..	..	8 39	..	11 43	..		2 55	..	..	5 47	6 56		..		9 5		Sats. only.	..	..	..
38¼	Iron Bridge and Broseley	..	..	8 45	..	11 50	..		3 1	..	..	5 54	7 2		..		9 10			..	..	..
39¾	Buildwas 138	..	..	8P55	..	11 55	..		3 8	..	..	6 0	7 8		..		9 15			..	..	..
43¾	Cressage ¶ [492	..	..	9 1	..	12 2	..		3 13	..	..	6 6	7 14		..		9 21			..	..	..
47¾	Berrington [488, 490,	..	..	9 11	..	12 13	..		3 23	..	..	6 17	7 24		..		9 31			..	..	..
52	**Shrewsbury B 108**, arr.	..	..	9 21	..	12 25	..		3 35	..	..	6 28	7 37		..		9 43			..	..	..

Miles	Up.	Week Days.																		Sundays		
		mrn	mrn	mrn	mrn	mrn	mrn	aft	aft	aft	aft	aft		aft	aft	aft	aft	aft	aft			
	Shrewsbury (Gen.) dep.	..		..	8 15	..	1125		1 50	..	..	5 30		..	7 45				1030	..	..	..
4¼	Berrington ¶	..	Mondays only.	..	8 25	..	1135	Saturdays only.	2 0	..	..	5 40		..	7 54	Except Sats	Saturdays only.	Sats. only.	1039	..	..	..
8¼	Cressage	..		..	8 35	..	1145		2 9	..	..	5 50		..	8 3				1049	..	..	..
12¼	Buildwas 138	..		..	8F50	..	1156		2 16	..	..	5 58		..	8 13				1056	..	..	..
13¾	Iron Bridge and Broseley	..		..	8 57	..	12 3		2 22	..	..	6 5		..	8 19				11 0	..	..	..
15¾	Coalport **H 487**	..		..	9 2	..	12 8		2 27	..	..	6 11		..	8 25				11 5	..	..	..
18¼	Linley	..		..	9 8	..	1214		2 33	..	..	6 17		..	8 30				1111	..	..	..
22½	**Bridgnorth** arr.	..		..	9 15	..	1221		2 40	..	m	6 25		..	8 37	m		..	1118	..	..	..
	Bridgnorth dep.	..	7 0	..	9 18	..	1224		2 48	..	4 35	6 34		..	8 48	9 5	10 5	..	1120	..	..	..
24¾	Eardington	..	..	..	9 23	..	1230		2 54	..	4 40	6 39		..	8S55	..	..	..	..	..	..	..
27	Hampton Loade	m	7 10	..	9 28	..	1235	m	2 59	..	4 45	6 44		..	8Y57	9 15	1015	..	1130	..	..	..
29¼	Highley	6 15	7 16	..	9 33	..	1241	1 45	3 5	3E43	4 50	6 50		..	9Y2	9 21	1020	1115	1135	..	..	..
31¼	Arley	6 21	7 21	..	9 40	..	1248	1 51	3 12	3E49	5 4	6 56		..	9Y9	9 28	1026	1122	1140	..	..	..
35¼	**Bewdley 135, 138** arr.	6 27	7 28	..	9 46	..	1255	1 58	3 18	3E55	5 10	7 3		..	9Y16	9 35	1033	1128	1147	..	..	..
38¾	**139** Kidderminster arr.	6 40	7 40	..	9 53	..	1 10	2 21	3 30	4E8	5 20	7 15		..	9U39	9Z49	1043	1137	1156	..	..	..
57¾	**118** Birmingham (S.H.) "	8 6	8 40	..	10 50	..	2 27	3 25	4 30	5E30	6 23	8L45		..	11S12	11 12	..	..	m	..	..	..
—	**Bewdley** ¶ dep.	7 1	..	7N45	..	11N0	1 0	2 0	3N20	4 58	5 58	7N10	7 45	8 17	9 24	..	..	..		..	..	..
37¾	Stourport-on-Severn	7 8	..	7N55	..	11N8	1 9	2T14	3N27	5 7	6 4	7N20	8 0	8 24	9 32	..	..	..		..	..	..
40¾	Hartlebury 118 arr.	..	..	8N3	..	11N15	1 16	2 22	3N34	5 14	..	7N27	8 7	8 31	9 39	10A32	..	..	Sats. only	..	..	..
	Hartlebury 118 dep.	..	..	8 16	..	11 29	1 29	2 31	3S53	5 23	6A1	8 4	8 9	..	9 45	10A33	..	..		..	..	..
43	Cutnall Green	..	..	8 22	..	11 34	..	2 37	3S58	..	6A9	..	8 14	..	..	..	..	..		..	..	..
46½	Droitwich Spa **660**	..	..	8 31	10A46	11 42	1 41	2 43	4S6	..	6A16	8 13	8 21	8 41	9 54	10A42	..	..		..	..	..
49½	Fernhill Heath [137, **656**	..	..	8 37	..	11 48	..	2 49	4S12	5 41	6A22	..	8 27	..	Aa	..	..	..		..	..	..
52	**Worcester A 117, 122**, ar	..	..	8 42	10B56	11 53	1 50	2 55	4S17	4B55	6B0	8K22	8 32	8 50	10 4	10B51	..	..		..	..	..

A Shrub Hill.
A Via Kidderminster.
Aa Stops to set down on informing the Guard at Droitwich Spa.
B General; about ½ mile to Abbey Station.
B Worcester (Foregate Street) via Kidderminster.
Bb Stops to set down.
E Except Sats.
F Arr Buildwas 8 40 mrn.
H About 200 yards to L. M. & S. Station.
J Via Hartlebury.
K Worcester (Foregate Street)
L Arr 8 37 aft on Sats.
m Rail Motor Car, one class only.
N Rail Motor Car, one class only.
P Arrives Buildwas at 8 49 mrn.
S Saturdays only.
T Arr. 2 8 aft.
U Rail Motor Car, one class only. Arr 9 55 aft on Sats by Train.
V Via Hartlebury Dep 2 30 aft Sats.
Y 4 mins. later on Sats.
Z 5 mins. later on Thurs.
¶ "Halt" at Burlish, between Stourport-on-Severn and Bewdley, and at Cound, between Cressage and Berrington.

For Local Trains

Worcester and Hartlebury...... 118
Hartlebury and Bewdley....... 138

For other Trains

Worcester and Droitwich....... 660

The Winter 1934/5 timetable gave the train service as it was immediately prior to the introduction of the diesel railcars which came to dominate services for twenty-five years at the Southern end of the line. With five trains a day in each direction, the through service to and from Shrewsbury was not ungenerous but the overall speeds of around 20 mph cannot have aroused much excitement in Worcester.

The compilers were anxious to give the impression of a through Worcester - Shrewsbury service and remained silent about the change of trains required at Hartlebury and, in some cases, at Bewdley as well.

LOCOMOTIVE ALLOCATION SUMMARY : SHREWSBURY (84G)

Class	Oct-50	Oct-51	Oct-52	Oct-53	Oct-54	Oct-55	Oct-56	Oct-57	Oct-58	Oct-59	Oct-60
8F 2-8-0 (1935)	8	12	12	13	13	16	16	16	14	13	12
8F : WD 2-8-0 (1943)	11			3	4	3	3	6	2	1	1
8F : 28xx 2-8-0 (1903)	1	2	3	5	2					1	1
7P : CASTLE 4-6-0 (1923)	9	5	4	4	4	3	4	3	4	4	6
7F 0-8-0 (1892/1921)	5	6	6	5	4	8	8	7	3		
7F : ROD 2-8-0 (1917)				1	1						
6MT: COUNTY 4-6-0 (1945)		2	7	5	5	6	6	6	7	7	7
5P : STAR 4-6-0 (1907)	5	3	2								
5MT: MANOR 4-6-0 (1938)		1	3	3	2	3	3	2	2	2	2
5MT: GRANGE 4-6-0 (1936)					1						
5MT 4-6-0 (1951)				8	14	12	12	10	12	14	16
5MT 4-6-0 (1934)	19	12	8	8	8	8	8	8	8	8	8
5MT : MOD-HALL 4-6-0 (1944)	3	3	1	1	1	1	1	2	5	3	3
5MT : HALL 4-6-0 (1928)	4	2	4	4	5	5	6	5	5	5	8
5MT : 56xx 0-6-2T (1927)	5	5	3	3	3	2	2	3	3	3	
4MT: 45xx 2-6-2T (1927)										1	1
4MT 4-6-0 (1951)		8	10						1		
4MT : 51xx 2-6-2T (1928)	3	3	3	4	3	3				2	
4MT : 43xx 2-6-0 (1911)	4	3			4	4	7	9	7	8	5
4F: 94XX 0-6-0T (1949)							1	2	5	6	5
3P 2-6-2 (1935)					1	1	1	1	1		2
3P 2-6-2 (1930)	4	4	4	4	4	4	4	4	2		
3MT 2-6-2T (1952)						3	3	3	2		
3MT : 2251 0-6-0 (1930)	7	8	7	6	4	3	1	1	3	2	2
3F 0-6-0 (1909)	1	1									
3F 0-6-0 (1906)					1	1	1	1	1		
3F 0-6-0 (1889)	3	2									
3F 0-6-0 (1885)	8	8	8	7	10	8	8	8	4		
3F : 57xx 0-6-0T (1933)	11	11	10	10	10	9	8	8	8	8	8
2F 0-6-2T (1882)	2	2	2	2	1	1	1	1			
2F 0-6-0 (1878)	2	2	5	5	5	3	2	2	2	1	1
2F 0-6-0 (1875)			1	1	2						
2F 0-6-0 (1873)	4	4									
1F 0-6-0T (1878)	1	1	1	1	1						
1F : 27xx 0-6-0T (1896)	1										
0F: S.H.T 0-4-0T (1911)								1	1	1	1
0F: Diesel 0-6-0						3	5	5	5	4	6
0F Sentinel (1929)	1	1	1	1	1	1	1				
0F 0-4-0ST (1885)	1										
TOTAL	**104**	**99**	**93**	**88**	**97**	**111**	**112**	**114**	**88**	**93**	**95**

Although the joint shed at Coleham (Shrewsbury) had a very large allocation, its interest in the Severn Valley was confined to a pair of 51xx 2-6-2T's (later BR 3MT 2-6-2T's) and the 43xx 2-6-0's responsible for the daily Hartlebury goods. The allocation summary indicates why Shrewsbury was such an attraction for enthusiasts when BR was operated by steam.

Normally the Bewdley - Woofferton branch saw only one steam-hauled passenger service but when Worcester was short of Railcars a 57xx and a pair of coaches would be run as a substitute. 57xx 0-6-0PT 4629 of Kidderminster passes Foley Park with a Woofferton to Kidderminster steam substitute on 2nd July 1960. (B. Moone: KRM)

Most GWR 2-6-2T's were in the blue route classification which restricted them somewhat at Kidderminster since they were limited to 25 mph between Bewdley and Woofferton. The smaller 44xx and 55xx 2-6-2T's had a slightly wider (yellow) classification and this allowed them to work over the Woofferton branch a speeds of between 40 and 50 mph. 5518 of Kidderminster emerges from Bewdley tunnel with a down Severn Valley train on 4th August 1959. (Brian Moone: KRM)

The LMS 'Crab' 2-6-0's were barred from working express trains timed to anything but the most basic of running times which effectively restricted the class passenger activities to excursion duties; a form of work that occasionally brought members of the class onto the Severn Valley with special trains from the Birmingham (LNW) lines. 42933 had just been transferred to Nuneaton from Crewe South when on 3rd August 1959 it was used to work a Rugeley - Stourport excursion. The service is seen approaching Bewdley where it reversed, the engine running round and working tender-first for the final two-mile section. (Brian Moone: KRM)

Goods trains were no trifling affair on the Severn Valley and the sixteen wagons being worked above fell far short of the forty-five that were permitted by most trains. A view from the brakevan of 51xx 2-6-2T 4175 and the 11.30 Kidderminster - Woofferton goods. Under certain circumstances sixty wagons could be worked between Kidderminster and Foley Park provided the train contained two brakevans and was propelled by the train engine. Another peculiarity of the Severn Valley was the fact that the engine of all goods trains, irrespective of class or speed, exhibited the headcode - one lamp in the centre of the buffer beam - for a light engine (G.E.S.Parker: KRM)

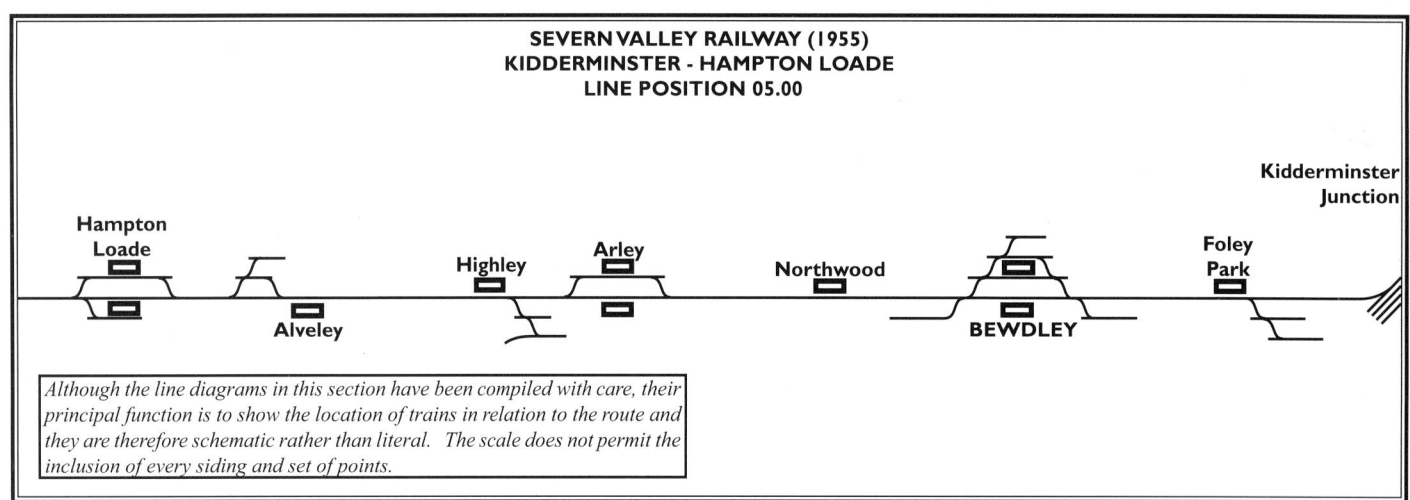

Although the line diagrams in this section have been compiled with care, their principal function is to show the location of trains in relation to the route and they are therefore schematic rather than literal. The scale does not permit the inclusion of every siding and set of points.

CONTROLLER'S LOG: The curse of overseeing operations on lines such as the Severn Valley revolves around the hours of operation. A two shift operation means taking duty at five in the morning to ensure that all preparations are in hand for the first train and it is at times like this that the romantic appeal of the line is rather difficult to locate.

The first train on the section will be a set of empty stock from Kidderminster to Arley homecoming passengers tend to be spread over a far wider range of hours than is the case in the morning when all three can be guaranteed to be well filled.

As well as ensuring that all is clear for the passenger service, a check has to be made of all goods traffic on hand together with a review of the volume expected during the coming ten hours or so. This is usually achieved by looking at the peg board - a note pinned to each changed its mind about the number of empties it is to bring, there is still time to amend the train.

With Highley Colliery being only sixteen miles from the power station at Buildwas, it is sometimes presumed that the one serves the other yet in fact the bulk of Highley's output is taken to either Stourport - where there is also a power station - or to Worcester. Highley occasionally sends coal to Buildwas but the bulk of the latters' requirements come from

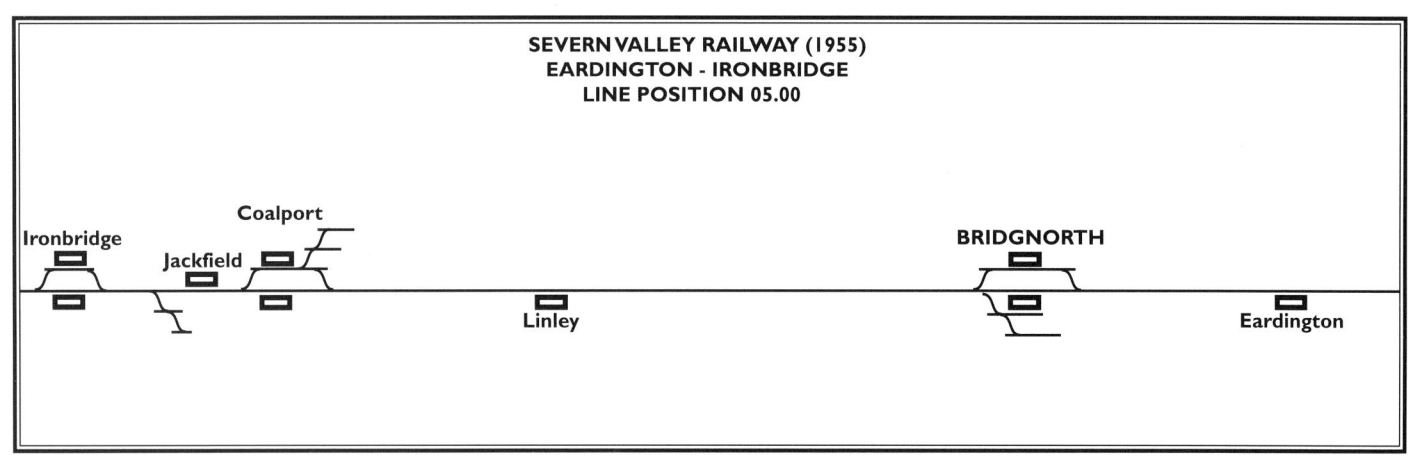

to form the 05.50 Arley to Birmingham (Snow Hill) and a few quiet words on the telephone circuit quickly establishes that all the signalmen are present and that the line is clear.

Through trains between the Severn Valley and Birmingham are not a regular feature of the line but three are provided for the morning rush-hour, leaving Arley at 05.50 and Bewdley at 07.25 and 08.00. All three are worked by 51xx 2-6-2T's but interestingly there is no corresponding service in the evening since group of sidings gives brief details of the traffic on hand - and confirming the details shown with the signalman or shunter concerned. Since the line has been closed for the last six hours it is unlikely that any fresh traffic will have materialised although overnight surprises are not entirely unknown. A little more attention is paid to Highley Colliery since traffic fluctuations can occur with very little notice. The first train for the colliery will leave Stourport in just over an hour and if during the night Highley has Wednesbury via Wolverhampton, Lightmoor Junction and the Wellington branch. Typically a pair of such trains will operate on an ad-hoc basis whilst once or twice a week a train of coal will run from either Highley or Shrewsbury. The output from coal mines and the demand by power stations rarely remains static and adds greatly to the fascination of running trains. To allow some of the flexibility needed, one of the regular services from Stourport has sufficient time at Arley to work a fill-in turn to Buildwas.

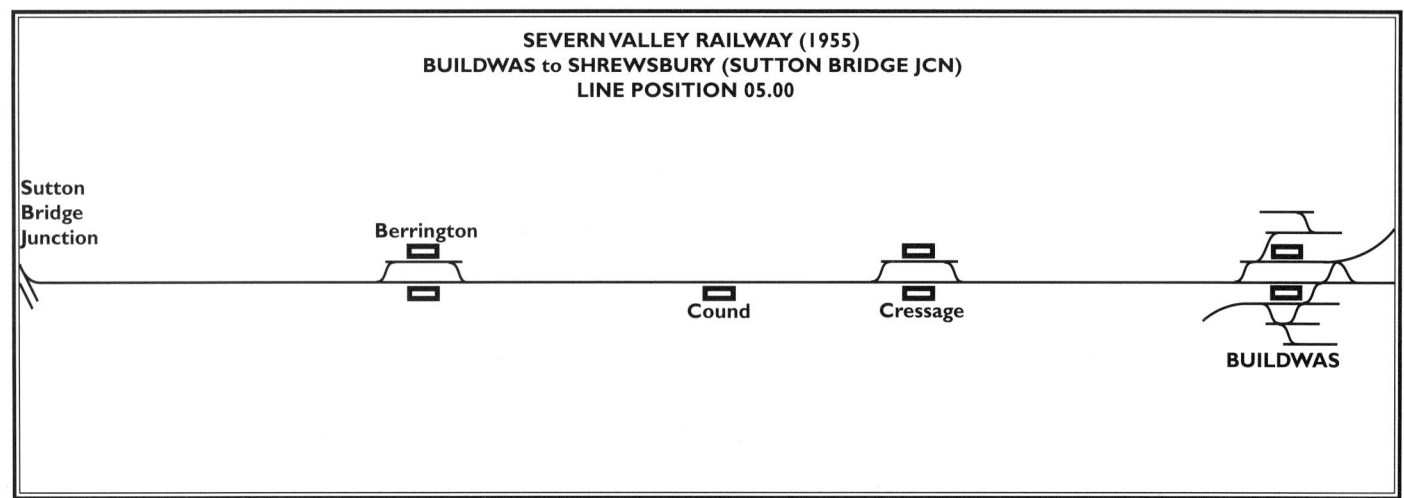

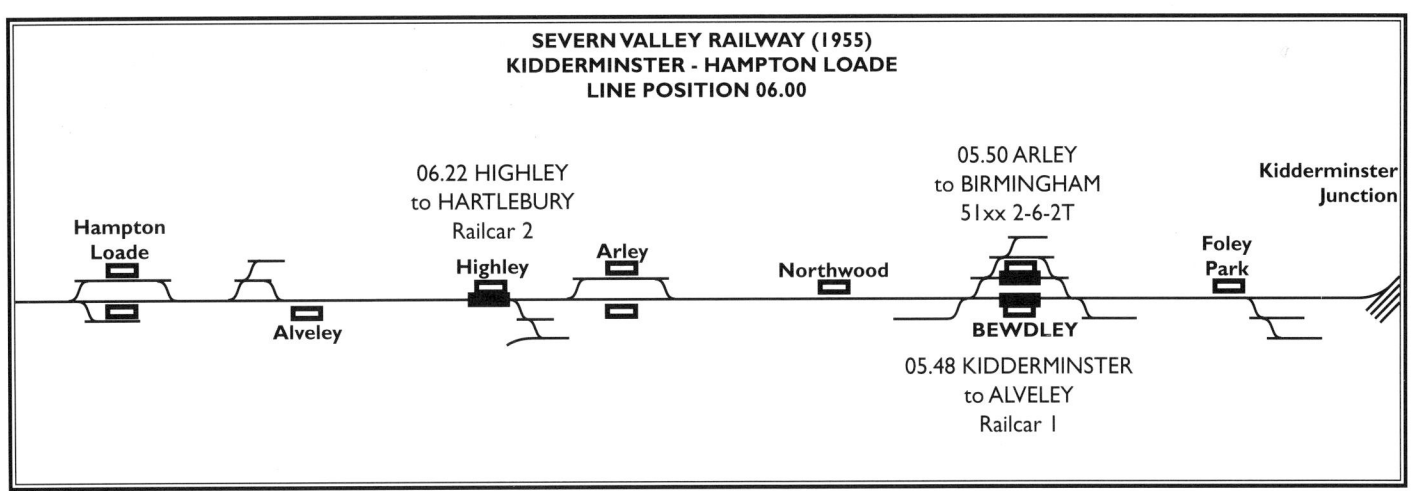

CONTROLLER'S LOG: Slowly, the line wakes and comes to life as three passenger trains work the southern end of the section whilst further down the line the Wellington - Much Wenlock branch starts to make its presence felt.

The constraints of the single line are amply demonstrated by current events; the punctuality of one train being heavily dependant on the running of another.

The key train at the moment is the 05.48 Kidderminster to Highley which has to clear the section to Bewdley before the 05.50 Arley to Birmingham can continue its journey. Under coin!

Although the lion's share of season ticket travel gravitates to Birmingham on account of its size - hence the through trains - Worcester, a very large town only fifteen miles away has a relatively poor service which, since no through trains are provided, requires a change at Hartlebury and often quite a long wait. The first train for passengers travelling in this direction is the 06.22 ex Highley although it caters more for the local workforce of Stourport than it does for those of Worcester. The latter in fact have to undergo a sort of dance macabre as they alight change direction in much less time than is normal. Three of Worcester's railcars - there are times when there seem to be more - are employed on the Severn Valley with almost all their duties being at the Bewdley end of the line. The chief exception to the rule is one of the Kidderminster to Shrewsbury workings which is worked by a railcar instead of a 51xx 2-6-2T.

Surprisingly, GWR auto-trains are entirely absent from the route apart from a morning and evening appearance on a local train between Tenbury Wells and Woofferton.

While the service south of Hampton might

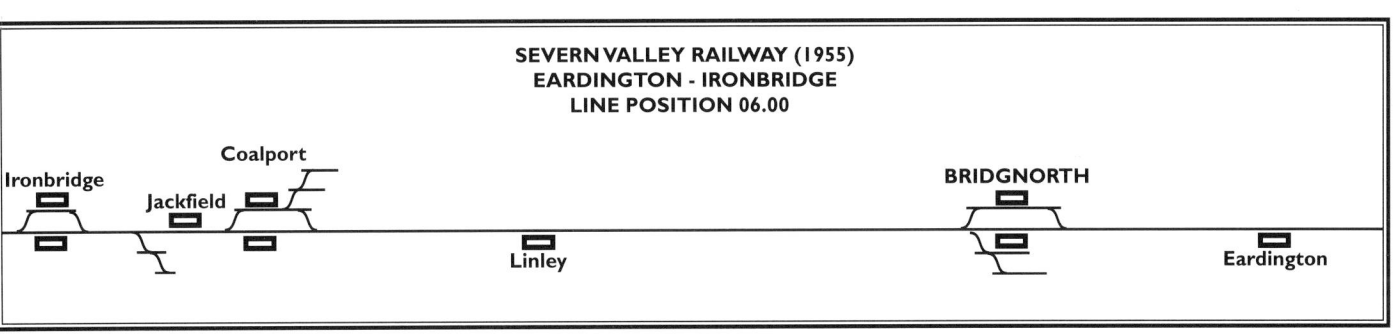

the normal rules of engagement if the down train ('Up' is towards Kidderminster) is more than five minutes late in starting, the Birmingham train will be given priority and the 05.48 held at Kidderminster until 06.08.

The problem, however, is not so easily resolved and while the Birmingham service is a train of more than ordinary importance, the 05.48 ex Kidderminster works two very hurried trips between Alveley and Hampton Loade before forming the 07.00 Hampton to Bewdley.

Thus when delays occur, one can either summon the wisdom of Solomon or toss a at Hartlebury at 06.54 and then wait thirty-five minutes for their Worcester connection which is worked by the same train that they arrived in Hartlebury with. (In the interim it has run empty to Kidderminster to form the 07.22 to Worcester and Henwick).

On a system that is almost wholly steam-worked, the local service is at times exceptional in that many of its workings are operated by GWR diesel railcars; five of which are based at Worcester. Cheaper to operate than a conventional train, the railcars match the population level North of Bewdley and can be described as adequate, it is generous in comparison with that given to those to the north which have over three hours to wait until the first up service. The exception can be found at Buildwas where the Severn Valley bisects the Wellington - Much Wenlock branch. The 05.20 Workman's from Wellington arrived a few minutes ago; its 57xx 0-6-0T has run round the two-coach set and is positioned to return to Wellington at 06.00. While this is being prepared for departure, a second 57xx 0-6-0 rumbles through, running light from Wellington to work the 06.50 from Much Wenlock.

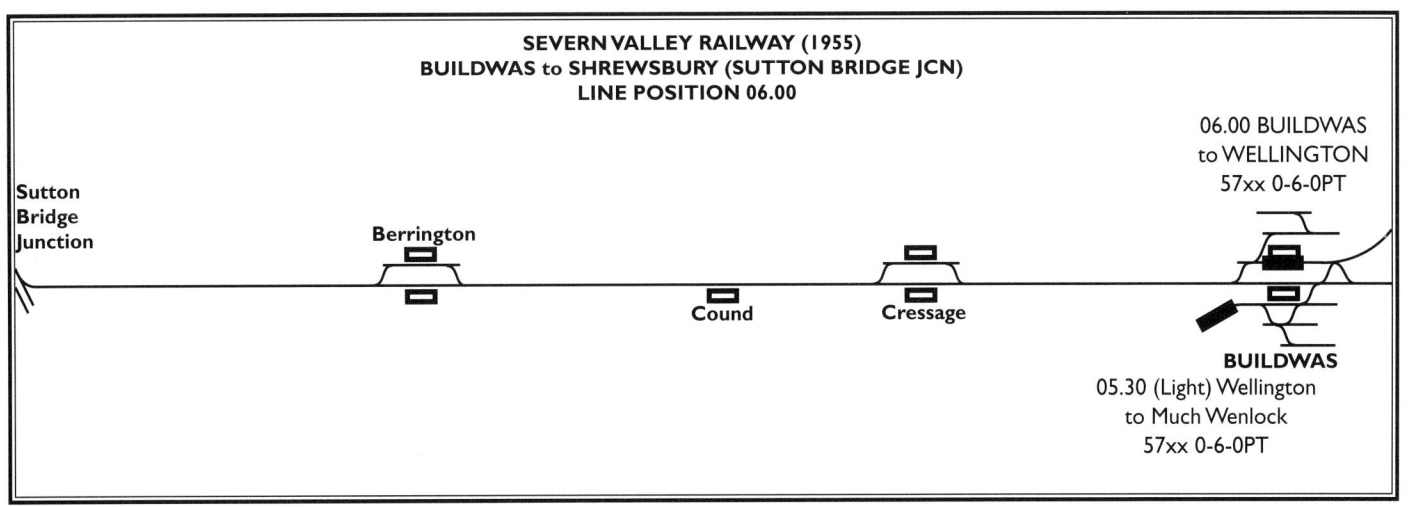

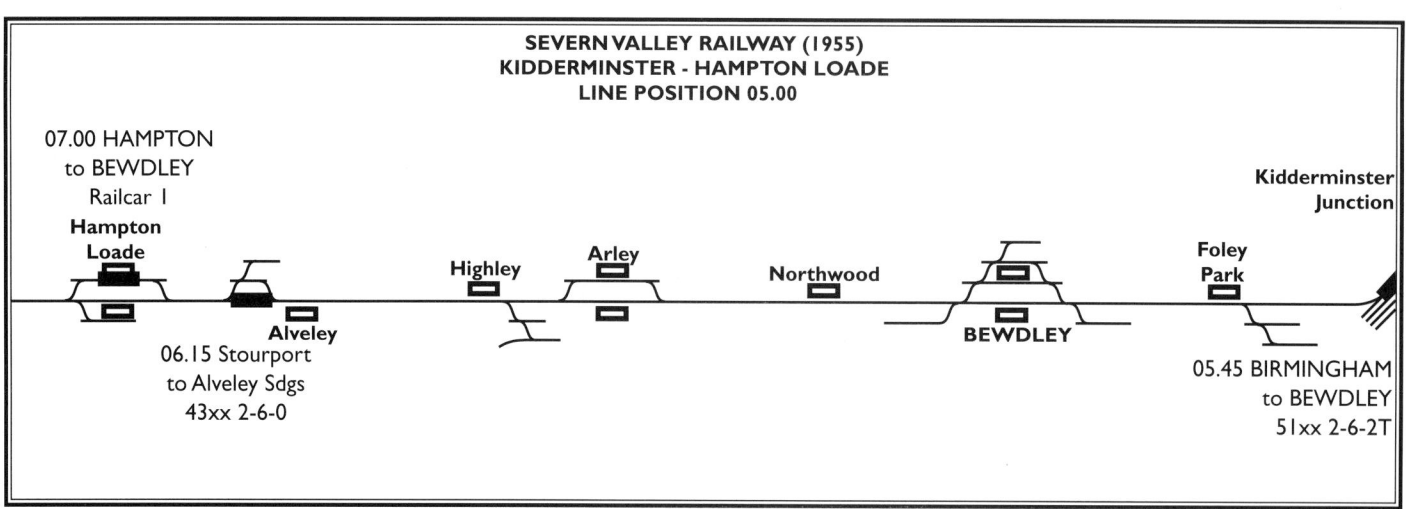

CONTROLLER'S LOG: Suddenly the Wolverhampton Controller comes on the line.

"- I've nothing for the five o'clock Wednesbury. Do you want the engine and men?"

"- Not unless you're desperate for empties."

"- Right. Cancelled then."

What he means is that there is no traffic - coal - on hand for the 05.00 Wednesbury to Buildwas and as a matter of routine courtesy was asking whether we wanted the engine sending light for the return working. Since the latter is the 10.40 train of empties from Buildwas to Wednesbury and he is not short of empties, he has cancelled the train and is in all probability arranging for the engine and men to work a special to Chester or Banbury. There are no preliminaries or formalities and nothing is put in writing. Thus is the fluidity of modern railway operating.

There are two booked trains from Wednesbury to Buildwas, the 05.00 and the 12.30, and on some days both will run whilst on others neither will make an appearance. It all depends on the arrival of coal at Wednesbury and the extent of stocks at Buildwas. When they do run, the trains are an impressive sight; a 43xx 2-6-0 and forty-five wagons of coal making quite a contrast to the workaday 57xx Pannier Tanks. In the return direction the 2-6-0's can take up to sixty mineral empties which means that every fourth service returns light engine to Wolverhampton. The large 28xx 2-8-0's are also permitted to work the Buildwas trains but by a quirk of the loading calculations cannot load as heavily over the route as a 2-6-0.

Current activity at Buildwas is provided by a pair of 57xx 0-6-0's; one about to pull away from the High Level platform with the 06.50 Much Wenlock to Wellington and the other engaged in shunting the yard after arriving engine and brakevan from Wellington. In just over half an hour it will run with its brakevan to Kemberton on the Shifnal branch to work a local goods back to Buildwas.

On the Severn Valley, a sigh of relief is

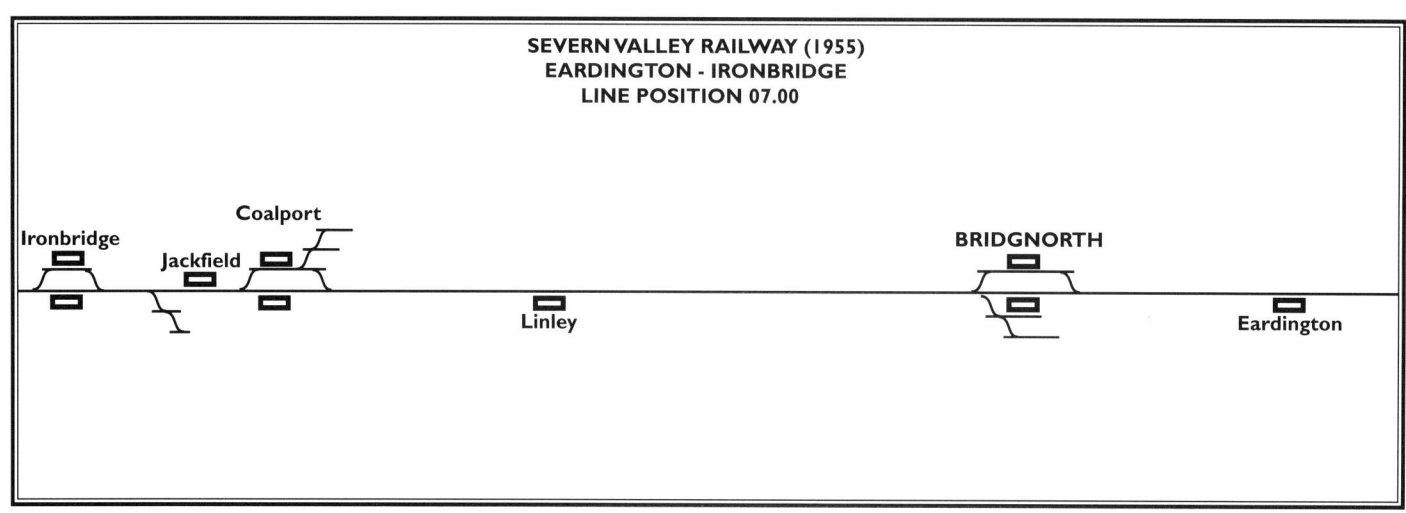

given as the down goods shuts itself in the yard at Alveley a minute before the up diesel is booked to leave Hampton Loade. It is a timing rather too tight for comfort, especially as the diesel has a four minute connection at Bewdley into the 07.25 through service for Birmingham. The inward working of the latter is just leaving Kidderminster.

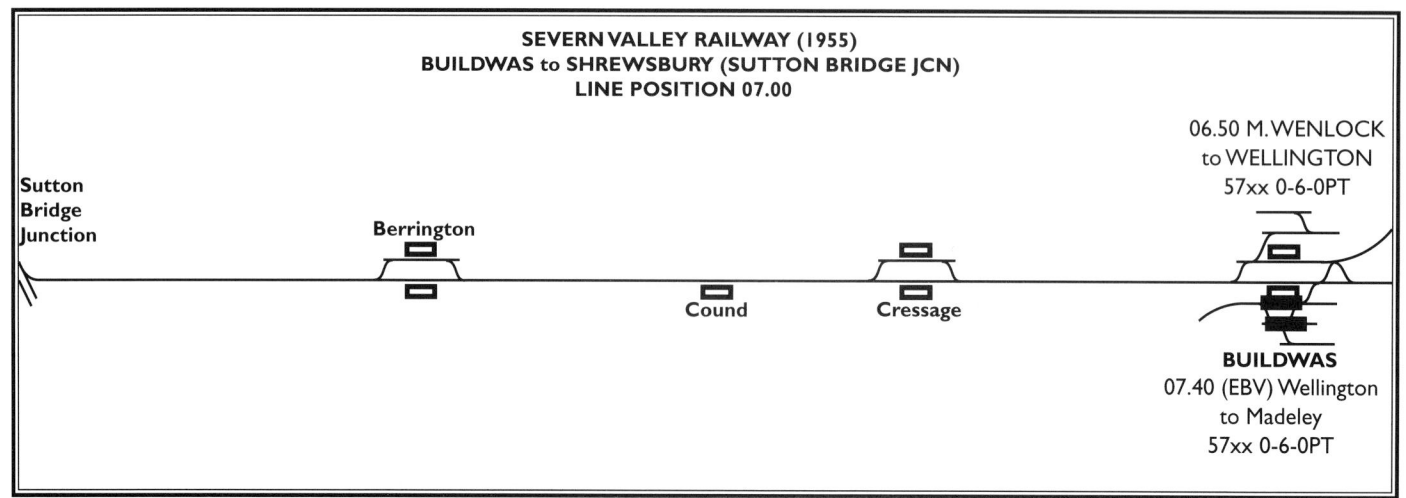

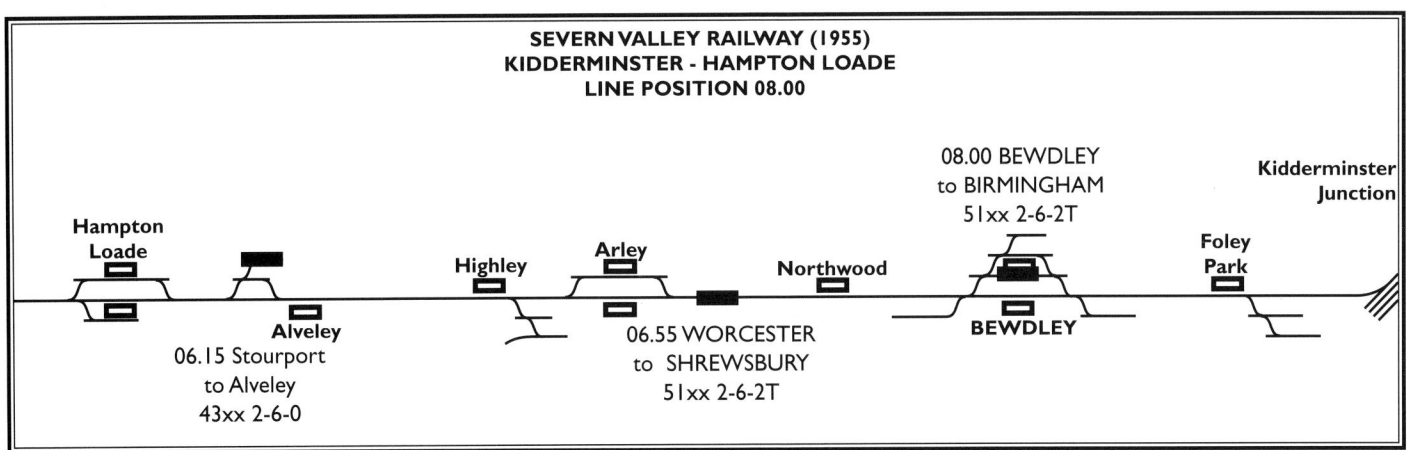

CONTROLLER'S LOG: Express trains are not a feature of the Severn Valley and the closest one can get to them are the through trains to Shrewsbury which, if not exactly express - they tend to stop at most stations - have the sense of being long distance services if for no better reason than the two hours they take to cover the forty miles of the Severn Valley.

One of the services in question is in section between Northwood and Arley and is notable for starting at Worcester as opposed to Hartlebury or Kidderminster. Pleasing as it doubtless must be for the locality of Worcester to have a through train to Shrewsbury, one suspects the gratitude might be reflected in greater booking office receipts if the service ran at a more civilised hour. Journeys made at more convenient times of day require a change of trains at Hartlebury (and often Bewdley as well) and it is surprising that better use is not made of the Severn Valley and its Railcars to give the important centres of Worcester and Shrewsbury a faster and more direct service. In point of fact the starting of the 06.55 at Worcester has little if anything to do with commercial affairs and exists to allow Worcester shed - partly through motive power politics and partly to retain route knowledge - to have a through working to Shrewsbury. The engine is a 51xx 2-6-2 tank; the standard for the line although 57xx Pannier tanks are often substituted since the ten coaches maximum of the latter are well in excess of normal loadings.

In one respect the 57xx 0-6-0T is a more suitable engine for the Shrewsbury service than the larger 51xx since the latter are restricted to 25 mph between Bewdley and Ironbridge. However the short distances between stations on this section together with the presence of several ordinary restrictions puts the line maximum of 50 mph beyond the reach of most engines.

Although Railcars play a prominent part in the workings local to Bewdley, the Shrewsbury service is very largely steam operated. The exceptions to the rule are the 10.35 ex Kidderminster and the 13.45 from Shrewsbury which are worked by one of the Worcester Railcars. No benefits - at least in terms of speed - accrue from the use of the railcar and when on Saturdays the train is worked by a 51xx 2-6-2T, the running times are identical to those of a weekday.

Goods traffic is very quiet at the moment. The 43xx 2-6-0 that worked the 06.15 empties from Stourport is shunting the yard at Alveley and putting a train of coal together which it will work to Hartlebury at 10.45. Gradients on the line are steep and none more so than at Alveley where the line climbs at 1 in 100 towards Highley. To counter this, coal trains for the south are backed out of the sidings onto the

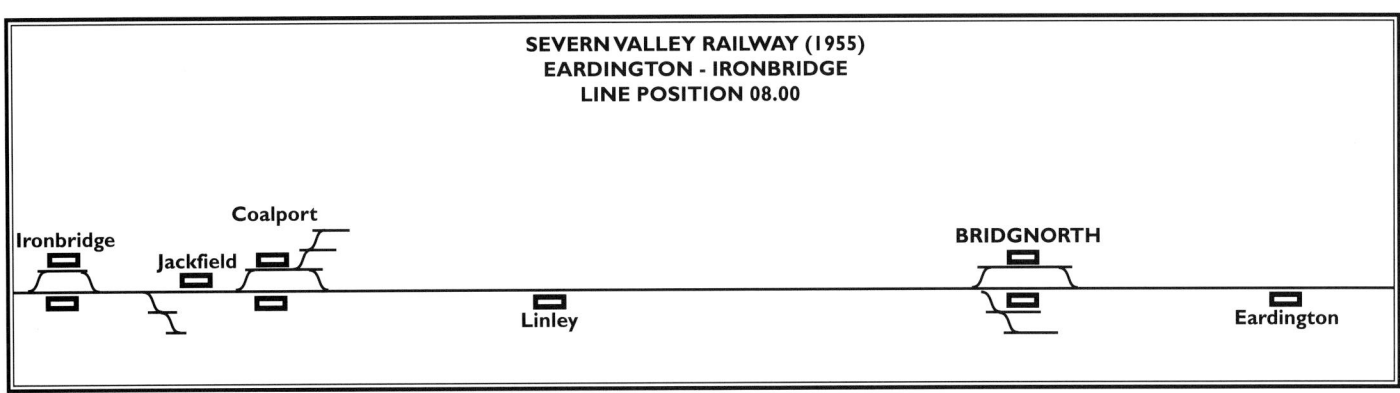

main line where a short easing of the gradient allows them to take a run at the bank. Using this ploy a 43xx is allowed to take 36 wagons of coal as opposed to a maximum of 25 when starting straight from the yard.

Buildwas Yard is also being attended to; the 57xx which arrived three-quarters of an hour ago is putting together a train of empties for the Wolverhampton area which it will work to Hollinswood at 10.40.

Of more immediate concern is the 08.15 Shrewsbury - Stourbridge Junction which has to cross the 06.55 Worcester - Shrewsbury at Buildwas and it does no harm to check that it is going to leave Shrewsbury on time.

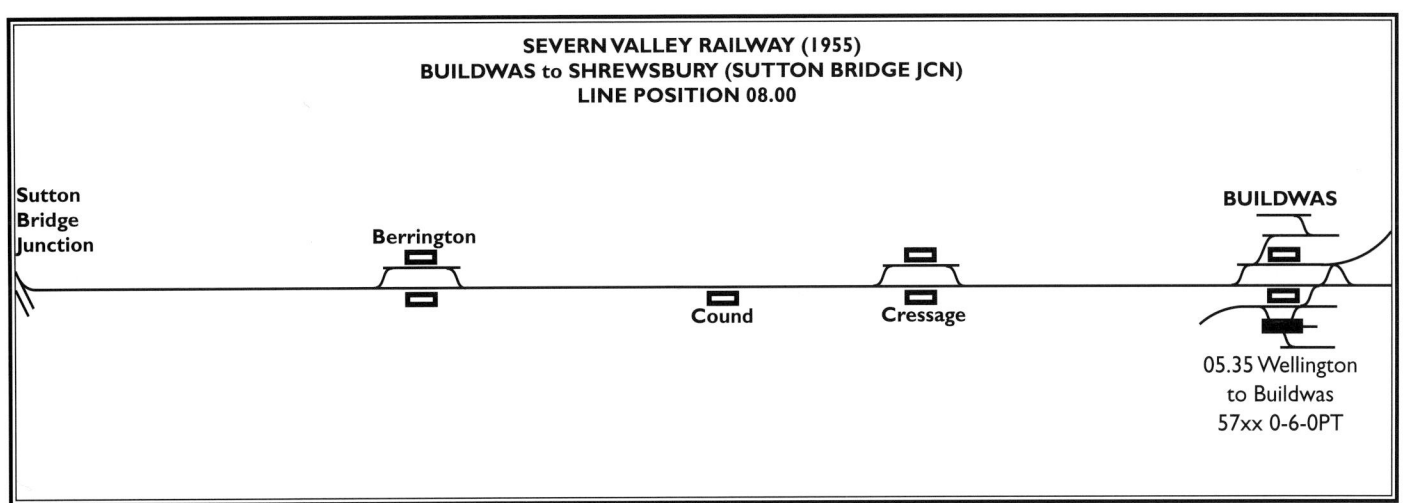

Bewdley was the focal point for passenger services with trains arriving from Kidderminster and Hartlebury to the south and from Shrewsbury and Woofferton in the north. An especial feature of the line was its dependence on GWR railcars with three of the Worcester allocation being used daily. These diesels came in especially useful on trains such as the 17.48 Kidderminster to Bewdley which turned round and returned to Kidderminster in two minutes. Most of the diesel workings were to the south of either Woofferton or Bridgnorth but one of the Shrewsbury services was worked by one of the railcars. On Saturday 19th September 1959 W19 in BR 'blood and custard' livery prepares to leave Bewdley with a down train as W29 (green livery) arrives from the north.

In an effort to find gainful employment for the class, some of BR's Standard 3MT 2-6-2T's were used on the Severn Valley, examples being allocated to Shrewsbury, Kidderminster and Wellington from time to time. 82007 of Shrewsbury is seen approaching Bewdley with the 08.15 Shrewsbury - Stourbridge Junction on Saturday 4th August 1956. The line on the far side of 82007 is the independent Bewdley - Woofferton branch. (Brian Moone: KRM)

In spite of its rural atmosphere, coal was very much the lifeblood of the Severn Valley with several train loads a day being worked from Alveley sidings to Stourport, Kidderminster and Worcester. Traffic flows were handicapped by a limit of forty-five wagons per train whilst 43xx 2-6-0's were restricted to thirty-six loaded vehicles. The 57xx 0-6-0 pannier tanks which shared in the coal traffic were limited to twenty-seven wagons. The engines which would have come very close to moving a full load - the 28xx 2-8-0's - were barred from the Bewdley - Ironbridge section. 43xx 2-6-0 6314 runs parallel with the Woofferton branch as it approaches Bewdley with an up coal train from Alveley. (Brian Moone: KRM)

Standing-in for a 2-6-2T, 57XX 0-6-0T 9656 of Shrewsbury calls at Northwood on Saturday 6th February 1960 with an up Severn Valley service. In some respects these diminutive engines were better suited to the Severn Valley line than the 51xx 2-6-2T's since the latter were subject to a number of speed restrictions between Bewdley and Ironbridge. (G.E.S. Parker: KRM).

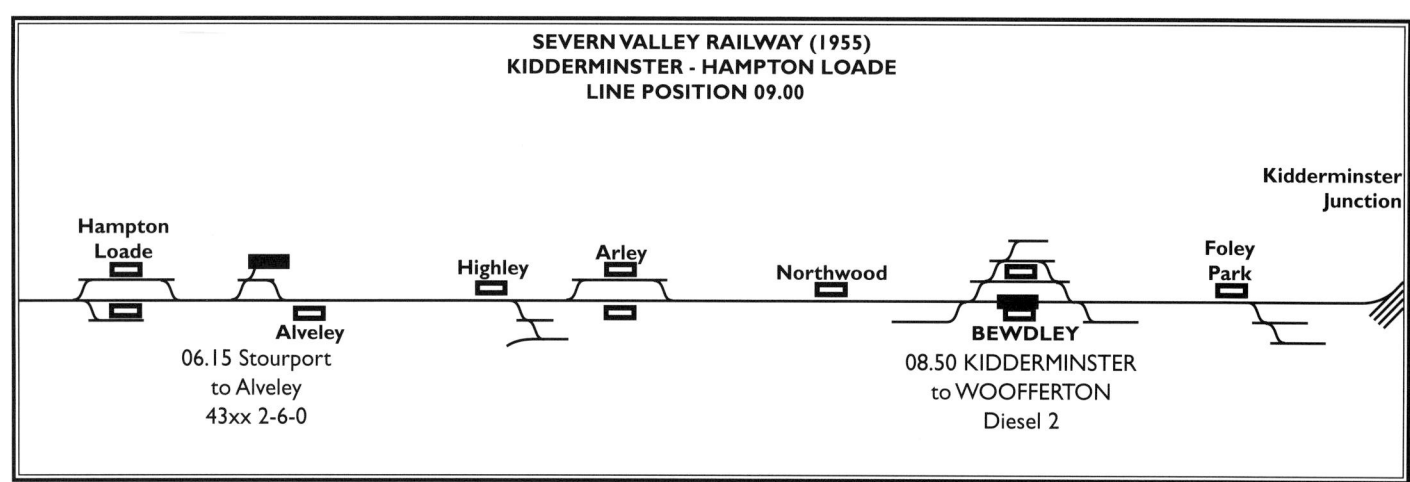

CONTROLLER'S LOG: The reason for asking Shrewsbury whether the 08.15 Salop - Stourbridge Junction was likely to leave on time - Shrewsbury could have been planning to hold the train to connect with a late-running North & West express - was to get the earliest possible intimation that the crossing at Buildwas with the 06.55 Worcester - Shrewsbury will not go as planned.

Unpunctuality is to be deplored on any railway but on single lines it is a major problem since trains can only cross at locations equipped with a passing loop.

Although railway timetables tend to reflect the more optimistic side of their compilers' nature, a good deal of flexibility is built into the Severn Valley schedules in order to counter a reasonable level of late running.

The 06.55 ex Worcester - now getting away from Buildwas after crossing the 08.15 from Shrewsbury - has five minutes at Hartlebury, six at Bewdley and seven at Bridgnorth: eighteen minutes that reduce considerably the possibility of its arriving late for its appointment at Buildwas. For its part the 08.15 ex Shrewsbury arrived in Buildwas no less than twelve minutes before the down train was due. Under these rather expansive arrangements, punctuality is all but assured.

There are, of course, times when crossing arrangements have to be adjusted and the guiding principal is that the train that is on time (or closest to it) will take priority. Thus, if the 06.55 ex Worcester had been running late from Bridgnorth, the 08.15 from Shrewsbury would have been allowed to leave Buildwas on time with the crossing being effected at Coalport.

Under normal circumstances the crossing of Shrewsbury trains is liberally distributed with Buildwas doing two crossings a day and Cressage, Arley and Bridgnorth one each.

Buildwas has enjoyed a relatively busy period of late and in addition to crossing the two Shrewsbury trains, it has played host to the Severn Junction's 08.16 Wellington to Much Wenlock. The engine is one of four 57xx 0-6-0PT's that work between Wellington and Much Wenlock although this particular example has the distinction of being the only engine of the day to work West of Much Wenlock; its next duty being the 09.35 goods from Much Wenlock to Longville. The latter was situated on the branch from Much Wenlock to Craven Arms and lost its passenger service in December 1951 after which the line's service was reduced to a single daily goods and parcels train.

The loss of the Craven Arms service did not entirely eliminate connections between the Severn Valley and the North & West main line since the line from Bewdley to Woofferton remains in use and provides an alternative route to Shrewsbury which, in spite of having to change trains at Woofferton, takes very little longer than the direct Severn Valley line. A Woofferton-bound waits to leave Bewdley with the 08.50 ex Kidderminster.

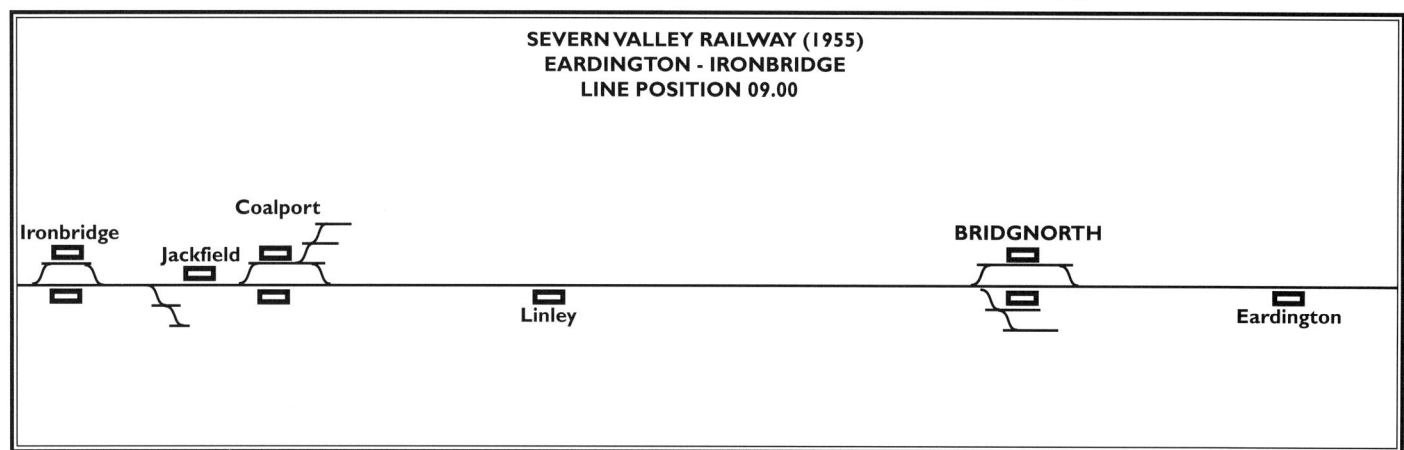

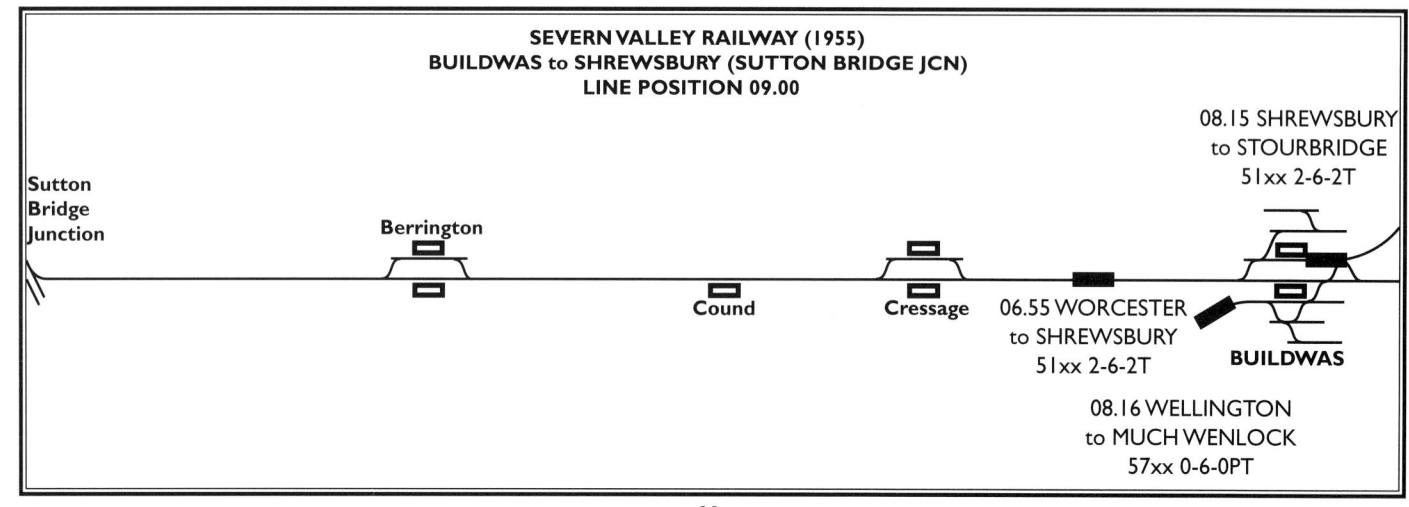

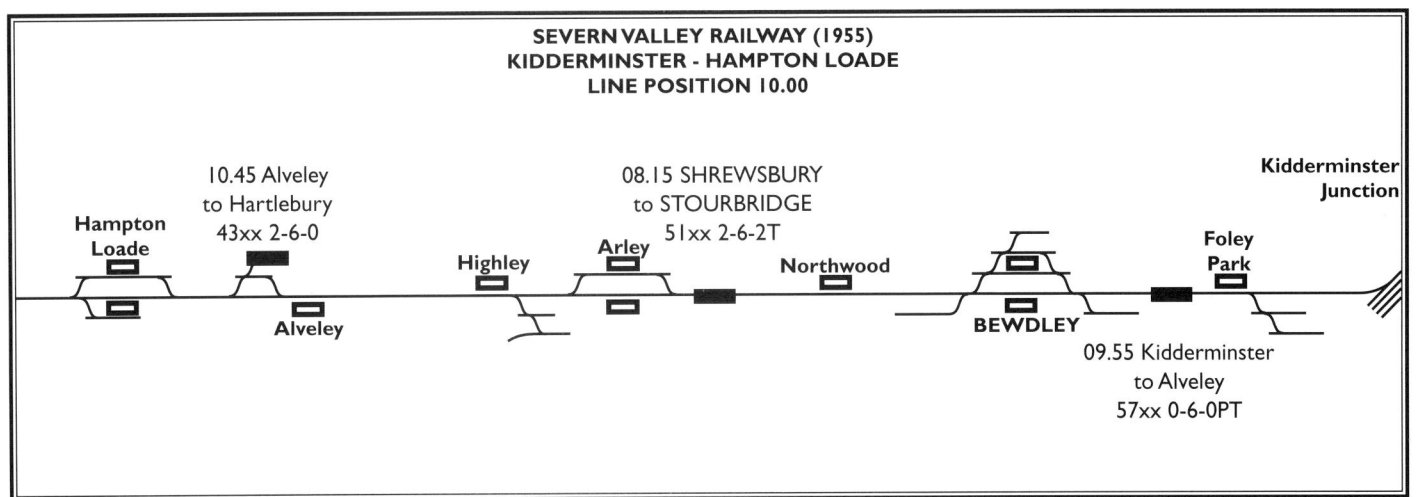

CONTROLLER'S LOG: Kidderminster Yard report the departure of the 09.55 goods to Alveley - engine 4641, 45 equal 45 empties - and a few minutes later Kidderminster Junction reports the train coming onto the branch. The train will reach Alveley in half an hour and will then work a couple of trips to Stourport. So far as the crew are concerned the turn is something of a mystery trip since between arriving at Alveley and leaving with the 14.20 to Worcester, that nearly 900 examples have been built. If, however, they have a weakness it is that they are not quite powerful enough for colliery work on heavily graded routes. The maximum length of any goods train on the Severn Valley is forty-five wagons and provided a train consists of ordinary goods traffic, forty five vehicles can be handled by something as small as a tiny 64xx 0-6-0T. However, coal is a great deal heavier than everyday goods and the most a 57xx can convey

The 57xx - which will have barked all the way up the 1 in 120 bank from Kidderminster Junction and will have laid a smoke screen over the greater part of Foley Park, is probably being driven on the presumption that the sooner it gets to Bewdley, the better its chances of a clear path through the station. Ironically, a clear path is more likely when the 57xx takes things easily up the bank since it cannot get onto the Bewdley - Arley section until the 08.15 Shrewsbury

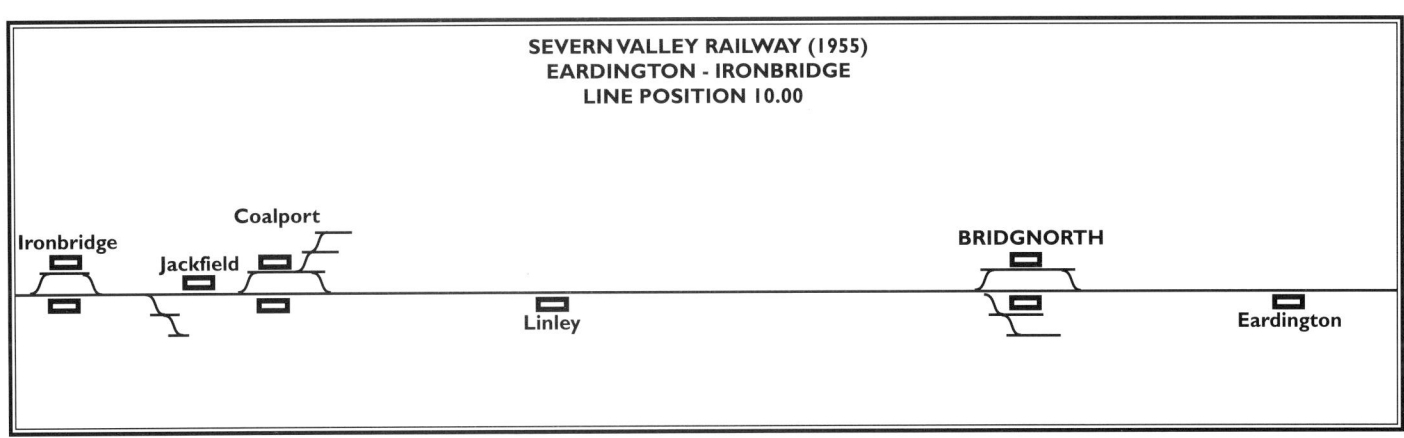

which they work as far as Hartlebury, they are at the Controller's disposal, to do as he wishes so long as they are back at Alveley in time for the Worcester train.

On four days a week the engine and men more often than not are given a train of Stourport coal, returning with empties whilst on the other days, usually Tuesdays and Fridays, they work a load of coal down to Coalport and Buildwas.

No-one can deny the usefulness of the 57xx engines, especially on routes such as the Severn Valley where they can be used for almost any duty that has to be covered. Little wonder southward from Alveley is a mere twenty-seven wagons which is not much more than half a train. Even a 43xx 2-6-0 can only handle thirty-six and it is therefore not difficult to understand why, at busy times, attempts are made to work certain 57xx diagrams with larger engines.

One would like to see a 28xx 2-8-0 used on the Alveley coal trains but although Blue engines are permitted to work over the Severn Valley, eight-coupled engines are prohibited from the Bewdley - Ironbridge section. This restriction is a drawback since a 28xx would be allowed to work forty-four wagon services.

passenger has arrived in Bewdley and that will not be until 10.06.

On the Severn Junction, the Kemberton colliery trip is running into Buildwas behind another 57xx. Upon arrival the engine will shunt its train out: part of the load being coal for the power station whilst the remainder is general coal and goods to be picked up later in the day by other services. Its shunting done, the engine will then perform a rather curious manoeuvre by running light down the Severn Valley to Shrewsbury to work the 11.50 goods from Coton Hill yard to Wellington.

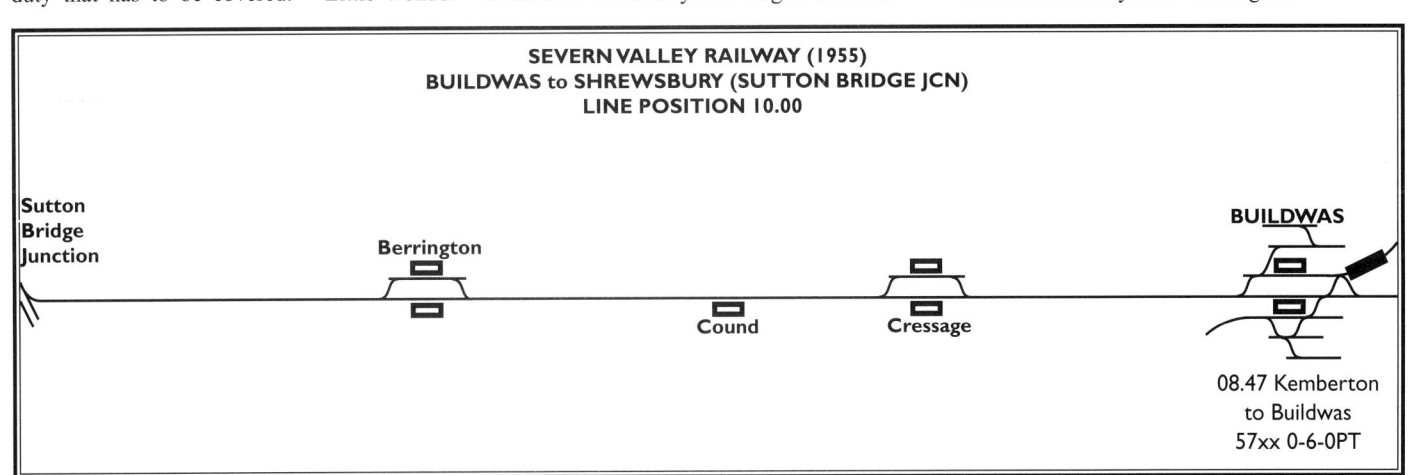

WORKING TIMETABLE - PASSENGER & GOODS

HARTLEBURY - BEWDLEY - WOOFFERTON (1955)

Train	05.05	Coupled			06.45		06.55			08.50			10.18		10.10		11.30
From	Worcs				Worcs		Worcs			Kidd			Kidd		H'bury		Kidd
Class	ECS	Light	Light	K	ECS	Auto	K	Pass	Pass	Auto	Pass	K	Pass	Pass	K	K	K	K
Shed	Worc 2	K 105	K 106	K 106	Worc 3	Leo 1	K 107	W 451	Worc 1	Leo 1	Worc 2	K 105	Worc 1	Worc 3	K 108	K 108	K 105	K 109
Engine	Diesel	57xx	43xx	43xx	Diesel	14xx	57xx	51xx	Diesel	14xx	Diesel	57xx	Diesel	Diesel	57xx	57xx	57xx	57xx
HARTLEBURY	05/25	05.39	05.39		07/02		07.10	07.22	08.10			08.22	09.22		10.10		10.40	
Sand Siding																		
Stourport		05.45	05.45				07.20	07.28	08.16			08.37	09.28		10.20	(10.20)	10.55	
Stourport	05/33			06.15	07/09			07.33	08.17				09.29		(10.35)	10.35		
Burlish								07.35	08.19				09.31					
BEWDLEY				06.26				07.40	08.24		08.59		09.36	10.27		10.45		11.40
BEWDLEY	05/40			06.36	07/14			07.53	08.25		09.00		09.39	10.29		11.05		11.50
Wyre Forest	(To			(To				(To	(To		09.11		(To	10.40		(To		
C. Mortimer	Highley)			Aveley)	07/26			Salop)	Arley)		09.18		Kidd)	10.47		B'nth)		12.17
Stop Board																		
Neen Sollars					07/31						09.25			10.55				
Newnham Bridge											09.30			11.01				
TENBURY WELLS					07.40						09.36			11.07				
TENBURY WELLS						07.58				08.45	09.40			11.09				
Easton Court						08.03				08.50	09.45			11.14				
WOOFFERTON						08.08				08.55	09.50			11.19				
Destination										Leo'mtr								

WOOFFERTON - BEWDLEY - HARTLEBURY (1955)

Train	06.22			08.35						10.45	11.15		11.25		14.20		
From	Highley			Arley						Alveley	Alveley		Salop		Alveley		
Class	Pass	Pass	Auto	Pass	Pass	Auto	EBV	K	Pass	K	K	Light	Pass	Pass	K	Pass	Pass
Shed	Worc 2	Worc 1	Leo 1	Worc 3	Worc 1	Leo 1	K 105	K 107	Worc 2	K 105	K 106	K 110	K 110	W 451	Worc 3	K 110	Worc 3	Worc 1
Engine	Diesel	Diesel	14xx	Diesel	Diesel	14xx	57xx	57xx	Diesel	57xx	43xx	57xx	57xx	51xx	Diesel	57xx	Diesel	Diesel
WOOFFERTON					07.35				08.30			10.05				12.22		15.47
Easton Court					07.41				08.36			10.11				12.27		15.53
TENBURY WELLS					07.45				08.40			10.15				12.32		15.57
TENBURY WELLS				07.57								10.20				12.33		16.00
Newnham Bridge				08.05								10.28				12.40		16.08
Neen Sollars				08.11								10.34				12.46		16.14
C. Mortimer				08.20								10.48				12.51		16.23
Wyre Forest				08.25								10.53				12.56		16.28
BEWDLEY	06.36			08.33	08.43							11.02	11.27			12.53	13.04	16.36
BEWDLEY	06.40	07.42		08.34	08.44							11.03	11.37	11/57		12.55	13.05	15/00	16.38	16.42
Burlish	06.46	07.47	(To		08.49									(To		13.01	(To	(To	16.47
Stourport	06.47	07.49	Kidd)		08.52			Kidd)			11.49	12.10		Kidd)		13.03	Kidd)	Kidd)	16.49
Stourport	06.48	07.50			08.53		09.00	10.20			11.50	12.00		12.20	13.05		15.25		16.50
Sand Siding																		
HARTLEBURY	06.54	07.57			08.59		09.10	10.30			12.00	12.10		12.28	13.12		15.35		16.56
Destination																Worc		

HARTLEBURY - BEWDLEY - WOOFFERTON (1955)

Train	11.30	11.30	11.30					14.10						16.48		18.25		
From	Kidd	Kidd	Kidd					Kidd						Kidd		Kidd		
Class	K	K	K	K	Light	K	Light	Pass	Pass	K	K	Pass	Auto	Pass	Pass	Pass	Pass	K
Shed	K 109	K 109	K 109	K 110	K 106	K 106	LM	Worc 3	K 117	SY 150A	K 105	Worc 1	Leo 1	K 110	Worc 1	Worc 3	SY 101	K 107
Engine	57xx	57xx	57xx	57xx	43xx	43xx	4F 0-6-0	Diesel	51xx	43xx	57xx	Diesel	14xx	57xx	Diesel	Diesel	51xx	57xx
HARTLEBURY				12.30		12.40		14.00	14.15		15.00	16.07			17.30		18.25	19.30
Sand Siding																		
Stourport				12.40				14.06	14.25		15.15	16.13			17.36		18.31	19.45
Stourport					12.40	13.10			14.08	14.40		16.14			17.42		18.34	
Burlish												16.16			17.44		18.36	
BEWDLEY				12.50		12.50		14.10	14.15	14.50		16.21			16.57	17.49	18.34	18.41
BEWDLEY				13.00		13.20	13.14	14.26	14.24	15.02					16.59	18.02	18.43	18.45
Wyre Forest				(To		(To	(To	14.37	(To						17.10	(To	18.54	(To
C. Mortimer	12.55			Alveley)		Alveley)	Kidd)	14.44	Salop)	Salop)					17.18	Highley)	19.00	Salop)
Stop Board	12.59																	
Neen Sollars	13.09	13.19						14.51							17.25		19.07	
Newnham Bridge		13.27	13.47					14.56							17.30		19.13	
TENBURY WELLS			13.57					15.02							17.36		19.19	
TENBURY WELLS				14.35				15.10						16.46	17.40		19.20	
Easton Court								15.15						16.51	17.45		19.25	
WOOFFERTON				14.50				15.20						16.56	17.50		19.30	
Destination															Leo'mtr			

WOOFFERTON - BEWDLEY - HARTLEBURY (1955)

Train		15.35	16.05	15.35	15.35		10.15	18.20	18.20	20.10		
From		W'ton	C. Arms	W'ton	W'ton		Salop	Leo'tr	Leo'tr	Kidd		
Class	K	K	K	Auto	K	K	K	SY 150	Pass	Pass	Pass	Light
Shed	K 109	K 109	Leo 1	K 109	K 109	K 105	SY 150	K 110	K 110	Tys	Worc 3	K 107
Engine	57xx	57xx	14xx	57xx	57xx	43xx	57xx	57xx	51xx	Diesel	57xx	
WOOFFERTON	15.25		16.30					18.35			19.50	
Easton Court			16.36					18.41			19.56	
TENBURY WELLS	15.39		16.40					18.46			20.00	
TENBURY WELLS		16.25							19.23		20.02	
Newnham Bridge		16.35		16.50					19.31		20.10	
Neen Sollars									19.37		20.16	
C. Mortimer				17.11	17.41				19.46		20.26	
Wyre Forest											20.31	
BEWDLEY				18.01	18.21				19.57	20.19	20.39	
BEWDLEY				18.11		18.45			19.59	20.28	20.41	
Burlish						(To			(To	20.33	(To	
Stourport						Kidd)	18.57		Kidd)	20.35	Kidd)	
Stourport				18.45	19.06					20.36	21.05	
Sand Siding												
HARTLEBURY				18.55	19.15					20.43	21.13	
Destination										Worcs		

24

For many years a Bristol (Bath Road) engine, LMS 2MT 2-6-2T 41202 moved to Shrewsbury in the early 1960's and took its turn in the working of the Severn Valley service. It is seen at Hartlebury on Saturday 7th April 1962, having arrived with the 13.45 ex Shrewsbury. The engine has run-round the stock and is preparing to dispose of the empty stock. On weekdays this was a turn for a diesel railcar. (Brian Moone: KRM)

43xx 2-6-0 5386 of Tyseley (Birmingham) approaches Woofferton with a main-line service from Shrewsbury to Hereford on Saturday 27th July 1957. The Bewdley branch can be seen diverging to the right. (V. R. Webster: KRM)

TENBURY WELLS

14xx 0-4-2T 1455 of Gloucester (out-based at Leominster) waits to leave Tenbury Wells with the Leominster Auto, the full details of which are given below.

By all appearances Tenbury Wells was one of many common or garden Great Western branch stations, comprising an up and down platform, a passing loop and a small goods yard. In fact it was one of the most unlikely border posts since the Bewdley - Woofferton branch upon which the station lay was not a continuous route but was formed of two separate lines which made an end-on Junction at Tenbury Wells. The situation arose from the fact that the first railway to Tenbury Wells had been the Tenbury Railway which opened in August 1861 as a branch of the Shrewsbury & Hereford which from 1862 became the joint property of the Great Western and London & North Western Railways. Three years later the Tenbury and Bewdley Railway opened and was absorbed by the Great Western Railway in 1869. Since joint railways remained outwith the scope of the 1923 grouping, Tenbury Wells remained a border post - in name if not in fact - until 1948.

As though fearing some legal nemesis, it took the Great Western something like thirty years to incorporate the Bewdley - Woofferton train service into one public timetable although ninety years after the route opened some trains continued to terminate at Tenbury. Why the morning empty railcar from Worcester to form the 07.57 Tenbury to Kidderminster could not have run through to Woofferton or, better still, Leominster is a question that will probably never be answered.

One lucrative but occasional source of revenue came from cattle traffic which could be heavy enough to warrant a special train. When this occurred a train of empty wagons would leave Stourbridge Junction at 13.10 to reach Tenbury at 14.41. Loading took most of the afternoon and the train would leave at 18.25, arriving back in Stourbridge Junction at 20.14.

TENBURY WELLS STATION WORKING : 1955			
Train	Arr	Engine	Dep Destination
06.45 ECS Worcester	07.40	Railcar: Worcester 3	
07.22 Ludlow	07.45	Leo 1 : Auto	
		Railcar: Worcester 3	07.57 Kidderminster
		Leo 1 : Auto	07.58 Woofferton
08.30 Woofferton	08.40	Leo 1 : Auto	
		Leo 1 : Auto	08.45 Leominster
08.50 Kidderminster	09.36	Railcar: Worcester 2	09.40 Woofferton
10.05 Woofferton	10.15	Railcar: Worcester 2	10.20 Kidderminster
10.18 Kidderminster	11.07	Railcar: Worcester 3	11.09 Woofferton
12.22 Woofferton	12.32	Railcar: Worcester 3	12.33 Kidderminster
11.30 Kidderminster (Goods)	13.57	57xx: Kidderminster 109	14.35 Woofferton
14.10 Kidderminster	15.02	Railcar: Worcester 3	15.10 Woofferton
15.25 Woofferton (Goods)	15.39	57xx: Kidderminster 109	
15.47 Woofferton	15.57	Railcar: Worcester 3	16.00 Kidderminster
		57xx: Kidderminster 109	16.25 Kidderminster (Goods)
16.05 Craven Arms	16.40	Leo 1 : Auto	
		Leo 1 : Auto	16.46 Woofferton
16.48 Kidderminster	17.36	57xx: Kidderminster 110	17.40 Leominster
18.20 Leominster	18.46	57xx: Kidderminster 110	
18.25 Kidderminster	19.19	Railcar: Worcester 3	19.20 Woofferton
		57xx: Kidderminster 110	19.23 Kidderminster
19.50 Woofferton	20.00	Railcar: Worcester 3	20.02 Kidderminster

LEOMINSTER 1 : 14xx 0-4-2T			
Arr	Station	Dep	Train
	Leominster MPD	06.30	Light
06.35	Leominster	06.45	Auto
07.36	Ludlow	07.22	Auto
07.45	Tenbury Wells	07.58	Auto
08.08	Woofferton	08.30	Auto
08.40	Tenbury Wells	08.45	Auto
08.55	Woofferton	08.56	Auto
09.08	Leominster		
	Work as Station Pilot		
	Leominster	15.15	Auto
15.48	Craven Arms	16.05	Auto
16.28	Woofferton	16.30	Auto
16.40	Tenbury Wells	16.46	Auto
16.56	Woofferton	17.53	Auto
18.01	Ludlow	18.15	Auto
18.33	Leominster	18.35	Light
18.40	Leominster MPD		

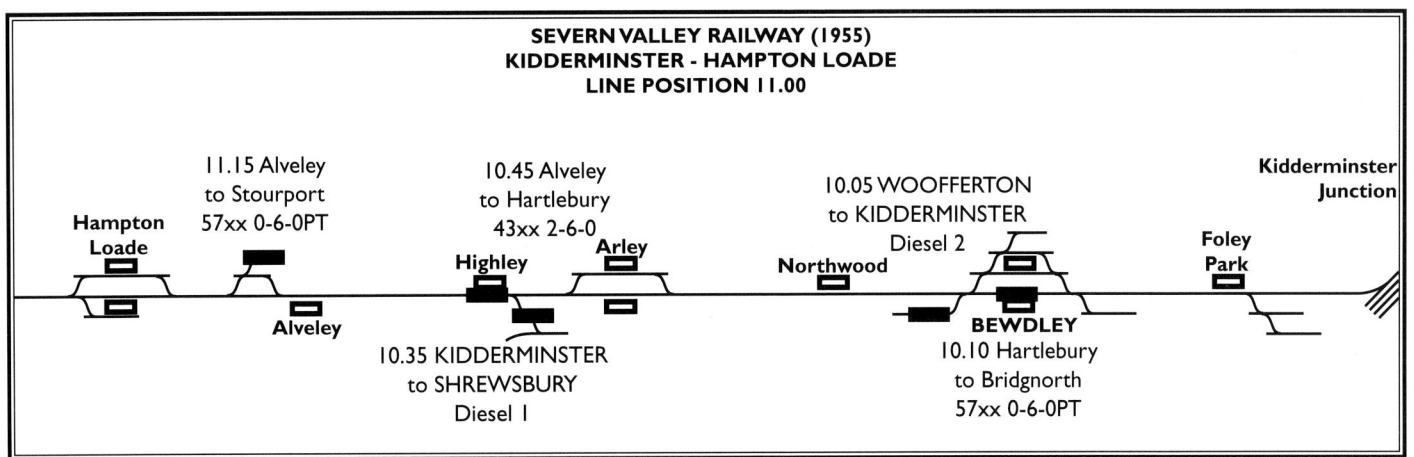

CONTROLLER'S LOG: As the Wellington 57xx which worked the Kemberton - Buildwas Goods disappears off the map at Sutton Bridge, the northern end of the Severn Valley - not to mention the Severn Junction - returns to its slumbers leaving the Southern section to shoulder the business of the moment, which is not inconsiderable.

Two single-line crossings are being executed, one at Arley and the other at Bewdley. The first of these involves an Alveley - Hartlebury based at Kidderminster.

The crossing is taking place at Highley chiefly because the goods is attaching traffic from the colliery connection there. One has to avoid the trap of thinking of Highley as a general crossing place since only two goods trains or a passenger and a goods are allowed to pass there. The crossing of two passenger trains is not allowed at Highley.

As remarked upon, the use of a railcar in a Shrewsbury service is unusual and it

The second crossing is being made at Bewdley where the 10.10 Hartlebury - Bridgnorth goods waits for the 10.05 Woofferton - Kidderminster Railcar.

The Woofferton service is almost entirely Railcar-worked and the only exceptions are a morning and evening 0-4-2T auto between Tenbury Wells and Woofferton plus the 16.48 Kidderminster - Leominster. The Railcar working the service now approaching Bewdley has been shuttling around the area for some

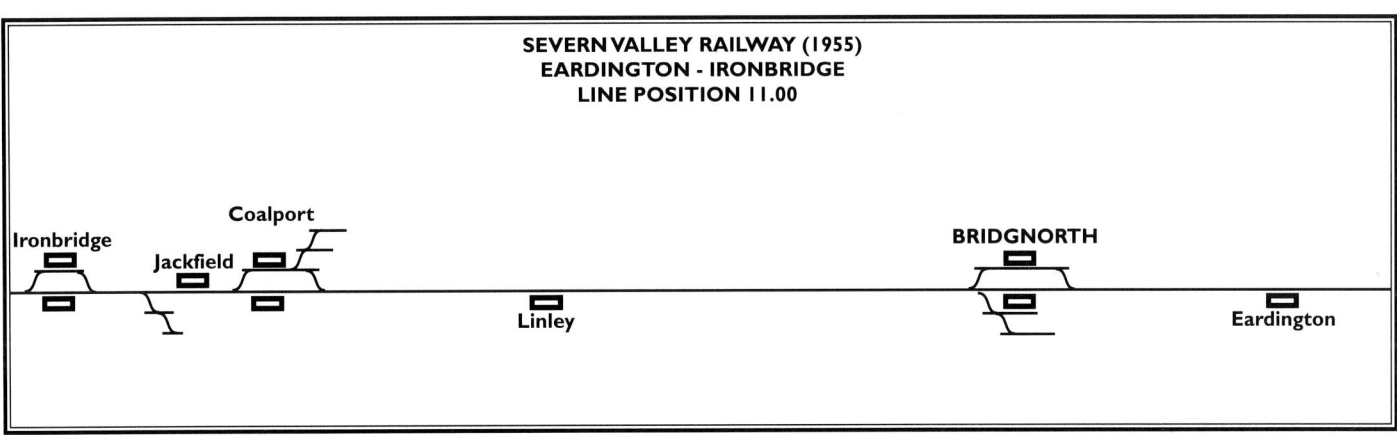

goods and the late-morning Kidderminster - Shrewsbury Passenger, the latter being the only Shrewsbury service to be worked by a GWR Railcar.

The goods is the return working of the 06.15 from Stourport, the engine of which will do another trip to Alveley in the afternoon. It is a working that generates more than its fair share of complaints at Kidderminster loco because of the amount of tender-first running involved. The result of the complaints was an increase from one to four in the number of 43xx engines demonstrates the range of workings to which these units can be put. In the course of an eighteen-hour day, the railcar works no less than twenty-three trains and although many of them are of very short duration, it is still an impressive performance. During the middle of the day demand for local travel tapers off and the diesel is free to fill in with a trip to Shrewsbury and back; the return trip being with the 13.45 Shrewsbury to Kidderminster.

Altogether three GWR Railcars can be seen at work on the Severn Valley.

hours but will not be seen again on the Severn Valley since it transfers to an interestingly varied set of workings that take in Malvern Wells, Honeybourne and Stratford-on-Avon.

Any minute now the guard of the train working at Aveley will call up and ask for the road for his 57xx 0-6-0T and train of 27 wagons of Stourport coal. If he can get it away by 11.15 then the engine can propel its load out onto the main line after the passage of the Shrewsbury Railcar and cross the down Bridgnorth Goods at Arley.

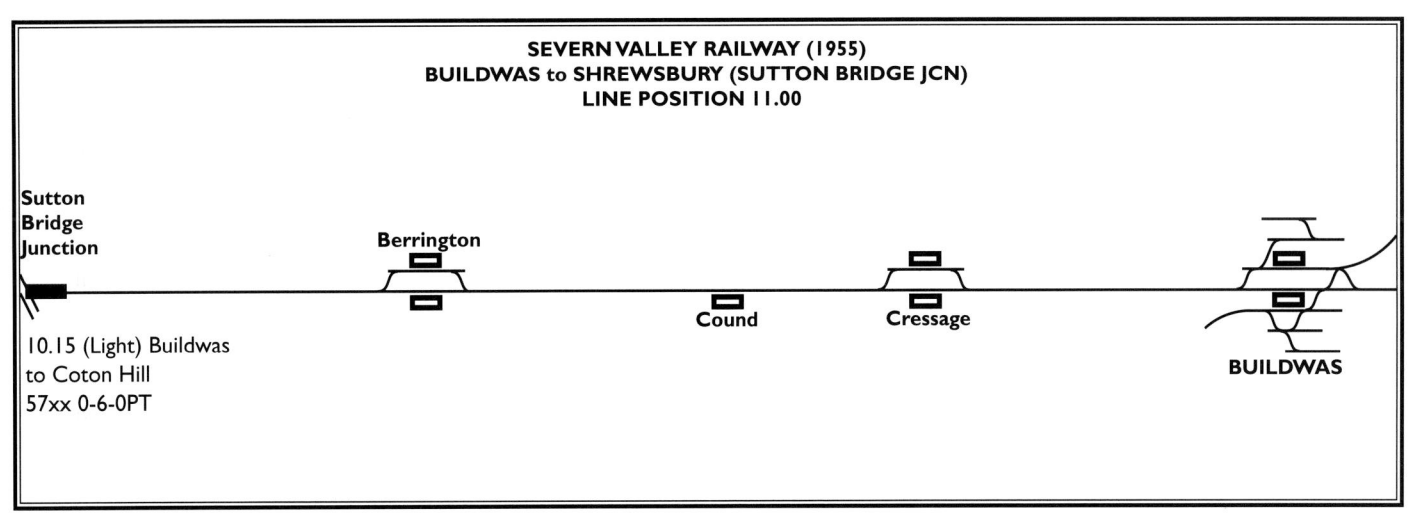

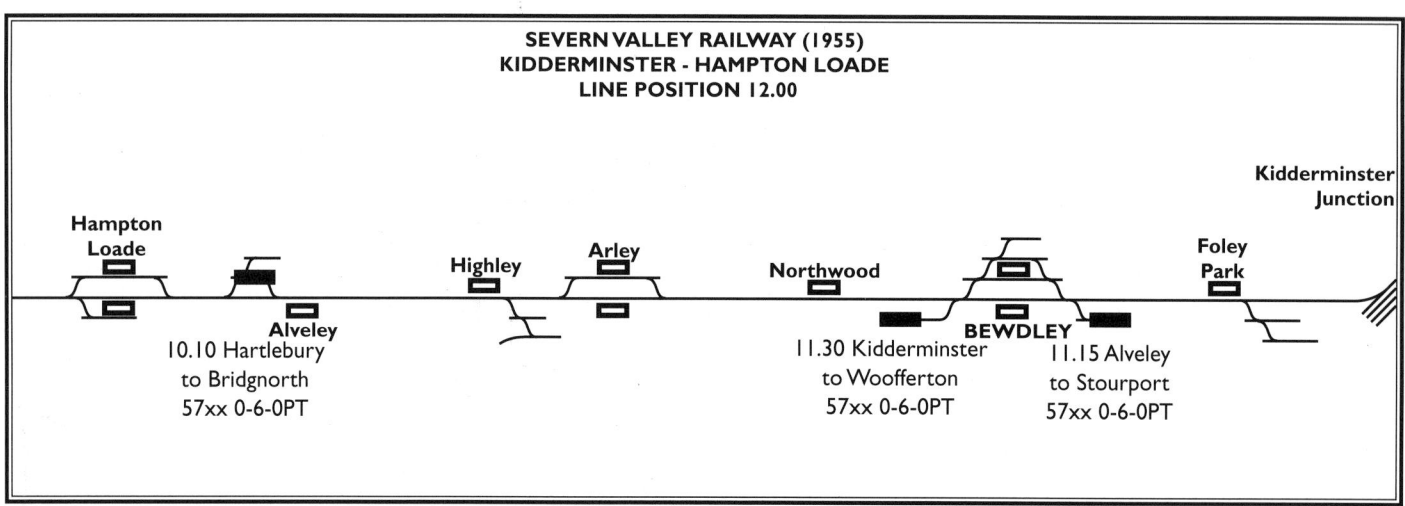

CONTROLLER'S LOG: Like a flare, Buildwas flashes into life and then fades away; the staff dealing with five trains in almost as many minutes. A pair of Shrewsbury trains - one diesel and the other a 2-6-2T - meet in the Severn Valley platforms whilst in the high level section of the station a couple of Severn Junction services pass. It may be thought that the Wellington - Much Wenlock service would be better served by diesel railcars rather than are standing back to back. To prevent corners from being cut, a member of the traffic staff has to be present to handsignal the operation whilst the Station Master also has to be present to supervise if at all possible.

Also present as Buildwas is the daily Shrewsbury to Hartlebury goods which has followed the Up Passenger from Cressage. The service can claim something of a record since it is timed to take exactly nine hours to cover Bewdley section with a trio of 57xx 0-6-0 PT's going their various ways. The 11.15 ex Alveley - the working that occasionally runs to Buildwas - has just crossed the 11.30 Kidderminster to Woofferton goods at Bewdley whilst the daily Hartlebury to Bridgnorth goods has gone inside at Alveley to drop off empties and pick up coal traffic for Bridgnorth and Hampton Loade. It will resume its journey north in about forty minutes time when the 11.25 Shrewsbury -

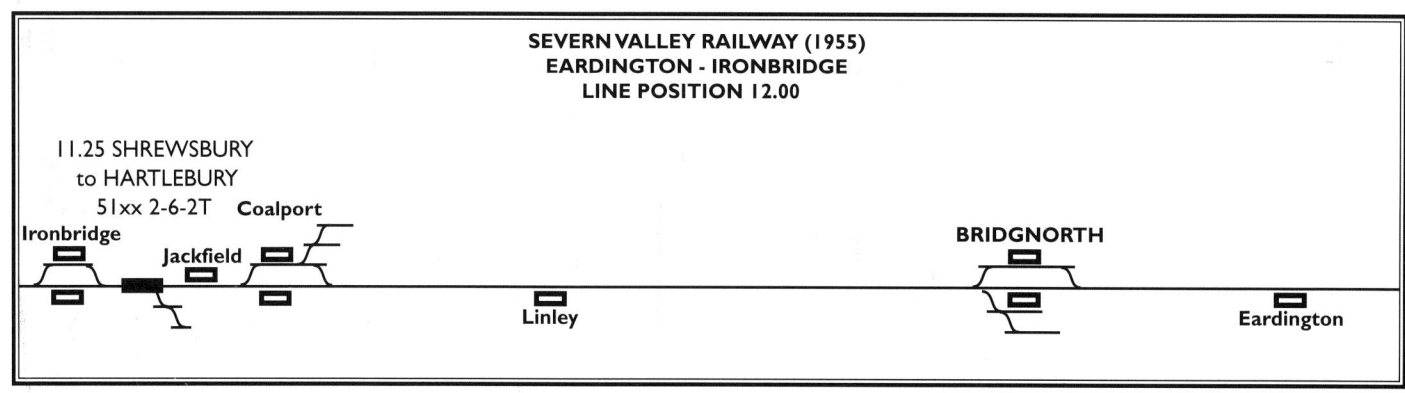

57xx Pannier Tanks which are associated more with goods work than passenger. In fact diesels were tried on the line during the late 1930's but were quite unequal to the Severn Junction gradients which are fearsome. For most of the distance between Wellington and Lightmoor Junction, the line climbs at about 1 in 45 whilst the section from Buildwas to Much Wenlock is even steeper. The railcars retired defeated!

The arrangements for crossing trains in the high level platform is unusual to say the least but the regulations allow a second train (from either direction) to run past the station on the loop and reverse into the platform so that both services the forty-one miles - four and a half miles per hour - between Coton Hill Yard and Hartlebury. Some of this time is attributable to the curious way in which the train doubles back on itself as it makes its way south.

Reaching Coalport at 13.13, the train reverses direction and runs back to Ironbridge, serving Maw and Jackfield Sidings en route. At 15.00 the service leaves Ironbridge for the second time and runs normally as far as Bridgnorth where it spends two hours in shunting and waiting to meet and change footplates with its opposite number, the 14.15 Hartlebury to Coton Hill.

Goods traffic is also in evidence in the Hartlebury Passenger clears the section from Hampton.

It may be noticed that freight traffic coming onto the line is not concentrated at Kidderminster but is worked from Hartlebury and Stourport as well. The relatively heavy flows from Stourport reflects the coal traffic between the power station and Alveley whilst that from Hartlebury consists largely of mineral empties for Alveley brought in from the outside world plus coal traffic for the local stations. Traffic from Kidderminster is generally for the Woofferton branch and worked by the 11.30 although a train of mineral empties is also run daily to Alveley.

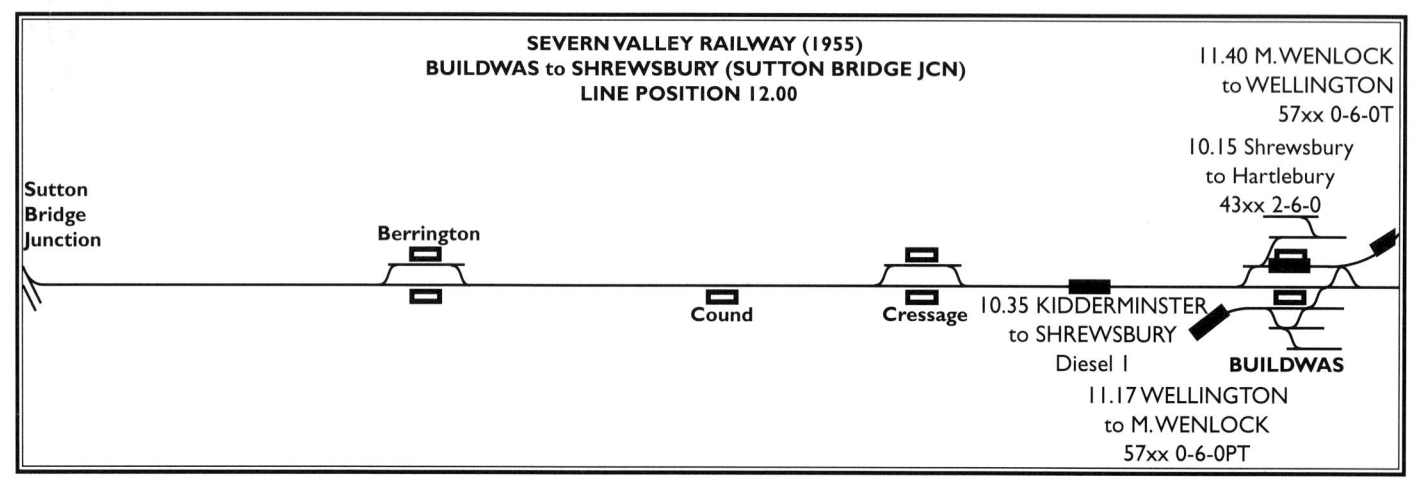

G.W.R. DIESEL RAILCARS

Externally the railcars fell into two broad categories: the early cars that were streamlined (the original Flying Banana's) and the later - post 1937 - vehicles which were much more angular in appearance. Internally all the railcars had a far closer resemblance to a bus than a train. W20, one of the later examples, waits at Newnham Bridge with a Woofferton to Kidderminster service. This was an especially well-travelled member of the class and not only did it spend some time during 1944 with the LNER at Newcastle but worked pre-dmu trials between Leeds City and Harrogate in 1952.

Although in many respects the Great Western Railway was a very conservative undertaking, there were instances when it demonstrated a talent for highly original thinking. Amongst these ideas were such things as corridor coaches, the first Pacific engine, 70' coaching stock and - perhaps the most far-sighted of all - diesel railcars and multiple units. Introduced in stages between 1934 and 1942, the Great Western eventually possessed thirty-eight diesel railcars, four of which worked in pairs on express services whilst the remainder were employed on a wide variety of branch and secondary work. Cutting running costs by about a third - only a driver and guard were needed - the wonder is that it took the rest of the country nearly thirty years to follow the GWR's example.

The degree to which railcars interacted with conventional workings varied. On some routes they were seen only a few times a day whilst on others they came close to having a monopoly of the service and this was very nearly the case on the Severn Valley where twelve of the eighteen northbound passenger trains from Bewdley were worked by railcars. Depressing as this state of affairs might have appeared a generation on, up to 1960 the railcars were viewed as novelties and were as much a part and parcel of the Great Western portfolio as the Pannier or 2-6-2 tanks. Most of the railcar workings were on the Woofferton branch - where they worked the majority of services - or over the southern half of the Severn Valley. Only one railcar penetrated the latter north of Bridgnorth; the through service to Shrewsbury being steam-worked except for one train in each direction. As can be judged from the table below, the railcars worked long hours and covered an impressive variety of trains. Observers at Bewdley were sometimes surprised to find that only three railcars were used on the Severn Valley and Woofferton services - there seemed to be more.

| Worcester (SH) GWR RAILCAR WORKINGS - 1955 ||||||||||
| RAILCAR 1. ||| RAILCAR 2 ||| RAILCAR 3 |||
Arr	Station	Dep	Arr	Station	Dep	Arr	Station	Dep
	Worcester (SH)	04.50 ECS		Worcester (SH)	05.05 ECS		Worcester (SH)	06.45 ECS
05.17	Kidderminster	05.48	05.51	Highley	06.22	07.40	Tenbury Wells	07.57
06.18	Alveley	06.20 ECS	06.36	Bewdley	06.40	08.43	Kidderminster	10.18
06.23	Hampton Loade	06.30	06.54	Hartlebury	07.07 ECS	11.19	Woofferton	12.22
06.33	Alveley	06.35 ECS	07.13	Kidderminster	07.22	13.13	Kidderminster	14.10
06.38	Hampton Loade	07.00	07.54	Henwick	08.04	15.20	Woofferton	15.47
07.21	Bewdley	07.42	08.38	Kidderminster	08.50	17.47	Kidderminster	17.48
07.57	Hartlebury	08.10	09.50	Woofferton	10.05	17.58	Bewdley	18.00
08.32	Arley	08.35	11.12	Kidderminster	11.35	18.10	Kidderminster	18.25
08.59	Hartlebury	09.22	12.28	Malvern W	13.05	19.30	Woofferton	19.50
09.36	Bewdley	09.39	13.30	Worcester (SH)	13.35	20.50	Kidderminster	21.02
09.48	Kidderminster	10.35	14.05	Evesham	14.40	21.27	Worcester (SH)	21.45 ECS
12.32	Shrewsbury	13.45	15.15	Stratford	16.00	22.05	Gt Malvern	22.15
15.45	Kidderminster	15.54	17.05	Worcester (SH)	17.18	22.48	Droitwich Spa	22.53 ECS
16.00	Hartlebury	16.07	17.45	Malvern W	18.10	23.05	Worcester (SH)	(06.45)
16.21	Bewdley	16.42	18.35	Worcester (SH)	19.45			
16.56	Hartlebury	17.30	20.05	Gt Malvern	20.14			
18.16	Highley	18.20	20.31	Worcester (SH)	21.20			
18.44	Kidderminster	19.20	22.10	Honeybourne	22.40			
19.44	Highley	19.55	23.16	Worcester (SH)	(05.05)			
20.10	Bewdley	20.26						
20.58	Bridgnorth	21.05						
21.45	Kidderminster	22.05						
22.33	Worcester (SH)	(04.50)						

STATION WORKING : BEWDLEY (1955)

Train	Arrive	Engine	Shed	Dep	Destination
05.10 Kidderminster ECS		51xx 2-6-2T	Kidd 100	05/19	Arley (05.25)
05.05 Worcester ECS		Diesel 2	Worcester	05/40	Highley (05.51)
05.50 Arley	05.58	51xx 2-6-2T	Kidd 100	05.59	Birmingham
05.48 Kidderminster	05.59	Diesel 1	Worcester	06.00	Highley (06.18)
06.15 Stourport (Goods)	06.26	43xx 2-6-0	Kidd 106	06.36	Alveley (06.59)
06.22 Highley	06.36	Diesel 2	Worcester	06.40	Hertlebury (06.54)
05.45 Birmingham	07.09	51xx 2-6-2T	Tyseley		
06.45 Worcester ECS		Diesel 3	Worcester	07/14	Tenbury Wells (07.40)
07.00 Hampton Loade	07.21	Diesel 1	Worcester		
		51xx 2-6-2T	Tyseley	07.25	Birmingham
06.55 Worcester	07.40	51xx 2-6-2T	Worc 451		(Fwd at 07.53)
		Diesel 1	Worcester	07.42	Hartlebury (07.57)
06.15 Birmingham	07.44	51xx 2-6-2T	Tyseley		
(06.45 Worcester)		51xx 2-6-2T	Worc 451	07.53	Shrewsbury (09.21)
		51xx 2-6-2T	Tyseley	08.00	Birmingham
08.10 Hartlebury	08.24	Diesel 1	Worcester	08.25	Arley (08.32)
07.57 Tenbury Wells	08.33	Diesel 3	Worcester	08.34	Kidderminster (08.43)
08.35 Arley	08.43	Diesel 1	Worcester	08.44	Hartlebury (08.59)
08.50 Kidderminster	08.59	Diesel 2	Worcester	09.00	Woofferton (09.50)
09.22 Hartlebury	09.36	Diesel 1	Worcester		
		Diesel 1	Worcester	09.39	Kidderminster (09.48)
09.55 Kidderminster (Empties)	10.03	57xx 0-6-0PT	Kidd 110	10.08	Alveley (10.30)
08.15 Shrewsbury	10.08	51xx 2-6-2T	Salop 100	10.09	Stourbridge Jcn
10.18 Kidderminster	10.27	Diesel 3	Worcester	10.29	Woofferton (11.19)
10.10 Hartlebury (Goods)	10.45	57xx 0-6-0PT	Kidd 108		(Fwd at 11.05)
10.35 Kidderminster	10.44	Diesel 1	Worcester	10.45	Shrewsbury (12.32)
10.05 Woofferton	11.01	Diesel 2	Worcester	11.03	Kidderminster (11.12)
(10.10 Hartlebury Goods)		57xx 0-6-0PT	Kidd 108	11.05	Bridgnorth (13.09)
10.45 Alveley (Mineral)	11.27	43xx 2-6-0	Kidd 106	11.37	Hartlebury (12.10)
11.30 Kidderminster (Goods)	11.40	57xx 0-6-0PT	Kidd 109	11.50	Woofferton (14.50)
12.10 Light ex Stourport	12.20	57xx 0-6-0PT	Kidd 107		(For 12.50 Goods)
12.30 Light ex Stourport	12.40	57xx 0-6-0PT	Kidd 105		(To Pilot 12.50 Gds)
		2 x 57xx	Kidd 105/107	12.50	Kidderminster Goods (13.00)
11.25 Shrewsbury	12.53	51xx 2-6-2T	Worc 451	12.55	Hartlebury (13.12)
12.40 light ex Hartlebury	12.58	4F 0-6-0	Aston		(Departs 13.14)
12.22 Woofferton	13.04	Diesel 3	Worcester	13.05	Kidderminster (13.13)
		4F 0-6-0	Aston	13.14	Kidderminster (Light)
13.10 Stourport (Empties)		43xx 2-6-0	Kidd 106	13/20	Alveley (13.40)
14.00 Hartlebury	14.15	51xx 2-6-2T	Kidd 110	14.24	Shrewsbury (15.58)
14.10 Kidderminster	14.19	Diesel 3	Worcester	14.26	Woofferton (15.20)
14.15 Hartlebury (Goods)	14.50	43xx 2-6-0	Salop 150A		(Depart at 15.02)
14.20 Alveley (Goods)		57xx 0-6-0PT	Kidd 110	15/00	Worcester
(14.15 Hartlebury Goods)		43xx 2-6-0	Salop 150A	15.02	Shrewsbury (21.14)
15.00 Alveley (Goods)		43xx 2-6-0	Kidd 106	15/23	Kidderminster (15.33)
13.45 Shrewsbury	15.34	Diesel 1	Worcester	15.36	Kidderminster (15.45)
13.45 Bridgnorth (Goods)	16.19	57xx 0-6-0PT	Kidd 108		(Departs 17.10)
16.07 Hartlebury	16.21	Diesel 1	Worcester		
16.23 Kidderminster	16.33	51xx 2-6-2T	Salop 100	16.38	Shrewsbury (18.15)
15.47 Woofferton	16.36	Diesel 3	Worcester	16.38	Kidderminster (16.47)
		Diesel 1	Worcester	16.42	Hartlebury (16.56)
16.48 Kidderminster	16.57	57xx 0-6-0PT	Kidd 110	16.59	Leominster
(13.45 Bridgnorth)		57xx 0-6-0PT	Kidd 108	17.10	Kidderminster Goods (17.20.)
15.50 Shrewsbury	17.22	51xx 2-6-2T	Salop 101	17.24	Kidderminster (17.34)
17.48 Kidderminster	17.58	Diesel 3	Worcester	18.00	Kidderminster
17.30 Hartlebury	17.49	Diesel 1	Worcester	18.02	Highley (18.16)
15.25 Woofferton (Goods)	18.01	57xx 0-6-0PT	Kidd 109	18.11	Kidderminster (18.22)
10.15 Shrewsbury (Goods)	18.21	43xx 2-6-0	Salop 150		(Departs 18.45)
18.20 Highley	18.34	Diesel 1	Worcester	18.35	Kidderminster (18.44)
18.25 Kidderminster	18.34	Diesel 3	Worcester	18.43	Woofferton (19.30)
18.25 Hartlebury	18.41	51xx 2-6-2T	Salop 101	18.45	Shrewsbury (20.17)
(10.15 Shrewsbury)		43xx 2-6-0	Salop 150	18.45	Hartlebury (19.15)
17.33 Shrewsbury	19.06	51xx 2-6-2T	Kidd 110	19.09	Kidderminster (19.18)
19.20 Kidderminster	19.29	Diesel 1	Worcester	19.30	Highley (19.44)
18.20 Leominster	19.57	57xx 0-6-0PT	Kidd 110	19.59	Kidderminster (20.08)
19.55 Highley	20.10	Diesel 1	Worcester		
20.10 Kidderminster	20.19	51xx 2-6-2T	Worcester		
		Diesel 1	Worcester	20.26	Bridgnorth (20.58)
		51xx 2-6-2T	Worcester	20.28	Worcester (20.10 ex Kidderminster)
20.20 Kidderminster ECS	20.31	57xx 0-6-0PT	Kidd 110		
19.50 Woofferton	20.39	Diesel 3	Worcester	20.41	Kidderminster (20.50)
		57xx 0-6-0PT	Kidd 110	20.50	Light to Kidderminster
21.05 Bridgnorth	21.34	Diesel 1	Worcester	21.35	Kidderminster (21.45)

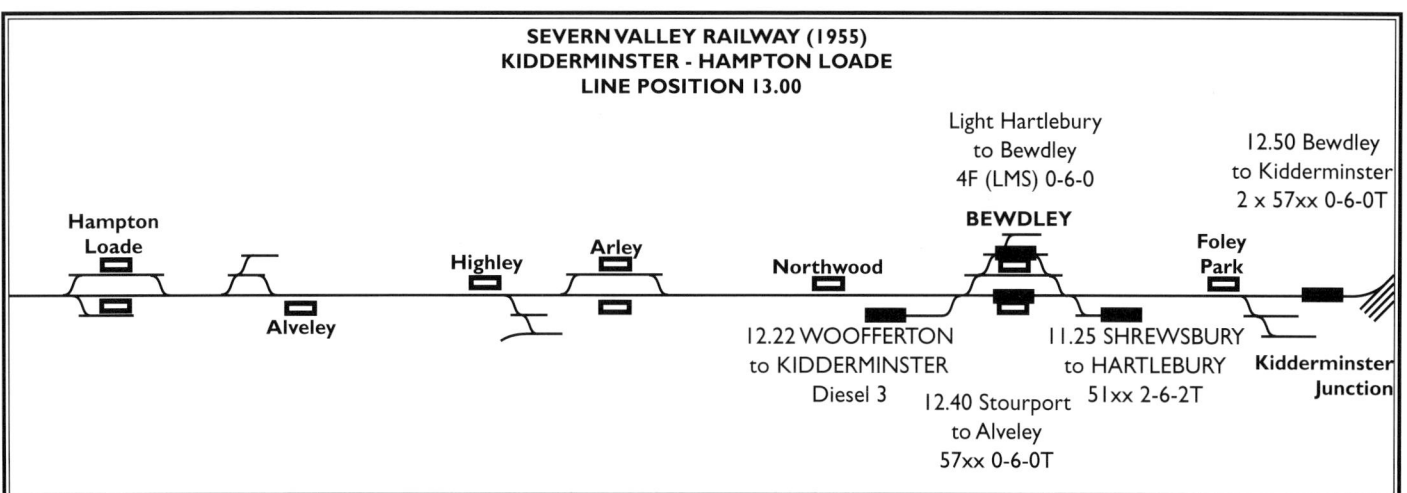

CONTROLLER'S LOG: Situated in the heart of the Great Western, foreign engines are not a regular feature of Severn Valley life and observers at Bewdley are likely therefore to be rather surprised at the object - an LMS 4F 0-6-0 goods engine - waiting for the road to Kidderminster.

Given the presence of the Midland at Worcester, only fifteen miles away, one's surprise is heightened by the fact the visitor is not from the Midland at all but the LNWR and is based at Walsall shed. The reason for its appearance is that some of the locally used coal is imported from the Nottingham pits and is brought by the Midland to Wichnor Junction, a few miles south of Burton on Trent, where it is handed over to the LNW. The latter work it as a through train to Hartlebury, routing it via Lichfield and Wednesbury to join the Great Western at Dudley. The engine returns with the 14.04 Hartlebury to Walsall but has to turn first which it does by running tender-first to Kidderminster Junction via Bewdley. It is the only booked instance of a non-GWR engine appearing on the Severn Valley.

Ahead of the LMS 4F is the 12.40 Stourport to Alveley, its 57xx 0-6-0 Pannier trailing a string of empties for Highley Colliery. It has been waiting for the 11.25 Shrewsbury - Hartlebury to clear the section and is now pulling ahead - and almost certainly rattling a few windows - in order to get across the Junction without delaying the 12.22 Railcar which is on its way up from Woofferton.

This is the 57xx's second trip of the day to Alveley - it earlier worked the 09.55 from Kidderminster - and will finish with the 14.20 back to Hartlebury.

By now it will be appreciated that in terms relative to the Severn Valley, Alveley is not only a location of some importance but is by quite a margin the most profitable point on the system. Two services have already taken out traffic to Hartlebury and Stourport and there will be another three departures before the yard staff finish work at 16.00.

The 12.40 ex Stourport will form the 14.20 to Worcester, changing engines at Hartlebury, while a 43xx 2-6-0 will arrive in about forty minutes time with the 13.10 empties from Stourport to work out with the 15.00 to Kidderminster. Traffic for local stations and anything left by the two services mentioned will be picked up by the Bridgnorth goods on its way back to Kidderminster. If anything is left behind then consideration will be given to running a special using the Stourport pilot.

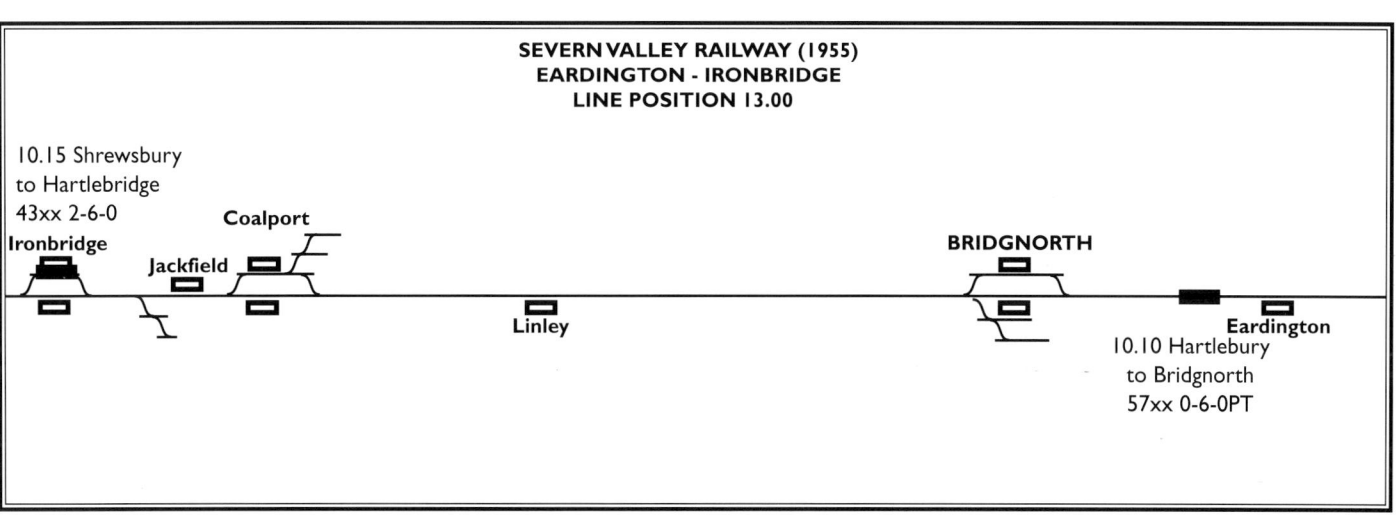

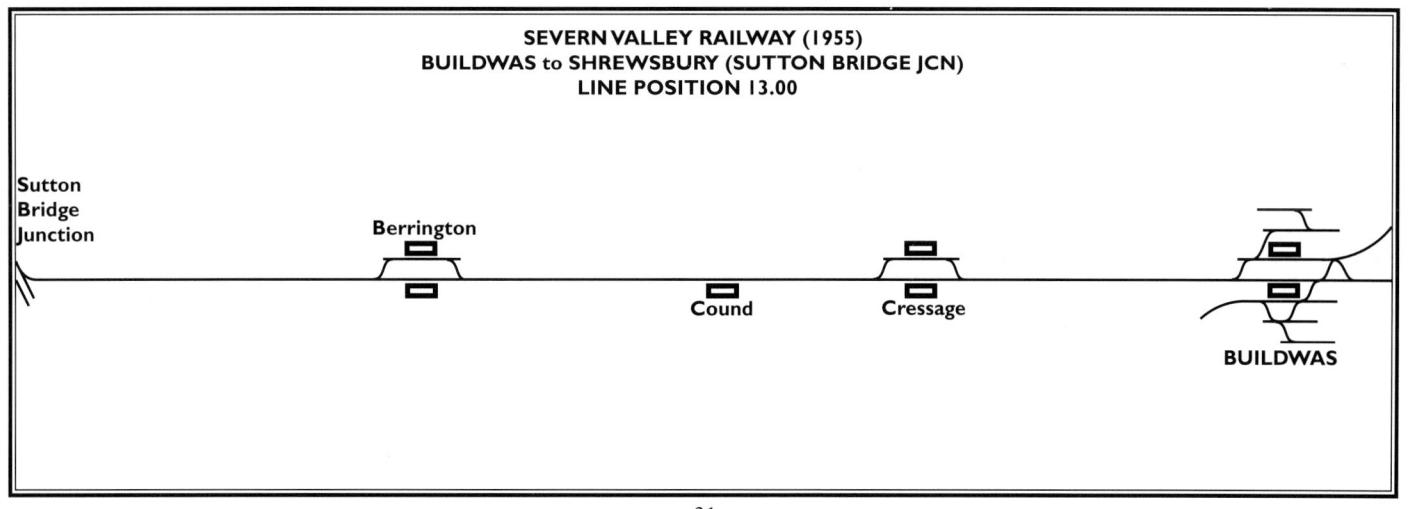

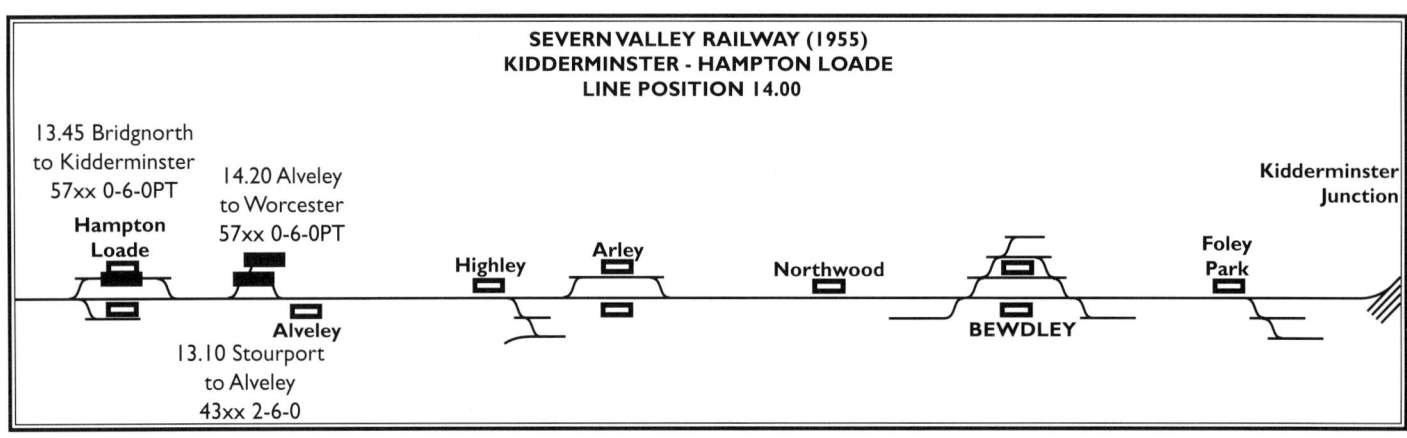

CONTROLLER'S LOG: In view of its importance, it might be thought that Alveley yard would be controlled by its own signalbox yet it is in fact situated in the block section between Highley and Hampton Loade and operated by ground frames at the north and south ends of the sidings. There is also an instrument cabin located between the two frames from where telephone communication with Hampton and Highley is available.

When a train arrives at Alveley, it is shunted clear of the main line and locked into the siding. The points are then restored to the main line placed in the instrument, the 3-5 signal is sent from Highley to Hampton after which the line is clear for through running.

Several trains can be accepted into Alveley sidings at the same time and at the moment the 14.20 and 15.00 services for Worcester and Kidderminster are both inside whilst the 13.45 Bridgnorth to Kidderminster may make a third when it arrives in a few minutes time.

When trains are ready to depart from Alveley, after making arrangements with the Hampton signalman, the brakevan is propelled onto the main line about a quarter of a mile whenever possible the yard will try and get the 14.20 to Worcester on its way before accepting the up Bridgnorth goods.

Elsewhere, the seemingly eternal up Salop goods is attaching and detaching in Jackfield Siding whilst en route from Coalport to Ironbridge. When it arrives at the latter it will combine its train with the wagons brought from Coton Hill and proceed forward to Hartlebury.

Passenger traffic is generally absent at the moment, the exception being the 13.45 Shrewsbury - Kidderminster (the return working of the 10.35 Kidderminster - Shrewsbury) which

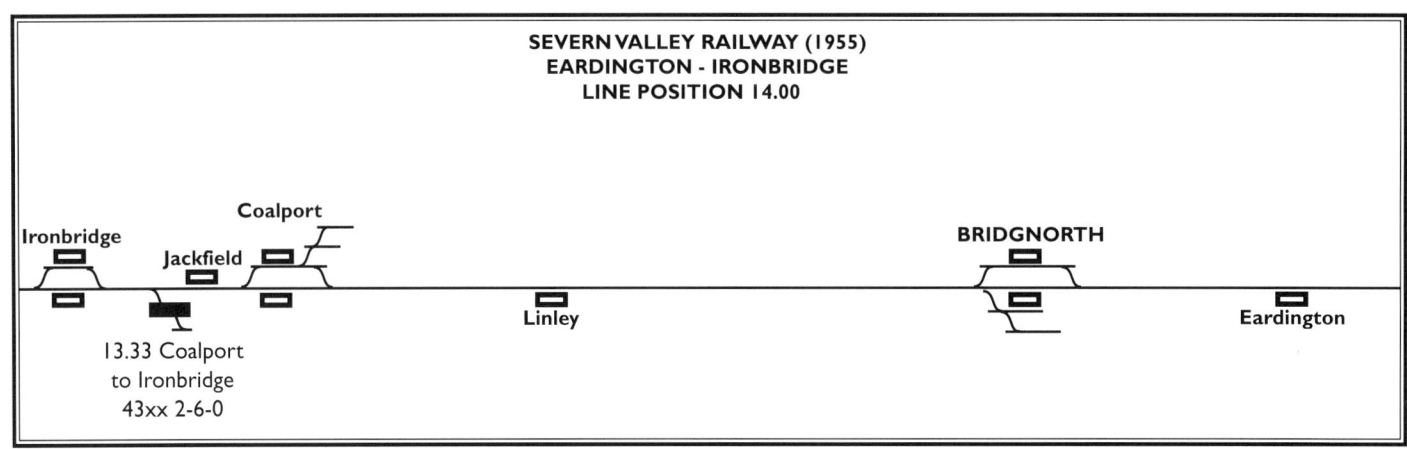

position, the token placed into the Alveley machine so that through running can be resumed between Hampton and Arley in the normal way. The signalling arrangements for a down train, as an example, require Highley to send the 2-5-5 block code to Hampton who respond with 3-5-5. The token is withdrawn by the Highley signalman and given to the driver of the train who can proceed forward once arrangements have been agreed with the Alveley shunter.

When a train has been shunted clear at Alveley, the main line restored and the token towards Hampton, the train then being backed onto it before reversing and heading towards Highley and Bewdley.

Generally trains enter the sidings at the south ground fame and depart from the north although much is left to the discretion of the shunter in duty. However, because of the steep rising gradient on the main line, in order for up trains to take a full load, they must exit via the north ground frame and reverse direction.

With three trains in Alveley at the same time, life can become a little too active and is approaching Cound Halt. Special attention has to be paid to the running of this service since it only has nine minutes at Kidderminster before forming its next working, the 15.54 to Hartlebury.

The Severn Valley is showing a little activity as the 57xx 0-6-0T which arrived a quarter of an hour ago with the 13.05 goods from Hollinsworth, shunts the yard before leaving with the afternoon Wenlock goods. Another 57xx approaches from the east with the Horsehay - Buildwas trip.

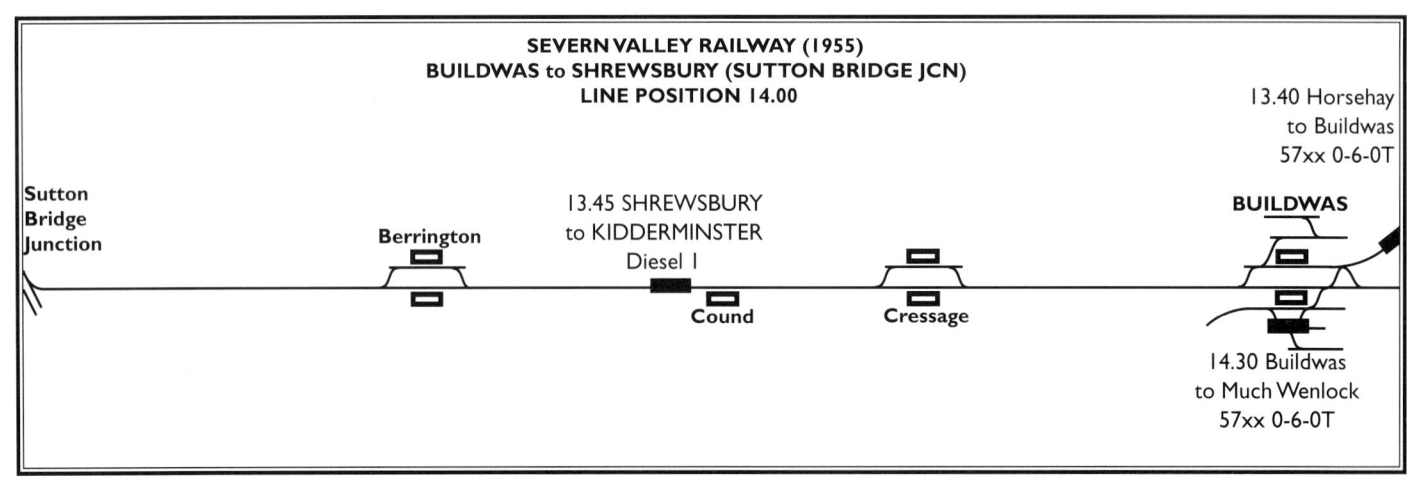

On weekdays the 10.40 Kidderminster to Shrewsbury was booked to be worked by a GWR Railcar but on Saturdays steam was substituted with a variety of engines and vehicles being used was illustrated on Saturday 4th June 1960 when 57xx 0-6-0PT 7700 of Gloucester was booked to the train - formed unusually of non-corridor stock - in lieu of the normal 2-6-2T. (Brian Moone: KRM)

Under normal circumstances the only trains that passed at Hampton Loade were the 15.50 Shrewsbury - Kidderminster and the 16.23 Kidderminster - Shrewsbury although when services were running late, the arrangements for passing trains would be modified with the facilities at Hampton Loade being used to advantage. This was the case in the above 1952 view when 5518 of Kidderminster made an unscheduled crossing at Hampton with a Shrewsbury-bound service.

SEVERN VALLEY ENGINE DIAGRAMS : 1955

Kidderminster 105
57xx 0-6-0PT

Arr	Station	Dep	Train
	Kidderminster MPD	05.30	Coupled
05.38	Hartlebury	05.39	Coupled
05.45	Stourport	07.45	Light
07.55	Hartlebury	08.22	Goods
08.37	Stourport	09.00	EBV
09.15	Hartlebury	10.40	Goods
10.55	Stourport	11.50	Goods
12.00	Hartlebury	12.10	Goods
12.15	Elmley	12.50	Goods
12.55	Hartlebury	15.00	Goods
15.15	Stourport	18.45	Goods
18.55	Hartlebury	19.03	Light
19.11	Kidderminster MPD	(05.30)	

Shunting during intermediate times

Kidderminster 106
43xx 2-6-0

Arr	Station	Dep	Train
	Kidderminster MPD	05.30	Coupled
05.38	Hartlebury	05.39	Coupled
05.45	Stourport	06.15	Goods
06.59	Alveley	10.45	Goods
12.10	Hartlebury	12.30	Light
13.40	Stourport	13.10	Goods
13.40	Alveley	15.00	Goods
15.33	Kidderminster Yard	15.40	Light
15.45	Kidderminster MPD		

Kidderminster 107
57xx 0-6-0PT

Arr	Station	Dep	Train
	Kidderminster MPD	05.50	Light
05.58	Hartlebury	07.10	Goods
07.20	Stourport	10.20	Goods
10.30	Hartlebury	11.30	Light
11.40	Kidderminster Jcn	12.10	Light
12.20	Bewdley	12.50	Goods
13.00	Kidderminster	13.30	
13.40	Kidderminster MPD	16.00	Light
16.15	Hartlebury		
	Yard Pilot		
	Hartlebury	19.30	Goods
19.45	Stourport		
	Yard Pilot		
	Stourport	21.05	Light
21.15	Hartlebury		
	Yard Pilot	23.15	Light
23.25	Kidderminster MPD		

Kidderminster 108
57xx 0-6-0PT

Arr	Station	Dep	Train
	Kidderminster MPD	05.50	Light
05.58	Hartlebury	10.10	Goods
13.09	Bridgnorth	13.45	Goods
17.20	Kidderminster Yard	17.30	Light
17.35	Kidderminster MPD		

Kidderminster 109
57xx 0-6-0PT

Arr	Station	Dep	Train
	Kidderminster MPD	11.15	Light
	Kidderminster Yard	11.30	Goods
14.50	Woofferton	15.25	Goods
18.22	Kidderminster Yard	18.30	Light
18.35	Kidderminster MPD		

Kidderminster 110
57xx 0-6-0PT

Arr	Station	Dep	Train
	Kidderminster MPD	09.35	Light
	Kidderminster Yard	09.55	Goods
10.30	Alveley	11.15	Goods
12.10	Stourport	12.20	Light
12.28	Hartlebury Jcn	12.30	Light
12.35	Stourport	12.40	Goods
13.22	Alveley	14.20	Goods
15.35	Hartlebury	16.00	Light
16.10	Kidderminster	16.48	Pass
18.04	Leominster	18.20	Pass
20.08	Kidderminster	20.20	ECS
20.31	Bewdley	20.40	Light
20.50	Kidderminster MPD		

Kidderminster 111
57xx 0-6-0PT

Arr	Station	Dep	Train
	Kidderminster MPD	14.00	Light
	Kidderminster Yard		
	Yard Pilot		
	Kidderminster Yard	16.00	Goods
16.05	Foley Park	16.15	Light
16.20	Kidderminster Yard		
	Yard Pilot		
	Kidderminster Yard	09.05	Goods
09.10	Foley Park	09.30	Light
09.35	Bewdley		
	Yard Pilot		
	Bewdley	12.50	Pilot
13.00	Kidderminster Yard		
	Yard Pilot		
	Kidderminster Yard	13.55	
14.00	Kidderminster MPD		

Kidderminster 117
51xx 2-6-2T

Arr	Station	Dep	Train
	Kidderminster MPD	13.40	Light
13.50	Hartlebury	14.00	Pass
15.58	Shrewsbury	17.33	Pass
19.18	Kidderminster	19.25	Light
19.30	Kidderminster MPD		

Kidderminster 118
57xx 0-6-0PT

Arr	Station	Dep	Train
	Kidderminster MPD	16.00	
	Yard pilot		
00.00	Kidderminster MPD		

Wellington 460
57xx 0-6-0PT

Arr	Station	Dep	Train
	Wellington Loco	05.00	Light
05.05	Wellington	05.20	ECS
05.51	Buildwas	06.00	Pass
06.36	Wellington	06.48	Pass
07.23	Buildwas	07.40	Mixed
07.57	Much Wenlock	08.35	Pass
08.44	Buildwas	08.56	Pass
09.34	Wellington	10.15	Goods
11.14	Horsehay	13.40	Goods
14.05	Buildwas	15.25	Pass
15.37	Lightmoor Jcn	16.05	ECS
16.08	Coalbrookdale	16.10	Pass
16.30	Much Wenlock	17.30	Pass
17.33	Buildwas	18.15	Goods
19.37	Wellington	19.45	Light
19.50	Wellington Loco		

Note: 15.25 to 17.33 applies during school term only

Wellington 461
57xx 0-6-0PT

Arr	Station	Dep	Train
	Wellington Loco	05.30	Light
06.05	Much Wenlock	06.50	Pass
07.35	Wellington	08.16	Pass
09.10	Much Wenlock	09.35	Goods
10.21	Longville	10.40	Goods
11.16	Much Wenlock	11.40	Pass
12.28	Wellington	12.40	Light
12.45	Wellington Loco	14.55	Light
15.00	Wellington	15.10	Pass
16.00	Much Wenlock	16.40	Pass
17.32	Wellington	17.50	Pass
18.34	Much Wenlock	19.05	Pass
19.52	Wellington	20.00	Light
20.05	Wellington Loco		

Wellington 462
57xx 0-6-0PT

Arr	Station	Dep	Train
	Wellington loco	05.20	Light
05.25	Wellington Yard	05.35	Goods
06.08	Horsehay	06.45	Goods
07.16	Buildwas	09.40	Goods
11.17	Hollinswood	11.27	Light
11.37	Wellington	15.05	Light
15.10	Wellington Yard	15.15	Goods
15.33	Ketley	17.30	Goods
17.42	Wellington Yard	17.47	Light
17.52	Wellington loco		

Wellington 463
57xx 0-6-0PT

Arr	Station	Dep	Train
	Wellington loco	05.55	Light
06.00	Wellington Yard	06.05	EBV
06.50	Buildwas	07.40	EBV
08.00	Madeley	08.08	Goods
08.12	Kemberton	08.40	Goods
09.58	Buildwas	10.15	Light
10.58	Shrewsbury (CH)	11.50	Goods
13.46	Wellington Yard	13.50	Light
13.55	Wellington loco		

Wellington 464
57xx 0-6-0PT

Arr	Station	Dep	Train
	Wellington loco	11.00	Light
11.05	Wellington	11.17	Pass
12.10	Much Wenlock	13.00	Pass
13.48	Wellington	16.30	
	Station Pilot		
	Wellington	16.30	Pass
17.20	Much Wenlock	17.45	Pass
18.37	Wellington	19.55	Pass
20.45	Much Wenlock	21.00	Light
	via Buildwas & Salop		
22.10	Wellington loco		

Wellington 467
57xx 0-6-0PT

Arr	Station	Dep	Train
	Wellington loco	07.00	Light
07.20	Hollinswood		
	Yard Pilot		
	Hollinswood	13.05	Goods
13.45	Buildwas	14.30	Goods
14.48	Much Wenlock	15.00	Goods
15.17	Buildwas	16.01	Goods
17.01	Hollinswood	17.17	Light
17.26	Wellington loco		

Wellington 468
57xx 0-6-0PT

Arr	Station	Dep	Train
	Wellington loco	06.55	Light
07.00	Wellington Yard	07.10	Goods
08.58	Shifnal		Goods
	Yard Pilot		
	Shifnal	10.37	Goods
13.42	Oxley	14.25	EBV
15.00	Hollinswood	15.10	Goods
16.50	Buildwas	17.06	Goods
17.56	Wellington Yard	19.40	Goods
20.00	Hollinswood	21.10	Goods
21.42	Wellington Yard	21.45	Light
21.50	Wellington loco		

Shrewsbury 100
51xx 2-6-2T

Arr	Station	Dep	Train
	Coleham loco	07.55	Light
08.00	Shrewsbury	08.15	Pass
10.18	Kidderminster	10.23	Pass
10.40	Stourbridge Jcn	11.00	Light
11.20	Kidderminster Loco	16.23	Pass
18.15	Shrewsbury	18.20	Light
18.25	Coleham loco		

Shrewsbury 101
51xx 2-6-2T

Arr	Station	Dep	Train
	Coleham loco	15.30	Light
15.35	Shrewsbury	15.50	Pass
17.34	Kidderminster	17.50	Light
17.56	Hartlebury	18.25	Pass
20.17	Shrewsbury	20.45	Pass
21.19	Ironbridge	21.35	Pass
22.17	Shrewsbury	22.25	Light
22.30	Coleham loco		

Shrewsbury 150
43xx 2-6-0

Arr	Station	Dep	Train
	Coleham loco	09.55	Light
10.05	Coton Hill	10.15	Goods
12.45	Ironbridge	13.05	Goods
13.13	Coalport	13.33	Goods
14.10	Ironbridge	15.00	Goods
19.15	Hartlebury	19.25	Light
10.33	Kidderminster Yard	20.12	Goods
20.59	Worcester	21.05	Light
21.10	Worcester loco		

Shrewsbury 150A
43xx 2-6-0

Arr	Station	Dep	Train
	Worcester loco	08.15	Light
08.20	Worcester	08.35	Goods
10.22	Kidderminster	10.40	EBV
10.50	Hartlebury	14.15	Goods
16.39	Bridgnorth	17.50	Goods
21.14	Shrewsbury CH	21.20	Light
21.30	Coleham loco		

Worcester 451
51xx 2-6-2T

Arr	Station	Dep	Train
	Worcester loco	06.30	Light
0635	Worcester SH	06.55	Pass
09.21	Shrewsbury	11.25	Pass
13.12	Hartlebury	13.50	Pass
14.18	Worcester loco		

Table 161 SHREWSBURY, BRIDGNORTH, HARTLEBURY and WORCESTER

Miles		Week Days																		Sundays		
		am	am	am	am	am	am	pm Saturdays only	pm D	pm	pm	pm	pm	pm	pm	pm	pm Except Saturdays	pm	pm	pm	pm	
—	**Shrewsbury** dep	..	..	..	..	**8 15**	**11 25**	..	**1 45**	..	..	**3 50**	..	**5 30**	..	..	..	**8 45**	..	..	..	..
4¼	Berrington	..	..	..	..	8 26	11 34	..	1 55	..	..	4 0	..	5 41	..	..	..	8 55	..	..	..	..
7	Cound Halt	..	..	..	..	8 32	11 40	..	2 0	..	..	4 6	..	5 47	..	..	..	9 1	..	..	..	..
8¼	Cressage	..	..	..	..	8 37	11 45	..	2 5	..	..	4 11	..	5 52	..	..		9 6	③	..	..	..
12¼	Buildwas	..	..	..	..	8V59	11v54	..	2 14	..	..	4 19	..	6† 3	..	..		9 13	9 30	..	..	..
13½	Iron Bridge and Broseley	..	..	..	..	9 6	11 59	..	2 21	..	..	4 25	..	6 9	..	..		9E19	9 35	..	..	..
15	Jackfield Halt	..	..	..	..	9 10	12 3		2 25	..	..	4 29	..	6 13	..	..		..	9 39	..	..	..
15½	Coalport	..	..	..	..	9 14	12 6		2 29	..	..	4 33	..	6 16	..	..		..	9 42	..	..	..
18¼	Linley Halt	..	..	..	..	9 20	12 12		2 35	..	..	4 39	..	6 22	..	..		..	9 48	..	..	..
22½	**Bridgnorth** arr	..	..	..	..	**9 28**	**12 19**		**2 42**	D	..	**4 46**	..	**6 29**	..	..	③	..	**9 55**	..	..	..
	Bridgnorth dep	..	..	..	..	**9 34**	**12 23**		..	**3 0**	..	**4 49**	..	**6 33**	..	..	**9 5**	..	**10 5**	..	**6 55**	..
24¾	Eardington Halt	..	..	③	..	9 39	12 28		..	3 6	..	4 54	..	6 38	..	..	zz	..	zz	..	7 0	..
27	Hampton Loade	..	③	7 0	..	9 44	12 33	③	..	3 11	..	5 0	③	6 43	③	..	9 15	..	1015	..	7 7	..
29¼	Highley	..	6E22	7 8	③	9 51	12 39	2 4	..	3 19	..	5 8	6 20	6 48	7 55	..	9 20	..	1020	..	7 14	..
31½	Arley	5 50	6E28	7 13	8 35	9 57	12 45	2 10	..	3 25	..	5 14	6 26	6 58	8 0	..	9 26	..	1026	7 5	7 22	..
33½	Northwood Halt	5 55	6E33	7 18	8 40	10 2	12 50	2 15	..	3 30	..	5 19	6 30	7 3	8 5	..	9 31	..	1031	7 10	7 28	..
35¼	**Bewdley** arr	**5 58**	**6E36**	**7 21**	**8 43**	**10 6**	**12 53**	**2 18**	..	**3 34**	..	**5 22**	**6 34**	**7 6**	**8 10**	..	**9 34**	..	**1034**	**7 15**	**7 34**	..
38¾	182 Kidderminster arr	6 8	..	7‡35	9 48	1018	1N13	2 30	..	3 45	..	5 34	6 44	7 18	8 50	..	9 45	..	1045	7 26	7 46	..
57¾	164 Birmingham (S.H.) arr	7 11	..	8‡37	1126	1151	2 51	4‡51	..	5B17	..	6 35	7‡51	9 15	11‡15	..	11‡15	..	..	8 33	8 53	..
—	**Bewdley** dep	..	**6 40**	**7 40**	**8 44**	Stop	**12 55**	..	..	..	D **4 42**	Stop	..	..	..	**8 28**	..	..	..	..	..	..
37¼	Burlish Halt	..	6 46	7 46	8 49	..	1 1	..	..	..	4 47	..	..	..	..	8 33	..	..	..	..	..	..
38	Stourport-on-Severn	..	6 48	7 50	8 53	..	1 5	..	..	..	4 50	..	..	..	..	8 36	..	..	..	..	..	..
40¾	Hartlebury arr	..	6 54	7 57	8 59	am	1 12	..	..	..	4 56	pm	..	..	..	8 43	..	..	Saturdays only	..	..	..
	Hartlebury dep	..	7 29	8‡ 7	..	9 35	1 25	..	..	..	..	5 17	..	..	..	8 44	..	..		..	..	..
43	Cutnall Green Halt	..	..	8‡12	..	9 40	..	..	..	..	..	5 22	..	..	..	..	..	..		..	..	..
46½	Droitwich Spa	..	7 39	8‡19	..	9 47	1 35	..	..	..	..	5 30	..	..	..	8 55	..	..		..	..	..
49½	Fernhill Heath	..	7 44	8‡24	..	9 53	..	..	..	..	..	5 36	..	..	..	..	..	..	..	..	..	..
52	**Worcester** (Shrub H.) arr	..	**7Y51**	**‡8Y31**	..	**9 58**	**1 46**	..	..	..	..	**5 41**	..	..	..	**9 5**	..	..	..	..	..	..

Miles		Week Days																		Sundays		
		am	am	am	am	am	pm	am Saturdays only	pm E	pm S	pm	pm	pm	pm ③	pm	pm	pm Except Saturdays	pm Saturdays only	pm	am		
—	**Worcester** (Shrub H.) dep	..	**6 55**	**7Y46**	..	**9 32**	..		**12 45**	**1 15**	**2 35**	..	..	**4‡52**	**5Y30**	..			..	..	..	..
2½	Fernhill Heath	..	7 1	..	..	9 38	..		12 51	1 22	..	..	..	4‡58	..	..			..	..	..	..
5½	Droitwich Spa	..	7 8	7 56	..	9 45	..		12 59	1 30	2 45	..	..	5‡ 5	5 40	..			..	..	..	..
9	Cutnall Green Halt	..	..	..	..	9 53	..		1 6	1 38	..	..	..	5‡13	..	..			..	..	..	..
11¼	Hartlebury arr	..	7 17	8 6	..	10 2	..		1 14	1 47	2 55	..	..	5‡22	5 50	..			..	..	..	..
	Hartlebury dep	..	7 22	8N10	..	..	③ 1210		2 0	2 0	..	D 4 5	..	5 30	6 25	..			..	..	..	..
14	Stourport-on-Severn	..	7 33	8N17	..	..	1217		2 8	2 8	..	4 12	..	5 42	6 33	..			..	..	..	..
14¾	Burlish Halt	..	7 35	8N19	..	..	1219		2 10	2 10	..	4 14	..	5 44	6 36	..			..	..	..	..
16¾	**Bewdley** arr	..	**7 40**	**8N24**	..	..	**1224**		**2 15**	**2 15**	..	**4 19**	..	**5 49**	**6 41**	..			..	..	..	..
—	164 Birmingham (S.H.) dep	③	6 15	..	D 9 45	..		③ 11‡20	12 45	1245	..	..	2 45	5‡ 0	5 40	③ 6y15	③ 6‡45	③ 6‡45	..	7 30	..	..
—	182 Kidderminster dep	5 48	7 35	..	10 35	..	Saturdays only	12p40	2N10	2N10	..	..	4 23	5 48	6N25	7 20	8‡10	8‡10	..	8 32	..	..
—	**Bewdley** dep	**6 0**	**7 53**	**8N25**	**10 45**	..		**1 0**	**2 24**	**2 24**	..	..	**4 38**	**6 2**	**6 45**	**7 30**	**8 26**	**8 26**	..	**8 44**	..	..
18½	Northwood Halt	6 3	7 56	8N28	10 49	..		1 4	2 27	2 27	..	..	4 41	6 6	6 48	7 34	8 30	8 30	..	8 52	..	..
20½	Arley	6 9	8 2	8N32	10 55	..		1 9	2 33	2 33	..	..	4 46	6 11	6 51	7 39	8 36	8 36	..	9 1	..	..
22¾	Highley	6 15	8 8	..	11 2	..		1 14	2 39	2 39	..	..	4 51	6 16	6 57	7 44	8 42	8 42	..	9 9	..	..
25	Hampton Loade	..	8 13	..	11 9	..	..	..	2 46	2 46	..	..	5 1	..	7 7	..	8 49	8 49	..	9 16	..	..
27¼	Eardington Halt	..	8 19	..	11 15	..	..	..	2 52	2 52	..	..	5 8	..	7 13	..	yy	yy	..	9 24	..	..
29½	**Bridgnorth** arr	..	**8 23**	..	**11 19**	..	..	..	**2 56**	**2 56**	..	..	**5 14**	..	**7 17**	..	**8 58**	**8 58**	..	**9 30**	..	..
	Bridgnorth dep	..	**8 30**	..	**11 22**	..	..	..	**2 59**	**2 59**	..	..	**5 15**	..	**7 20**	..	..	**9 0**	..	..	..	..
33¾	Linley Halt	..	8 38	..	11 30	..	..	..	3 7	3 7	..	..	5 23	..	7 28	..	..	9 7	..	..	..	..
36½	Coalport	..	8 43	..	11 37	..	..	..	3 13	3 13	..	..	5 29	..	7 34	..	..	9 13	..	..	..	..
37	Jackfield Halt	..	8 45	..	11 40	..	..	..	3 16	3 16	..	..	5 32	..	7 37	..	..	9 16	..	..	..	..
38½	Iron Bridge and Broseley	..	8 49	..	11 45	..	..	..	3 20	3 20	..	..	5 38	..	7 42	..	..	9 20	9E35	..	..	..
39¾	Buildwas	..	8 55	..	11Z56	..	..	..	3 26	3 26	..	..	5F45	..	7 48	..	..	9 24	9 40	..	..	..
43¾	Cressage	..	9 2	..	12 5	..	..	..	3 33	3 33	..	..	5 52	..	7 54	..	..	..	9 46	..	..	..
45	Cound Halt	..	9 6	..	12 10	..	..	..	3 37	3 37	..	..	5 56	..	7 58	..	..	..	9J51	..	..	..
47¾	Berrington	..	9 12	..	12 18	..	..	..	3 43	3 43	..	..	6 2	..	8 4	..	..	..	9 58	..	..	..
52	**Shrewsbury** arr	..	**9 21**	..	**12 32**	..	..	..	**3 58**	**3 58**	..	..	**6 15**	..	**8 17**	..	..	..	**10 17**	..	..	..

B Arr 4 52 pm on Saturdays, 9th July to 3rd September and 5 30 pm on 18th, 25th June, 2nd July, 10th and 17th September
D Third class only on Mondays to Fridays. First and Third class on Saturdays
E Except Saturdays
F Arr. 5 43 pm
J Thursdays only
N Third Class only for a portion of the journey
p pm
V Arr. 8 43 am
v Arr 11 52 am
Y Foregate Street Station
yy Stops to set down on notice to Guard at Hampton Loade
y First and Third class. Dep. 5 45 pm on Saturdays
Z Arr. 11 50 am
zz Stops to set down passengers only
③ Third Class only
† Arr. 6 0 pm
‡ First and Third class

The public view of The Severn Valley as shown by British Railways in 1955. It is interesting to note that Kidderminster scarcely rated a mention since the main line (sic) was reckoned as running from Bewdley to Hartlebury with Kidderminster being served by a branch even though six of the eight through trains originating from stations to the north of Arley ran to Kidderminster.

One wonders if the route might have garnered a greater share of long-distance traffic had it regarded itself as a through route between Shrewsbury and Worcester rather than a meandering West Midlands branch. Morning passengers from Shrewsbury had the choice of the 11.10 express via Wolverhampton or the 11.25 Severn Valley train with a change at Hartlebury; both reaching Worcester at 13.46. A diesel (or even steam) express service via Bridgenorth ought to have accomplished the journey in something like an hour and a half: an improvement of almost an hour over the stopping service. Whether there was sufficient demand at Shrewsbury and Worcester for such a service is not something that seems to have been put to the test.

In October 1955 Shrewsbury's allocation of GWR 2-6-2T's was transferred to South Wales in exchange for a trio of BR 3MT 2-6-2T's together with a miscellany of LMS 2MT and 4MT tanks. This resulted in an increase in foreign sightings on the Severn Valley, some specimens being far removed from the classic form familiar to the Great Western. The austere lines of the LMS Parallel Boiler 4MT 2-6-4T did not suggest an engine that was both powerful and free-running; qualities that were very useful on a switchback line such as the Severn Valley. 42420 came to Shrewsbury after spells at Monument Lane (Birmingham) and Stoke and is seen setting out from Bridgnorth for Bewdley and the South on Saturday 9th May 1959. (Kidderminster Railway Museum)

Railcar W19 (Worcester) waits in the down platform to cross a Shrewsbury - Kidderminster train at Bridgnorth on Saturday 19th September 1959 whilst the signalman stands on the up platform ready to exchange tokens. It is very much an everyday scene except for the fact that the engine approaching from the north is 45xx 2-6-2T 5547 of Swindon - a rare bird indeed on the Severn Valley. (V.R. Webster; KRM)

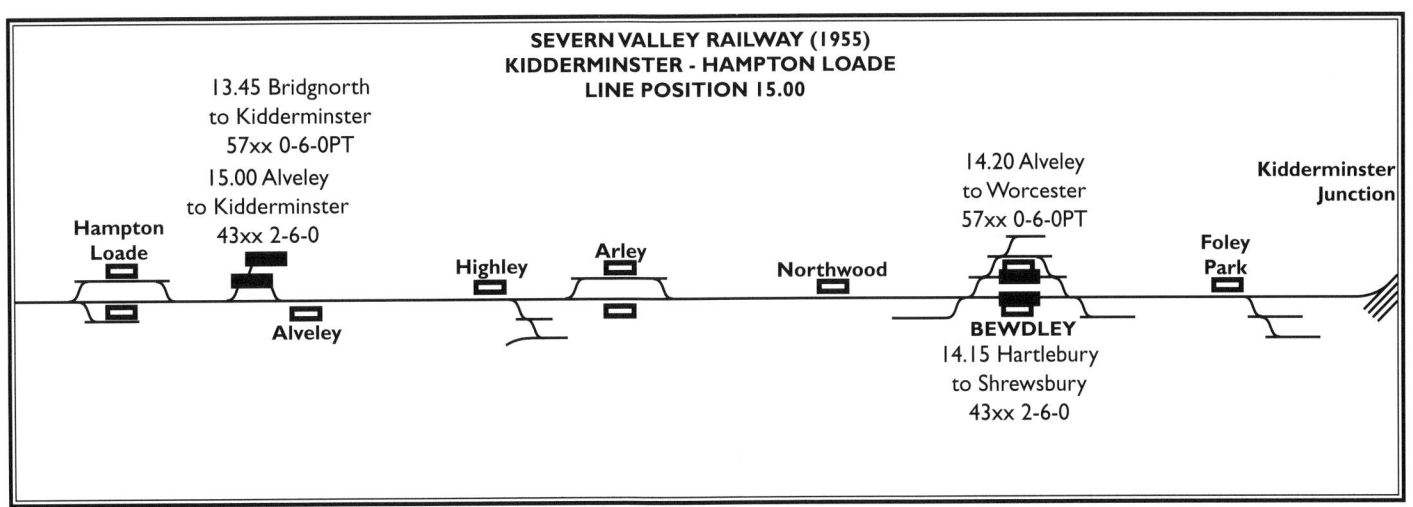

CONTROLLER'S LOG: In the short span of an hour, trains seem to have sprung up all over the place. The drums are banging.

"- Ironbridge speaking. The Salop goods is whistling up. 6317, forty-two with six Coalport and six Bridgnorth on the engine. Do you want me to hold it for the down passenger?"

" - Pull off and let him up to Coalport."

"- Bewdley North. Worcester goods up at fifty-nine. Can I let the down goods go?"

on this morning Wellington told me I came back with the six-thirty goods. They're telling me here at Buildwas that I got to work a Lightmoor train. What is going on?"

"- Three twenty-five passenger to Lightmoor. Empty stock to Coalbrookdale via the Junction. Then four-ten passenger back to Buildwas."

"- What train's that? They didn't tell me anything about that."

"- It's the school train. Doesn't run at

"- I've got ten Ironbridge just arrived. D'you want me to put them on?"

"- Up Shrewsbury passenger right time Coalport."

"- Down Salop goods arrived Arley thirteen. Up goods for Kidderminster through at fourteen."

"- No. They can go on the trip in the morning. Let it go with just the Coton Hill's - there's quite a bit to be picked up at Bridgnorth

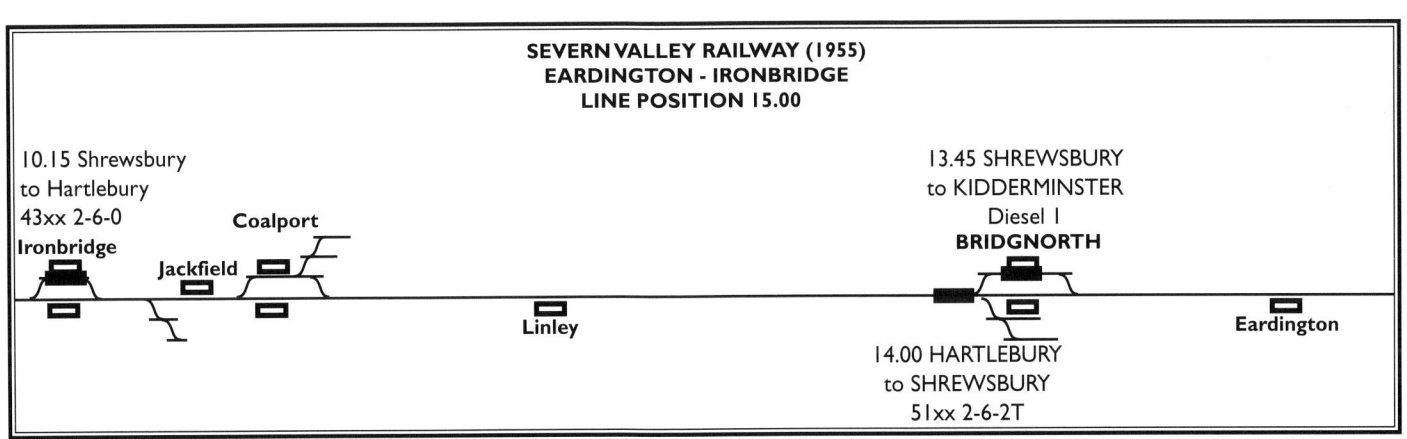

"- Yes."

"- Up and Down Salop right time from Bridgnorth."

"- Coalport? The Salop goods is on its way to you and wants to cross the down Shrewsbury passenger at you. There are six for you on the Salop engine; tell the guard to make the train up to forty-five with empties."

"- Kidderminster away from Alveley. 5394 thirty-six length of thirty-six, all Kidderminster."

"- Highley? Up and down goods to cross at you. Tell the guard of the down to changeover with the up Salop at Bridgnorth as booked."

" - Hello? Can you help? When I booked

holidays. Perhaps that's why Wellington thought it didn't run. Today is not a holiday though."

"- Oh. That must be it. I'll go and see the Foreman, then."

"- Up Shrewsbury right time Eardington."

"- Up Goods through Highley at seven."

"- Buildwas station here. There don't seem to be a guard for the school train."

"- He'll be there in two minutes."

"- Coalport box. Up Goods arrived at oh-nine."

"- Alveley? The down Salop goods is on its way. 5331 with 25 Coton Hill and 20 empties for you on the brake."

and Coalport".

"- The Colliery want fifty-four empties for tomorrow."

"- You've got forty on hand; the rest'll come down in the morning with the Stourport trip. You'll end up with more than they're asking for."

"- OK."

"- School train away from Buildwas on time."

"- You found the guard, I take it?"

"- First time out on his own. Just moved across from Carmarthen, Boyoh!"

"- Berrington speaking. The S&T want to disconnect my up home for half an hour......."

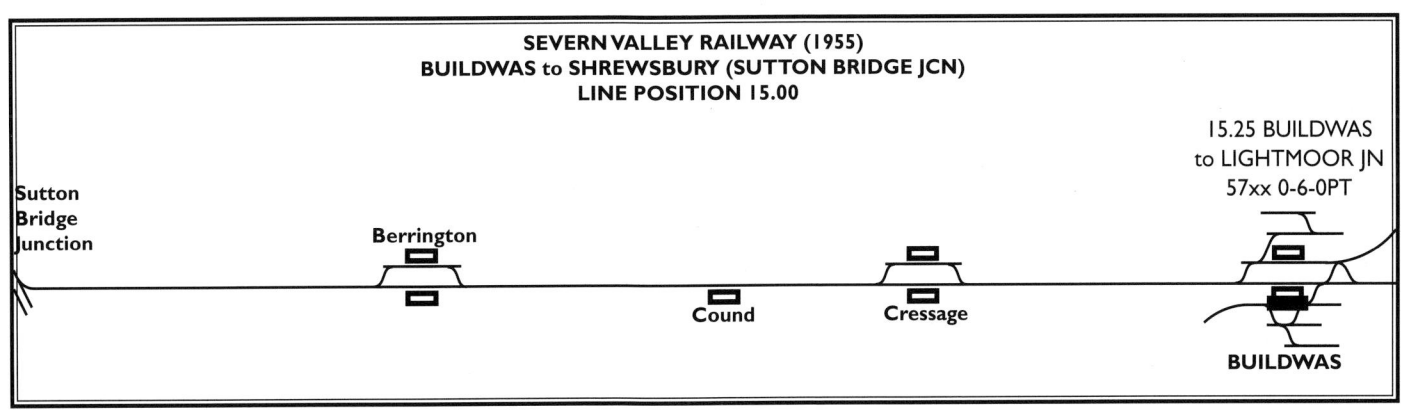

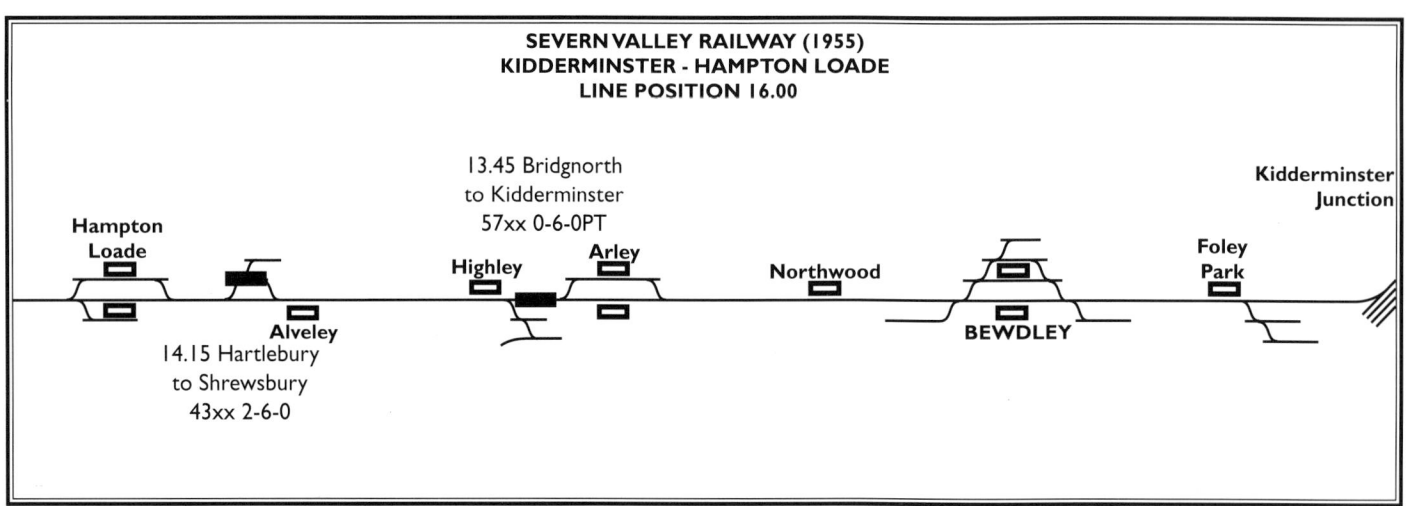

CONTROLLER'S LOG: As the dialogue on the preceding page suggests, even when matters are proceeding (more or less) normally, there is no lack of interest and there are certainly worse ways of getting a foothold on the management ladder than by being paid to watch trains and influence their destinies.

Matters have quietened down a little - not that affairs often approach the frenetic on the Severn Valley - as both the diesel railcars used in working between Stratford, Worcester and the Malverns.

The reason for this is that the evening rush-hour is far less compressed than the morning flow. In the latter the majority have to get to their places of work by 08.30 or 09.00 whilst in the evening finishing times are spread over three hours from 16.00 until 19.00 which makes it very difficult to decide when to run the 'key' trains. In the case of the Severn Valley the station an uncommonly busy period, having two goods trains and the Up Shrewsbury passenger to take care of.

The Bridgnorth - Kidderminster trip is running into Arley where it will pause to put off a wagon of coal before continuing forward. After that it will spend nearly an hour shunting and attaching traffic at Bewdley before reaching Kidderminster at 17.20.

On the Severn Junction, an 0-6-0 pannier

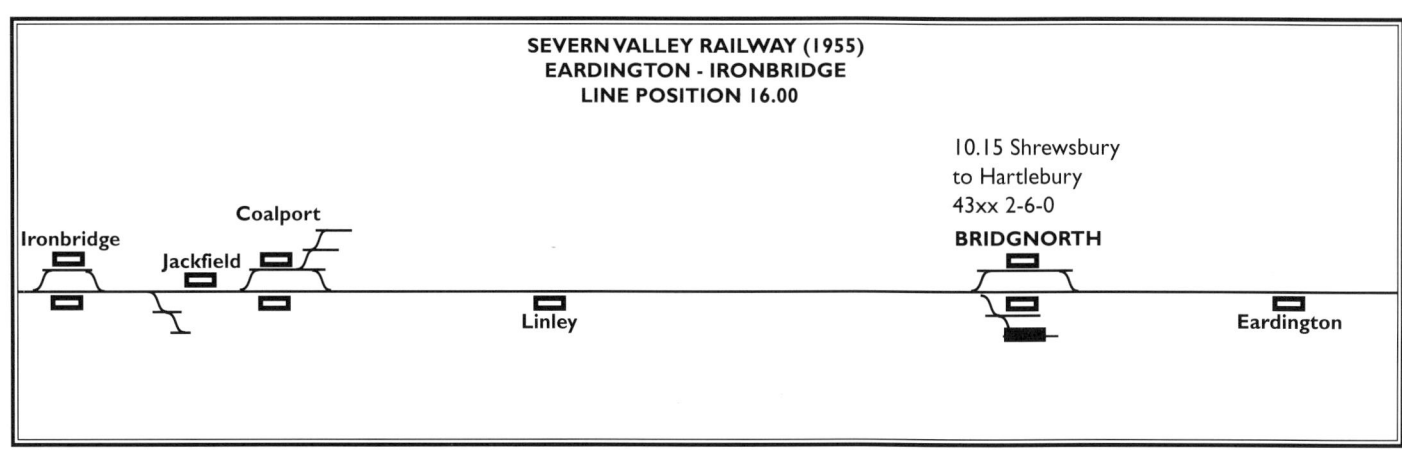

for the lines' passenger workings are for the moment 'off the map'. One is in the process of working the rather circuitous 15.54 from Kidderminster to Bewdley which is routed via Hartlebury and Stourport in order to maximise the use of the train albeit at the expense of through passengers whose normal ten minute journey is expanded to one of twenty-seven. The other railcar is at Tenbury Wells, en route from Woofferton to Kidderminster.

Unlike the morning rush-hour which involves through services to Birmingham and three GWR Railcars, the evening service is rather a muted affair with no Birmingham trains and only two Railcars; the third being engaged question is solved by not having an evening key train at all and passengers coming from Birmingham and Worcester have to change at either Kidderminster or Hartlebury.

Almost all the traffic on the Severn Valley at the moment is goods or mineral; the only exception being the late afternoon Shrewsbury - Kidderminster service which has just arrived at Berrington.

The 10.15 Coton Hill to Hartlebury goods has arrived at Bridgnorth where, after attaching and detaching traffic, it will wait to change footplates with the 14.15 Hartlebury to Shrewsbury. The latter is performing at Alveley and will get down to Bridgnorth in about forty minutes, giving the tank is pulling away with a goods train for Hollinswood. The latter is at the southern point of the Wellington - Lightmoor Junction - Hollinswood triangle and is a group of sidings used for traffic from the Severn Junction to the Birmingham region and the South. Traffic could of course be worked to the main line at Wellington were it not for the gradients between Lightmoor Junction and Ketley which restrict trains to 18 wagons of goods or 24 empties. By taking the easier route to Hollinsworth a 57xx can convey 27 goods or 30 empties. Through trains from Oxley to Buildwas use this route but have a concession to take 36 loaded minerals with a 2-6-0 engine.

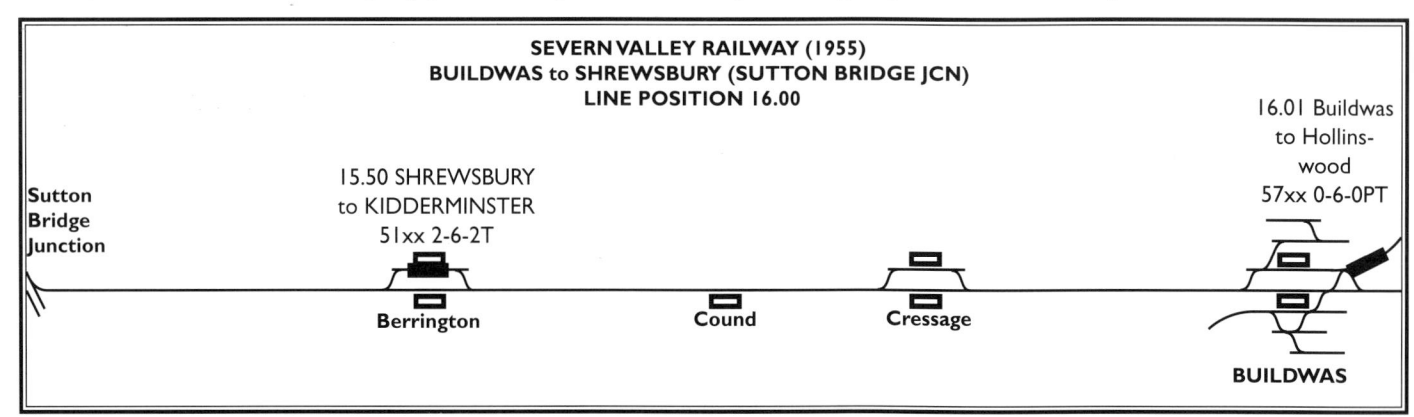

Buildwas Junction was the meeting point of the Severn Valley and Severn Junction Railways, the latter running East to West from Wellington to Much Wenlock and having its own platform at Buildwas. The latter can be seen on the left and was used by trains in both directions. On the right a Shrewsbury-bound service of the Severn Valley calls behind 51xx 2-6-2T 5547 of Swindon on Saturday 19th September 1959. (V.R. Webster: KRM)

Shortly after crossing the Severn Valley 57xx 0-6-0T 3732 (Wellington) brings a Wellington to Much Wenlock train into the Severn Junction platform at Buildwas. (V.R. Webster: KRM)

BUILDWAS STATION WORKING : 1955

Train	Arr	Engine	Dep	Destination
05.20 Wellington ECS	05.51	57xx 0-6-0PT: Well 460		
Light ex Wellington		57xx 0-6-0PT: Well 461	05/58	Much Wenlock (06.05)
		57xx 0-6-0PT: Well 460	06.00	Wellington (06.36)
06.05 Wellington (Engine & Brake)	06.50	57xx 0-6-0PT: Well 463		
06.50 Much Wenlock	06.59	57xx 0-6-0PT: Well 461	07.00	Wellington (07.35)
05.35 Wellington (Goods)	07.16	57xx 0-6-0PT: Well 462		
06.48 Wellington	07.23	57xx 0-6-0PT: Well 460		
		57xx 0-6-0PT: Well 460	07.40	(Mixed) Much Wenlock (07.57)
		57xx 0-6-0PT: Well 463	07.40	Engine & Brake Madeley (08.00)
08.15 Shrewsbury	08.43	51xx 2-6-2T: Salop 100		(Fwd at 08.59)
08.35 Much Wenlock	08.44	57xx 0-6-0PT: Well 460		(Fwd at 08.56)
08.16 Wellington	08.50	57xx 0-6-0PT: Well 461		(Fwd at 08.56)
06.55 Worcester	08.54	51xx 2-6-2T: Worcs 451	08.55	Shrewsbury (09.21)
(08.35 Much Wenlock)		57xx 0-6-0PT: Well 460	08.56	Wellington (09.34)
(08.16 Wellington)		57xx 0-6-0PT: Well 461	08.56	Much Wenlock (09.10)
(08.15 Shrewsbury)		51xx 2-6-2T: Salop 100	08.59	Stourbridge Jcn (
		57xx 0-6-0PT: Well 462	09.40	(Goods) Hollinswood (11.17)
08.47 Kemberton (Goods)	09.58	57xx 0-6-0PT: Well 463		
		57xx 0-6-0PT: Well 463	10.15	Light to Shrewsbury (10.58)
10.35 Kidderminster	11.50	Railcar: Worcs 1		(Fwd at 11.57)
11.40 Much Wenlock	11.50	57xx 0-6-0PT: Well 461		(Fwd at 11.55)
11.17 Wellington	11.51	57xx 0-6-0PT: Well 464		(Fwd at 11.56)
11.25 Shrewsbury	11.52	51xx 2-6-2T: Worcs 451	11.54	Hartlebury (13.12)
(11.40 Much Wenlock)		57xx 0-6-0PT: Well 461	11.55	Wellington (12.28)
(11.17 Wellington)		57xx 0-6-0PT: Well 464	11.56	Much Wenlock (12.10)
(10.35 Kidderminster)		Railcar: Worcs 1	11.57	Shrewsbury (12.32)
10.15 Coton Hill	12.00	43xx 2-6-0: Salop 150	12.40	Hartlebury (19.15)
13.00 Much Wenlock	13.09	57xx 0-6-0PT: Well 464	13.13	Wellington (13.48)
13.05 Hollinswood (Goods)	13.45	57xx 0-6-0PT: Well 467		
13.40 Horsehay (Goods)	14.05	57xx 0-6-0PT: Well 460		
13.45 Shrewsbury	14.13	Railcar: Worcs 1	14.15	Kidderminster (15.45)
		57xx 0-6-0PT: Well 467	14.30	(Goods) Much Wenlock (14.48)
15.00 Much Wenlock (Goods)	15.17	57xx 0-6-0PT: Well 467		
		57xx 0-6-0PT: Well 460	15.25	Lightmoor Junction (15.37)*
14.00 Hartlebury	15.25	51xx 2-6-2T: Worcs 451	15.26	Shrewsbury (15.58)
15.10 Wellington	15.45	57xx 0-6-0PT: Well 461	15.46	Much Wenlock (16.00)
		57xx 0-6-0PT: Well 467	16.01	(Goods) Hollinswood (17.01)
16.10 Coalbrookdale	16.14	57xx 0-6-0PT: Well 460	16.15	Much Wenlock (16.30)*
15.50 Shrewsbury	16.18	51xx 2-6-2T: Salop 101	16.20	Kidderminster (17.34)
15.10 Madeley Jcn (Goods)	16.50	57xx 0-6-0PT: Well 468		
16.40 Much Wenlock	16.50	57xx 0-6-0PT: Well 461	16.55	Wellington (17.32)
16.30 Wellington	17.05	57xx 0-6-0PT: Well 464	17.06	Much Wenlock (17.20)
		57xx 0-6-0PT: Well 468	17.06	(Goods) Wellington (17.56)
Light ex Much Wenlock	17.39	57xx 0-6-0PT: Well 460		
16.23 Kidderminster	17.43	51xx 2-6-2T: Salop 100	17.45	Shrewsbury (18.15)
17.45 Much Wenlock	17.54	57xx 0-6-0PT: Well 464		(Fwd at 18.02)
17.33 Shrewsbury	18.00	51xx 2-6-2T: Worcs 451		(Fwd at 18.04)
(17.45 Much Wenlock)		57xx 0-6-0PT: Well 464	18.02	Wellington (18.37)
(17.33 Shrewsbury)		51xx 2-6-2T: Worcs 451	18.04	Kidderminster (19.18)
		57xx 0-6-0PT: Well 460	18.15	(Goods) Wellington (19.37)
17.50 Wellington	18.18	57xx 0-6-0PT: Well 461	18.20	Much Wenlock (18.34)
19.05 Much Wenlock	19.14	57xx 0-6-0PT: Well 461	19.15	Wellington (19.52)
14.15 Hartlebury (Goods)	19.17	43xx 2-6-0: Salop 150A		(Fwd at 19.56)
18.25 Hartlebury	19.47	51xx 2-6-2T: Salop 101	19.48	Shrewsbury (20.17)
(Hartlebury Goods)		43xx 2-6-0: Salop 150A	19.56	Coton Hill (21.14)
19.55 Wellington	20.30	57xx 0-6-0PT: Well 464	20.31	Much Wenlock (20.45)
Light ex Much Wenlock	21.10	57xx 0-6-0PT: Well 464		
20.45 Shrewsbury	21.13	51xx 2-6-2T: Salop 101	21.14	Ironbridge (21.19)
		57xx 0-6-0PT: Well 464	21.15	Light to Wellington via Salop
21.35 Ironbridge	21.39	51xx 2-6-2T: Salop 101	21.40	Shrewsbury (22.17)

* *School term only*

51xx 2-6-2T 4147 of Kidderminster runs into the up platform at Buildwas with the 15.50 Shrewsbury - Kidderminster train on Saturday 21st July 1962. (Brian Moone: KRM)

An unidentified 57xx 0-6-0T arrives in the High Level (Severn Junction) platform at Buildwas with a Wellington - Much Wenlock service on Saturday 22nd July 1961. Although the Severn Junction had only one platform at Buildwas, the station working allowed trains to pass; Westbound (down) trains drawing up at the far end of the platform whilst the up train would run past the station on the loop to the right and then reverse into the station. Normally this movement would happen twice a day. (G.E.S. Parker: KRM)

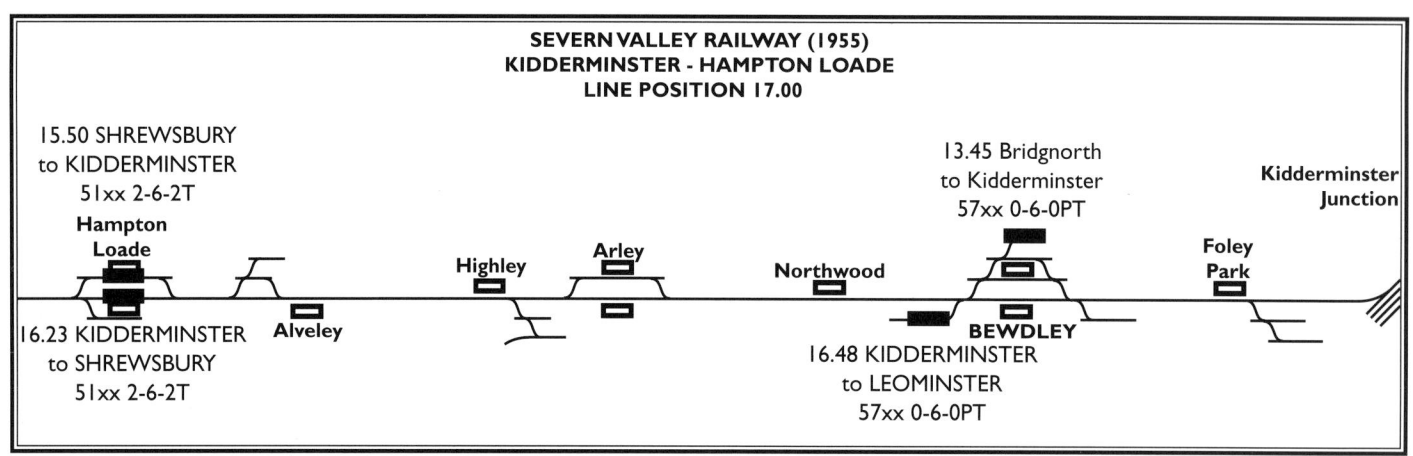

CONTROLLER'S LOG: The crews of the up and down Shrewsbury goods have exchanged footplates and are probably having a bite to eat before being let out onto the main line. The up train should leave first and although it is booked to leave at 17.45 and run non-stop to Bewdley, the guard will be urged to leave five or ten minutes early since the train has an extremely tight crossing at Arley with a down passenger. (Illustrating the optimistic world into which the compilers sometimes drift, the goods is booked to pass Arley at 18.11 whilst the 17.30 Hartlebury - Highley diesel stops for set off from Hartlebury at 10.10 this morning to work all goods yards to Bridgnorth and back. Although it serves Alveley sidings, the prime purpose of the train is to deal with goods rather than mineral traffic and any coal in its load will be for local coal merchants as opposed to power station fuel. It spends almost an hour shunting the yard at Bewdley and will depart in about ten minutes time with traffic to connect with the night services from Kidderminster.

With a pair of Shrewsbury passenger trains in each platform, Hampton Loade is having its moment of daily glory: this being the only the engine runs round the stock and returns to Kidderminster - with a stop of almost forty minutes at Tenbury Wells - at 18.20.

Useful as the service may be, it is doubtful if it contributes much to the season ticket traffic between Leominster and Birmingham since there is no corresponding morning service and it is impossible to reach Snow Hill before nine-thirty in the morning - and that with changes of train at Woofferton, Tenbury Wells and Kidderminster.

The 16.40 Much Wenlock to Wellington left the high level platform at Buildwas five minutes

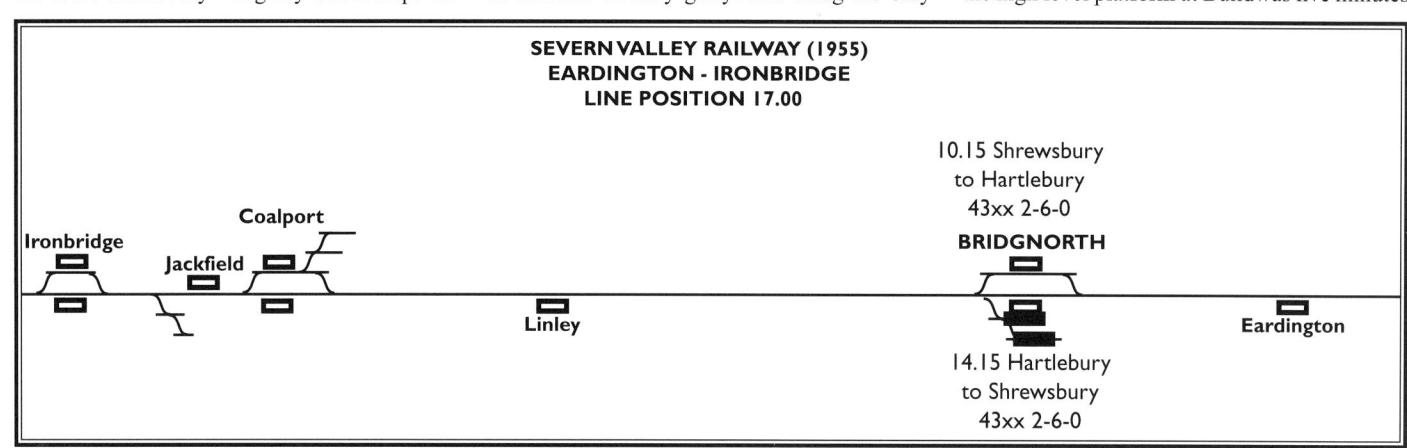

less than a minute at the same time. It is safer to play for safety by ensuring that the goods gets into the up loop a good five minutes before the passenger is due).

The Down Shrewsbury goods will leave at 17.50 in order to get to Coalport to cross the 17.33 Shrewsbury - Kidderminster.

A few miles to the south another goods train shunts at Bewdley before continuing forward to Kidderminster. This is the daily trip which time that two trains are booked to pass in its platforms.

Just leaving Bewdley in the down direction is a unique service: the only conventional train of the day to run over the Tenbury Branch. Worked by a 57xx 0-6-0T and formed of two non-corridor vehicles, the service operates as an extension of the Birmingham/Worcester rush hour and is extended down the GW/LNW joint line from Woofferton to Leominster. On arrival ago and the 17.06 coal empties for Wellington will leave as soon as the section to Coalbrookdale is clear. This clearance however cannot be given until the arrival of the 16.30 Wellington to Much Wenlock in Buildwas; the two passenger trains crossing either at Coalbrookdale or on the double-track section beyond to Lightmoor Junction. The 57xx on the 17.06 is unlikely to be unduly taxed since only 24 empties are allowed to be taken.

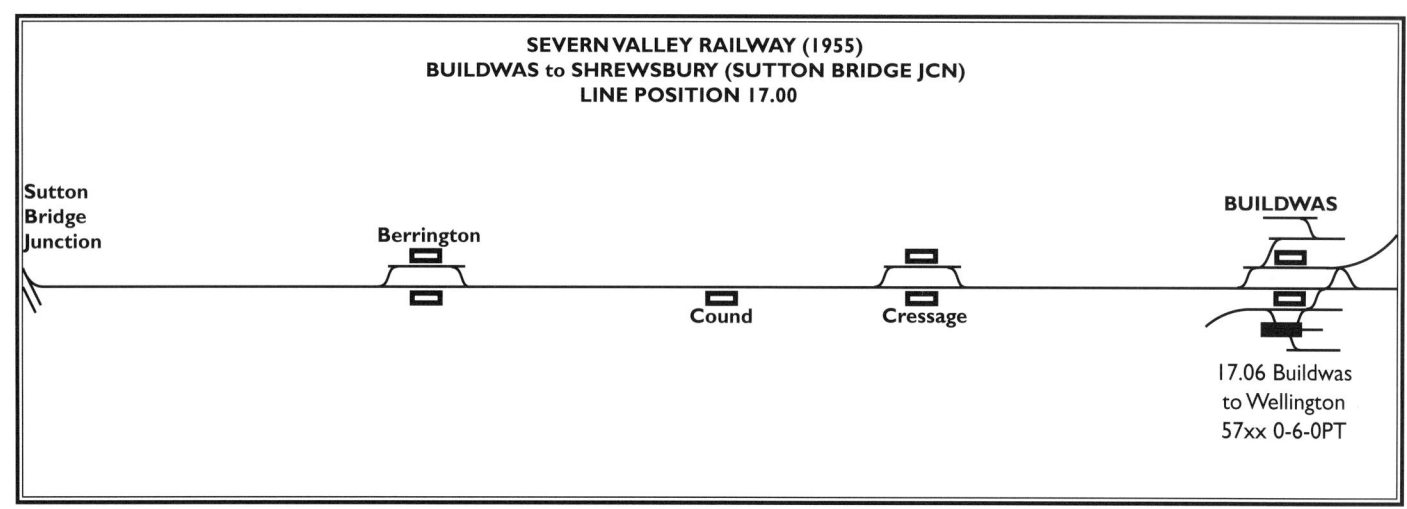

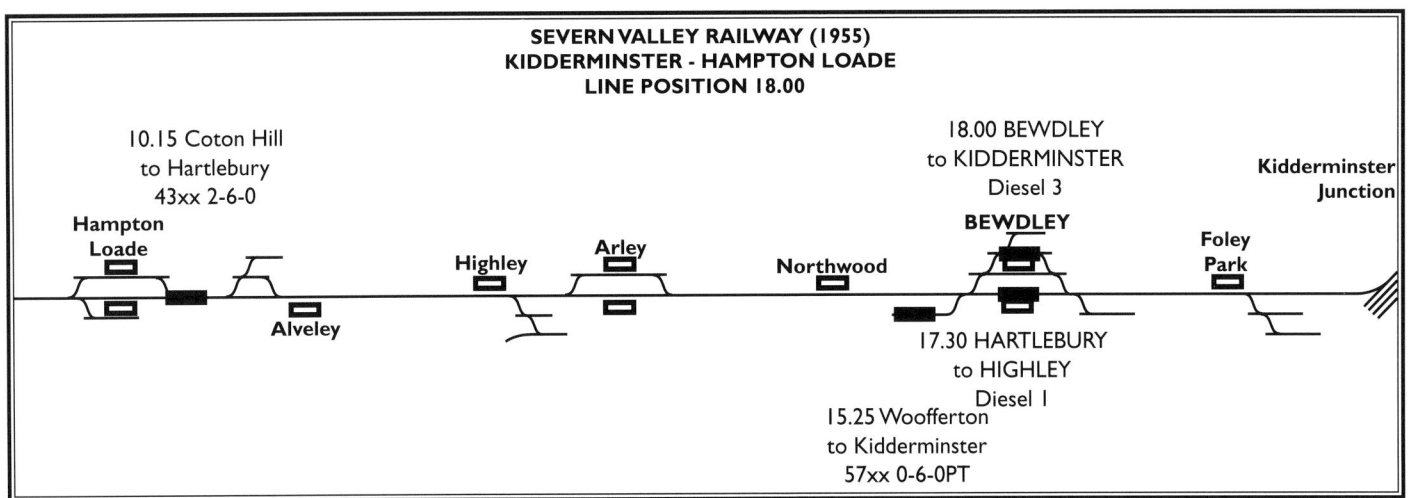

CONTROLLER'S LOG: It is an irony of history that the up Coton Hill Goods, which has just passed Hampton Loade, has been on the move for nearly eight hours yet is only twenty-seven miles from its starting point. The average speed of three and a half miles per hour is about a tenth of the maximum achieved by Stephenson's Rocket 126 years ago although, of course, the latter ran in a straight line and did not retrace its steps as the Salop goods has done. Neither did Rocket hang endlessly in sidings,

The lack of activity at Bewdley is in some degree compensated for by the complexity of the working that involves the two railcars which can be seen together in the station.

One, the 18.00 to Kidderminster, has just arrived from Kidderminster and, its driver having changed ends, is in the process of returning whilst the other, which arrived from Hartlebury eleven minutes ago, waits for connecting passengers. The scene has something of the flavour of the days before 1914

Woofferton - now approaching Bewdley - plays a critical part in the working of the rush hour since the 17.30 ex Hartlebury cannot continue its journey until the goods has cleared the six and a half mile section from Cleobury Mortimer. If the goods is not ready to leave Cleobury by its booked time of 17.41 then it has to be held back so that preference can be given to the down passenger.

For not the first time in the day, Buildwas is the busiest location of the system. The last

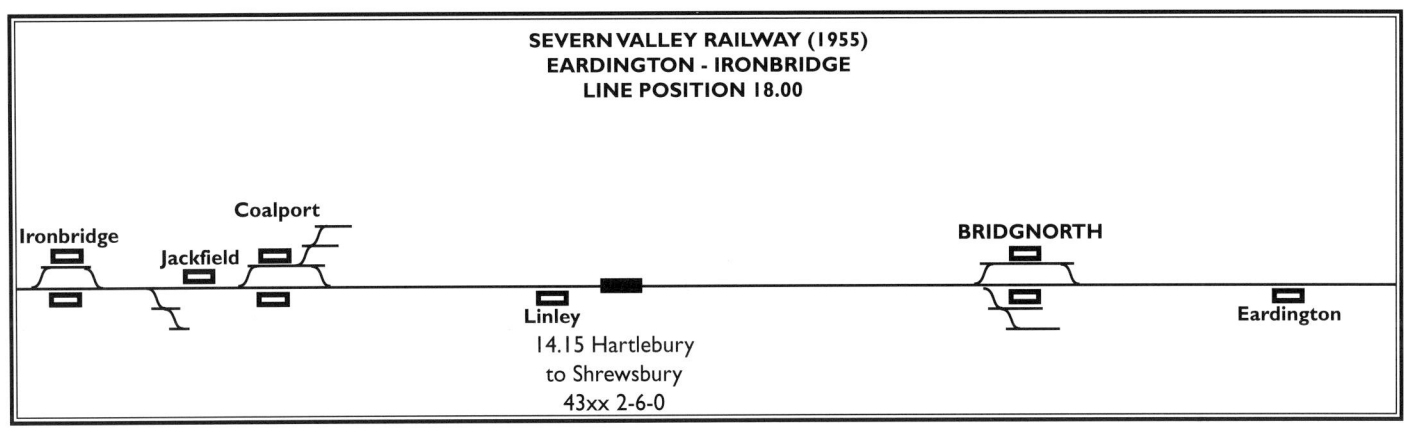

shunting and waiting for crew changeovers! Even so, by any reckoning the 10.15 Coton Hill to Hartlebury is a mightily slow train although after leaving Bridgnorth, its pace has accelerated somewhat with the train running non-stop to Bewdley where it will spend an hour putting off and attaching traffic.

The pace of its opposite number is not much faster as it approaches Coalport to do half an hour's shunting. More than three hours will pass before it sees the lights of Coton Hill Yard.

when trains from Kidderminster and Hartlebury not only connected at Bewdley but combined into one service. Edwardian memories recall the spectacle of the 17.48 Wolverhampton to Shrewsbury which married up to the 19.02 ex Hartlebury at Bewdley each evening. There were in fact three such combining operations daily with a similar number of divisions in which trains from Shrewsbury would split into Kidderminster and Hartlebury sections.

The running of the afternoon goods from

service of the day from Shrewsbury stands in the up Severn Valley platform whilst an Up Severn Junction train from Much Wenlock to Wellington connects in the High Level platform. In the adjacent yard a 57xx 0-6-0T which came in light from Wenlock a short time ago waits to follow with the Wellington Goods. This, because of the 1 in 45 drop between Horsehay and Ketley, is rather a short train and has to be limited to eighteen wagons of goods. Even then it has to stop to pin down brakes at Horsehay.

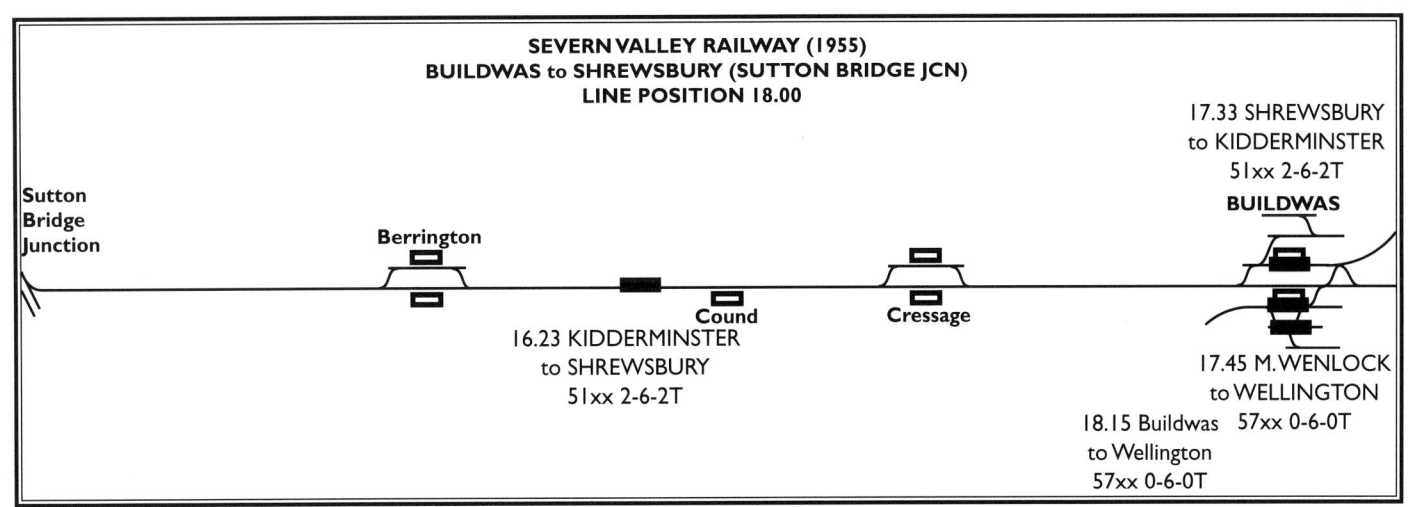

43

WORCESTER, BRIDGENORTH, IRONBRIDGE, AND MUCH WENLOCK,

To Shrewsbury, Chester, Liverpool, Holyhead, &c.

UP TRAINS.

Miles.		1	2	3	4	5	6	7	8	Sunday 1	Sunday 2
		A.M.	A.M.	A. M.	A. M.	A. M.					P. M
	KINGSTOWN					7 0					
	HOLYHEAD			1 50	7 30	11 40					
	LIVERPOOL (Landing Stage)			7 45	10 50	3 5					
	BIRKENHEAD			8 5	11 10	3 25					
	MANCHESTER			6 45	9 50						
	WARRINGTON			7 45	10 50						
	CHESTER			8 55	12 0	4 15					
		1,2,& Parl.		1 & 2	1 & 2	1,2,3					1,2,& Parl.
	Shrewsbury	7 30		10 55	3 20	6 15					5 5
4½	**Berrington**	7 40		11 5	3 29	6 25					5 15
8½	**Cressage**	7 50		11 15	3 38	6 35					5 25
12½	**Buildwas**	8 0		11 25	3 47	6 45					5 35
Much Wnlok Raily.	**Much Wenlock** Arrive	8 25		11 50	4 15	8 0					
	„ (Dep. for Up Tr.)	7 40		11 5	3 25	6 25					
13¾	**Ironbridge**	8 5		11 31	3 51	6 50					5 40
15¾	**Coalport**	8 11		11 37	3 57	6 56					5 46
18	**Linley**	8 18		11 45	4 6	7 3					5 53
22½	**Bridgnorth**	8 29		11 57	4 20	7 13					6 5
27	**Hampton Loade**	8 41		12 9	4 32						6 17
29	**Higley**	8 48		12 17	4 39						6 24
31½	**Arley**	8 55		12 25	4 46						6 34
35	**Bewdley**	9 5		12 35	4 54						6 44
37¾	**Stourport**	9 15		12 45	5 2						6 51
40½	**Hartlebury**	9 25		12 55	5 13						7 0
51½	**worcester**	10 10		2 0	5 58						7 30
	KIDDERMINSTER	9 45		1 10	5 30						7 15
	STOURBRIDGE	10 9		1 31	5 51						7 29
	DUDLEY	10 40		1 58	6 20						8 0
	Birmingham	11 30		2 45	7 5						8 45
	WOLVERHAMPTON	11 10		2 35	6 50						9 45
	MALVERN	10 50		2 30	6 35						8 5
	OXFORD	12 55		4 30	8 30						
	London (Paddington)	2 40		6 45	10 25						
	CHELTENHAM	10 52		4 1	7 33						
	GLOUCESTER	11 5		4 16	8 10						
	BRISTOL	12 20		5 35	10 0						

Will not run beyond Bridgnorth.

L Stops at Linley when required.

DOWN TRAINS.

Miles.		1	2	3	4	5	6	7	8	Sunday 1	Sunday 2
		A.M.	A.M.		P.M.	P M.				A.M.	
	BRISTOL Depart				11 15	3 30					
	GLOUCESTER		6 10		12 50	4 44					
	CHELTENHAM		6 30		1 12	5 0					
	London (Paddingtou)				9 30	1 0					
	OXFORD				11 20	3 5					
	MALVERN				1 27	5 5					
	WOLVERHAMPTON		8 10		1 25	4 15				8 0	
	Birmingham		7 50		12 20	4 0				7 45	
	DUDLEY		8 40		1 43	4 45				8 35	
	STOURBRIDGE		9 3		2 1	5 4				8 57	
	KIDDERMINSTER		9 25		2 15	5 24				9 20	
			1,2,& Parl.			1,2,3				1,2,& Parl	
	Worcester ... Depart		9 0		2 0	5 40				9 0	
11	**Hartlebury** . Depart		9 55		2 40	6 20				9 40	
13¾	**Stourport**		10 4		2 48	6 29				9 49	
16½	**Bewdley**		10 14		2 56	6 38				9 58	
20	**Arley**		10 24		A	6 48				10 8	
22½	**Higley**		10 32		—	6 55				10 15	
24½	**Hampton Loade**		10 40		—	7 2				10 22	
29	**Bridgnorth**	9 10	10 52		3 28	7 13				10 34	
33½	**Linley**	9 20	11 4		—	L				10 46	
36	**Coalport**	9 27	11 12		3 44	7 29				10 53	
38	**Ironbridge**	9 32	11 18		3 51	7 34				10 59	
39½	**Buildwas**	9 37	11 25		3 55	7 39				11 4	
Much Wnlck Raily.	**Much Wenlock** Arrive	10 0	11 50		4 15	8 0					
	„ (Dep for Down Tr.)	9 20	11 5		3 35	6 25					
43	**Cressage**	9 47	11 35		A	7 49				11 14	
47	**Berrington**	9 54	11 45		A	7 59				11 24	
51½	**Shrewsbury**	10 10	11 58		4 20	8 10				11 35	
	CHESTER	11 48	2 30		6 48	10 5					
	WARRINGTON	12 50			8 5						
	MANCHESTER	1 45			8 55						
	BIRKENHEAD	12 40	3 25		7 45	10 45					
	LIVERPOOL	1 0	3 45		8 5	11 0					
	HOLYHEAD	2 5	9 15		12 45	3 5					
	KINGSTOWN	6 5				7 5					

A Stops at Arley, Cressage & Berrington if required.

L Stops at Linley if required.

WELLINGTON AND SEVERN JUNCTION AND MADELEY BRANCHES

DOWN.

Starting from	Week Days 1	On Thursdays only.	Week Days 2	Week Days 3		Sundays	Sundays
	1, 2, 3 class.		1, 2, 3 class.	1, 2, 3 class.		1, 2, 3 class.	1, 2, 3 class.
	A.M.	A.M.	A.M.	P.M.		A.M.	P.M.
Birmingham . Depart			10 50	5 15			2 0
WOLVERHAMPTON			11 30	6 6		7 15	2 48
SHIFFNAL			12 50	6 45		7 55	3 20
MADELEY	7 5	11 40	1 8	7 3		8 13	3 37
LIGHTMOOR	7 15	11 45	1 13	7 8		8 18	3 42
HORSEHAY	7 25	11 55	1 23	7 18		8 28	3 52
LAWLEY BANK	7 30	12 0	1 28	7 23		8 33	3 57
KETLEY STATION	7 35	12 5	1 33	7 28		8 40	4 3
WELLINGTON ... Arrive	7 43	12 12	1 40	7 35		8 50	4 12
SALOP	8 20		2 28	8 35		9 15	4 40
Chester	10 3		4 10	10 5		11 15	6 50

UP.

Starting from	Week Days 4	Week Days 5	Week Days 6			Sundays	Sundays
	1, 2, 3 class.	1, 2, 3 class.	1, 2, 3 class.			1, 2, 3 class.	1, 2, 3 class.
	A.M.	P.M.	P.M.			A.M.	P.M.
Chester . . Depart	7 10	2 15	5 35				
SALOP	9 0	4 10	7 50			8 15	
WELLINGTON ... Depart	10 0	5 10	8 45			9 0	6 30
KETLEY STATION	10 10	5 20	8 55			9 10	6 40
LAWLEY BANK	10 15	5 25	9 0			9 15	6 45
HORSEHAY	10 20	5 30	9 5			9 20	6 50
LIGHTMOOR	10 30	5 40	9 15			9 25	7 0
MADELEY	10 35	5 45	9 20			9 30	7 5
SHIFFNAL ... Arrive	10 50	6 0				9 45	7 20
WOLVERHAMPTON	11 29	6 52				10 20	8 5
Birmingham	12 0	7 20				11 12	8 55

No. 1 TRAIN—Arrives at Wellington in time for 1st and 2nd Class Up Train to Birmingham and London; and 1st, 2nd, and 3rd Class Train to Shrewsbury, Chester, and Liverpool.

No. 2 TRAIN—Arrives at Wellington in time for 1st and 2nd Class Fast Train to Birmingham, &c., and London; and 1st and 2nd Fast Train to Shrewsbury, Chester, and Liverpool.

No. 3 TRAIN—Arrives at Wellington in time for 1st, 2nd, and 3rd Class Train to Wolverhampton, Birmingham, and 1st and 2nd Class to Leamington; and 1st and 2nd Class Train to Shrewsbury, Chester, and Liverpool. Passengers by Train leaving Liverpool at 3.5, and Chester at 4.15 p.m., for these Branches, go on to Shiffnal and down by the 6.45 Train.

No. 4 TRAIN—Arrives at Shiffnal in time for 1st and 2nd Class Fast Train to Birmingham, &c., and London; 1st, 2nd, and 3rd Class Train to Wolverhampton, Birmingham, &c., and London; and 1st and 2nd Class Train to Shrewsbury, Chester, and Liverpool.

No. 5 TRAIN—Arrives at Shiffnal in time for 1st and 2nd Class Train to Birmingham and London; and 1st and 2nd Class Train to Shrewsbury and Chester.

No. 6 TRAIN—Leaves Wellington on arrival of the 3rd Class Train from Liverpool, &c.; and 1st and 2nd Class Train from London, &c.

The 7.55 a.m. Down on Sundays arrives at Wellington in time for 1st, 2nd. and 3rd Class Train to Salop, Chester, Birkenhead, and Liverpool, &c. The 9.0 a.m. Up Train runs to Wolverhampton and Birmingham, &c. The 3.20 Down on Sundays reaches Wellington in time for a Train to Shrewsbury and the North; and the 6.30 Up Train on Sundays reaches Shiffnal in time for a Train to Wolverhampton and Birmingham.

The Classes refer to Trains on the Branch Lines only.

The passenger service for both the Severn Valley and Severn Junction lines in March 1864. There are numerous points of interest not the least of which is the independent Much Wenlock & Severn Junction Railway which operated between Much Wenlock and Buildwas. The Severn Junction line from Wellington had yet to complete its development and operated as a loop from Wellington to Shiffnal (sic), reversing at Lightmoor. In the ninety years between 1864 and 1954 much, of course, changed although the time taken to travel to London did not reflect the advances in modern locomotives, block signalling and bogie/corridor coaches. In 1864 the morning train from Bridgnorth to London took six hours and eleven minutes to reach Paddington yet nine decades later and in spite of all the improvements that had come to pass, the journey was only twenty-five minutes faster.

EVOLUTION OF THE SERVICE

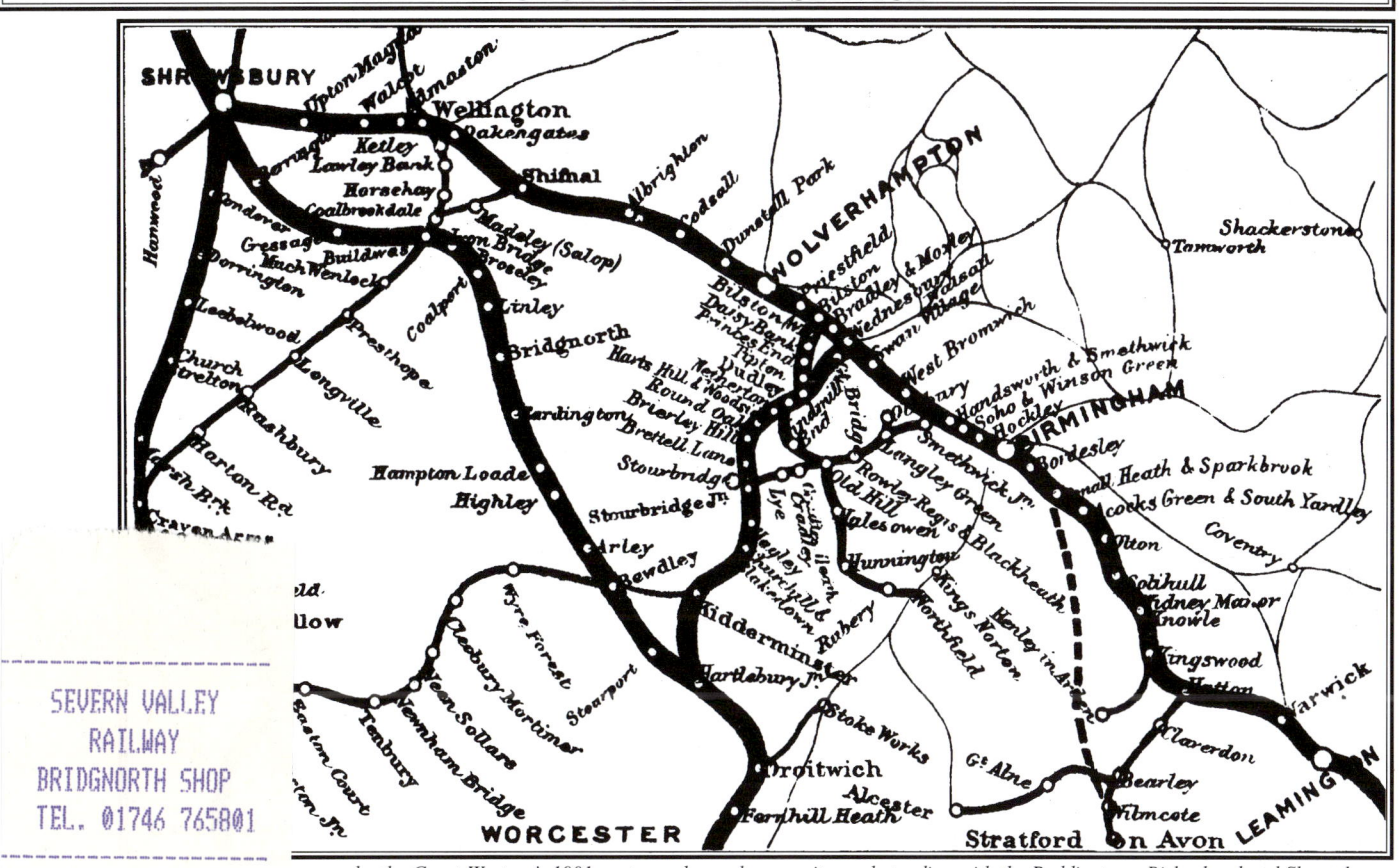

...as seen by the Great Western's 1901 cartographers who gave it equal standing with the Paddington - Birkenhead and Shrewsbury - ... It is interesting to note that the Bewdley - Kidderminster section (which survives as part of the preserved Severn Valley line) is shown ... the Bewdley - Hartlebury line is shown as a trunk line and in fact it was never easy to determine which of the two lines south of Bewdley ...ley; a quandary which remained until being settled by the preservation movement who now operate services between Kidderminster ...

The July 1910 timetable shows the pre-grouping Severn Valley passenger service at its busiest with five up and six down Shrewsbury trains, most consisting of separate Hartlebury and Kidderminster sections. Local trains in the Bewdley area - many which ran from Kidderminster to Hartlebury via Bewdley - relied heavily on steam 'motors' which were the precursors of the diesel railcars. The imbalance of Shrewsbury trains and the combing at Bewdley must have called for some very interesting carriage workings.

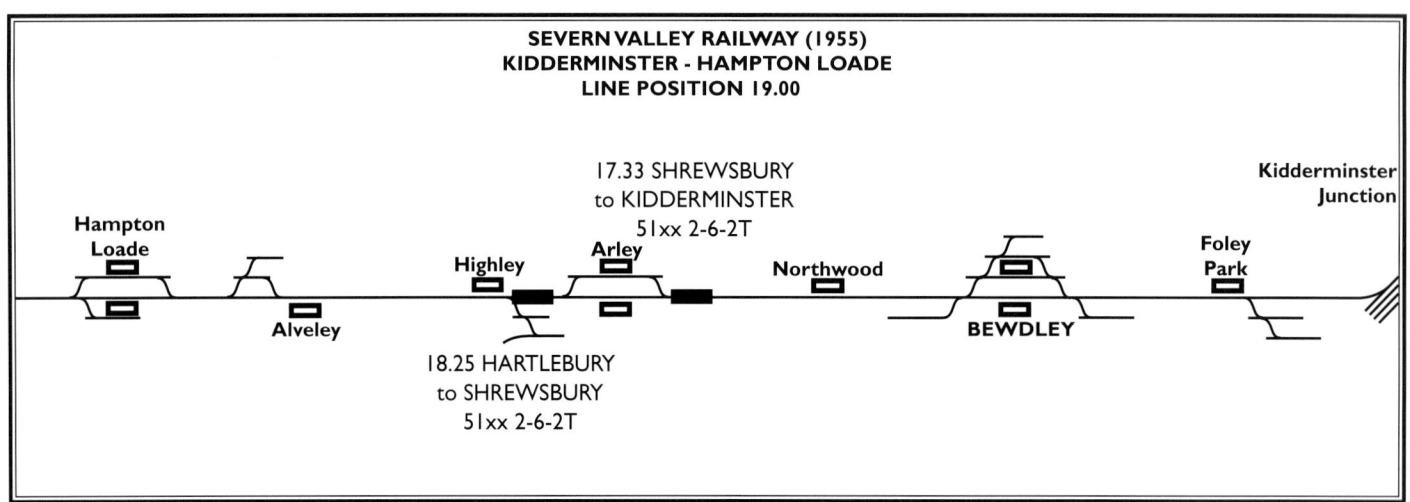

CONTROLLER'S LOG: As the line passes from afternoon to evening, the time arrives when it attracts a sizeable, if uncommercial, level of attention. At numerous points along its forty-mile length, a pleasant summer's evening will see a dozen or more elderly strollers ambling up to the lineside to view whatever activity there is to be seen. The more expert will have some idea of the timetable and will time their visit accordingly but most will turn up, armed with pipes, tobacco and Times crosswords, content to breath in the static tranquillity that is peculiar to the British branch line and those of the Great Western in particular. Those fortunate in their rendezvous will hear the squeal of a signal wire act as a prelude to the passage of a train whilst those particularly lucky in their timing may see two. Those especially blessed might catch sight of the Hartlebury - Coton Hill goods as it winds its way towards Buildwas and a good hour's shunting.

The area between Bridgnorth and Bewdley affords the best of an evenings viewing since the passing of the evening Shrewsbury to Kidderminster is followed, after not too long a pause, by the 18.25 Hartlebury to Shrewsbury. It is the most English of scenes: the teasing of crossword clues being interspersed with glances up and down the line to see whether anything is approaching. A signal falls and minutes later the clear and honest exhaust of a Swindon 2-6-2T echoes through hill and embankment heralding the approach of a train which passes with an amiable wave from the driver and a sensation of hot oil and sulphur. The watcher remains until the train is out of sight and sound before turning a reluctant back on the scene to head for a pint and bed.

Where, the observer might wonder, have the passengers in these trains come from? The answer in respect of the up train is that almost all will be local and few will be travelling further than Worcester. The down train is a different kettle of fish and some of its users will have come from far afield since it connects - after an hour's wait at Hartlebury - with the 13.45 Paddington - Wolverhampton express and since it is not uncommon to devote an entire day to travelling between London and Shropshire, the 17.33 does quite a good trade in long distance travel.

It is astonishing to realise that one has to leave Paddington as early as lunchtime in order to get to Berrington the same day; clearly Shropshire is a great deal further from London than it appears! It is however possible to get as

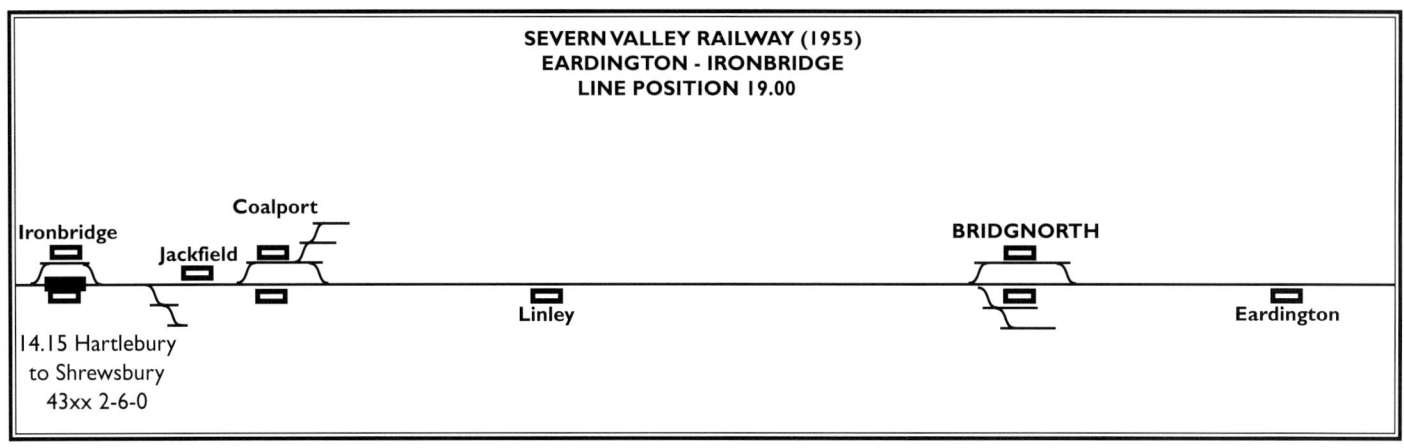

far north as Bridgnorth by leaving London in the 16.45 express which has a through portion for Wolverhampton via Kidderminster and arrives just in time to catch the 20.10 to Bewdley and the 20.26 beyond.

Although Buildwas is quiet at the moment, the Severn Junction still has a little life left in it. Goods traffic has finished for the day but there is still some passenger activity going on. A 57xx 0-6-0T is about to leave Much Wenlock with a service for Wellington whilst another 57xx is waiting at Wellington to complete a final round trip before the line shuts down for the night.

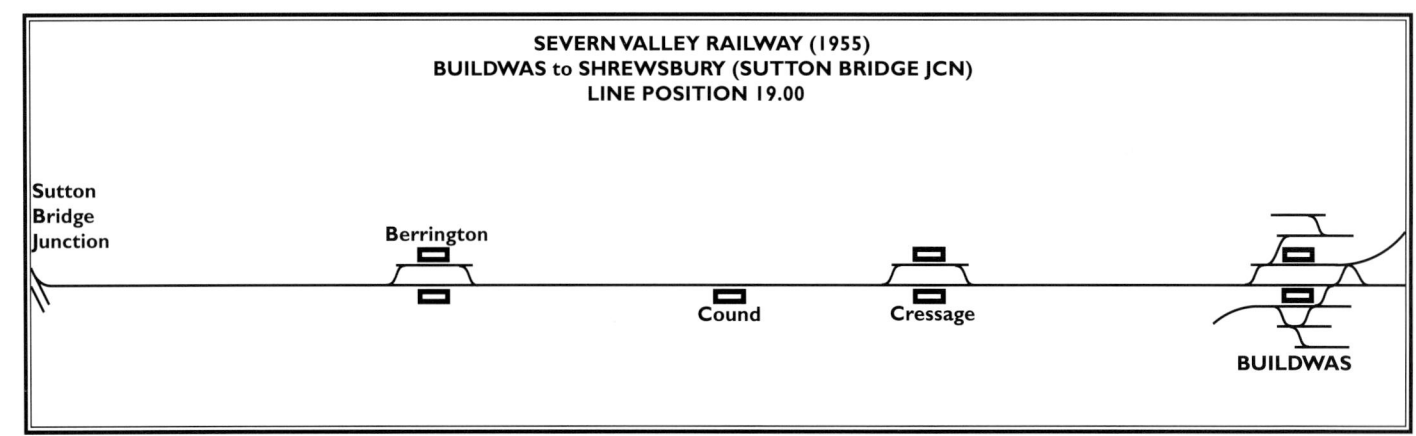

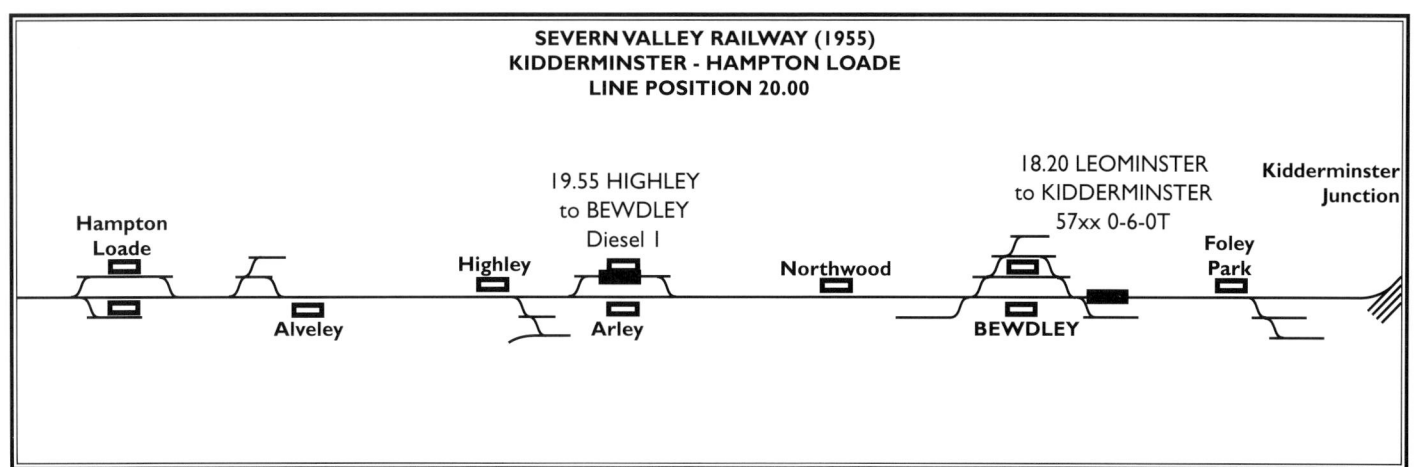

CONTROLLER'S LOG: Northbound passenger services on the Severn Valley finish early in the evening with the last train from Hartlebury being the 18.25 to Shrewsbury - now restarting from Cound Halt - whilst Kidderminster runs a Highley diesel at 19.20 and a Bewdley service at 20.10.

The diesel runs as a connection out of the 18.05 and 18.15 trains from Wolverhampton and Birmingham respectively and remains on the Severn Valley for some time, shuttling up and down the southern end of the line by working connects at Kidderminster with the 16.45 express from Paddington to Wolverhampton and the stop at Bewdley allows a connection to be made with the 20.26 Bewdley to Bridgnorth railcar.

One wonders sometimes if the intricate nicety of the working could not be improved by the substitution of a more basic but straightforward arrangement. If the 19.55 ex Highley were to be extended from Bewdley to Kidderminster, the 20.26 Bewdley to Bridgnorth would start back from Kidderminster at about Kidderminster to Worcester passengers; the normal twenty-five minute journey taking almost an hour.

Before the 20.10 is able to leave, it has to wait for the 18.20 ex Leominster to clear the section from Bewdley. On reaching Kidderminster the 57xx 0-6-0 pannier tank will run round its two-coach train and take it empty to Bewdley where it will stable, ready to be attached to the 08.00 Birmingham service in the morning. This train of empty stock will be the last Severn Valley service of the day to leave Kidderminster.

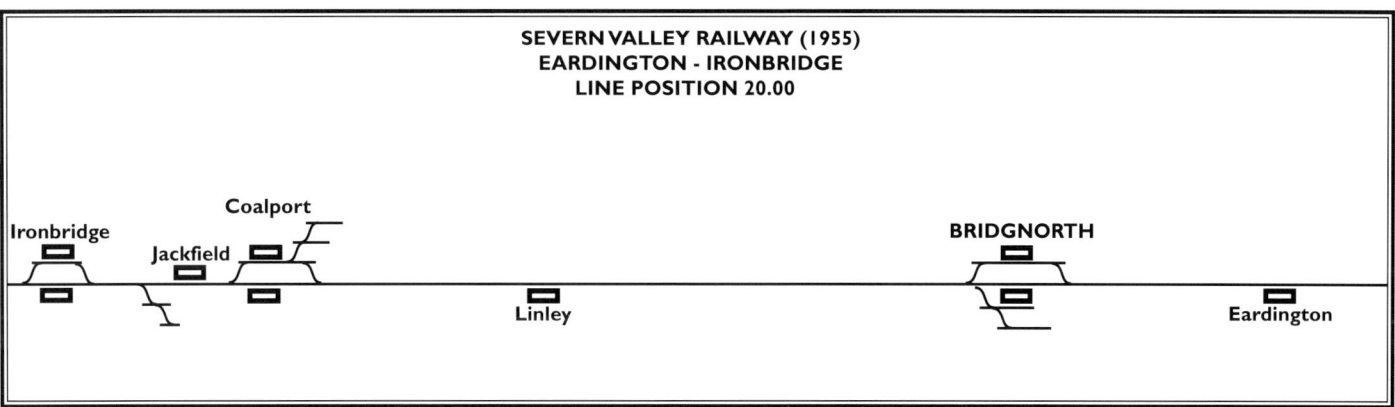

the 19.55 Highley to Bewdley followed by a trip to Bridgnorth and back.

The 20.10 from Kidderminster - the last Severn Valley passenger departure of the day - is a steam working of a very curious type since it is actually a through working to Worcester but is routed via Bewdley where the 51xx 2-6-2T engine has to run round its train. The circuitous routing of the service extends the normal twenty-five minute Kidderminster - Worcester journey time to one of fifty-five minutes.

The reason for the detour is that the 20.10 20.25 and would give a through service to Bridgnorth which would be a very agreeable alternative to passengers who had come all the way from London. Passengers from Highley to Worcester would connect with the 20.10 Birmingham to Hereford at Kidderminster whilst the 21.05 Bridgnorth to Worcester - the final working of the railcar - would run in its existing timings south of Kidderminster since the current arrangements allow it twenty minutes in Kidderminster. Needless to say, it is not a very agreeable arrangement for through

There is still a little freight activity left to monitor as the afternoon Hartlebury to Shrewsbury goods is still on the move, having just left Buildwas in the wake of the evening Hartlebury - Shrewsbury passenger. It has calls yet to make at Cressage and Berrington and will not get to Coton Hill yard for another hour and a quarter.

Lest the sight of two Shrewsbury-bound trains give the impression that the section north of Buildwas is shutting down for the night, there are one or two surprises to come.

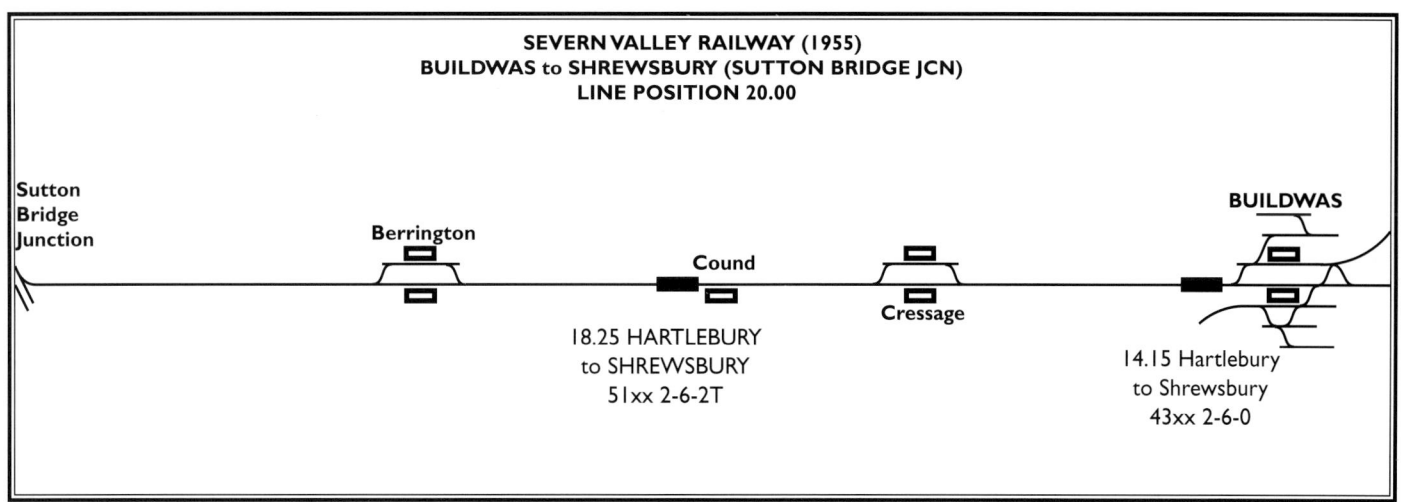

LOCOMOTIVE RESTRICTIONS

Section of line	King 4-6-0, 47xx 2-8-0	County 4-6-0, Castle 4-6-0, Hall 4-6-0, Grange 4-6-0, Mod Hall 4-6-0, 93xx 2-6-0, 72xx 2-8-2T	42xx 2-8-0T, 31xx 2-6-2T, 56xx 0-6-2T, 15xx 0-6-0T, 94xx 0-6-0T, 1101 0-4-0T	28xx 2-8-0, ROD 2-8-0	Manor 4-6-0, 43xx 2-6-0, 51xx 2-6-2T, 61xx 2-6-2T, 81xx 2-6-2T, 97xx 0-6-0T, BR4 4-6-0	51xx 2-6-2T	90xx 4-4-0, 1205 2-6-2T, 54xx 0-6-0T, 57xx 0-6-0T, 64xx 0-6-0T, 74xx 0-6-0T	2251 0-6-0, 45xx 2-6-2T
Kidderminster - Bewdley	X	20	20	Yes	Yes	Yes	Yes	Yes
Bewdley - Highley	X	X	X	X	25	25	Yes	Yes
Highley - Bridgnorth	X	X	X	X	25	25	Yes	Yes
Bridgnorth - Ironbridge	X	X	X	X	25	25	Yes	Yes
Ironbridge - Buildwas	X	X	X	X	25	25	Yes	Yes
Buildwas - Berrington	X	20	20	Yes	Yes	Yes	Yes	Yes
Berrington - Shrewsbury	X	20	20	Yes	Yes	Yes	Yes	Yes
Hartlebury - Stourport	X	20	20	Yes	Yes	Yes	Yes	Yes
Stourport - Bewdley	X	X	X	25	25	25	Yes	Yes
Bewdley - Cleobury M.	X	X	X	25	25	25	Yes	Yes
Cleobury M - Neen Sollars	X	X	X	25	25	25	Yes	Yes
Neen Sollars - Newnham Bge	X	X	X	25	25	25	Yes	Yes
Newnham Bge - Tenbury Wells	X	X	X	25	25	25	Yes	Yes
Tenbury Wells - Woofferton	X	X	X	25	25	25	Yes	Yes
Wellington - Lightmoor Jcn	20E	X	X	X	X	X	Yes	Yes
Lightmoor Jcn - Buildwas	20E	X	X	Yes	Yes	Yes	Yes	Yes
Buildwas - Farley	X	20*	20*	30	30	30	Yes	Yes
Farley - Much Wenlock	X	20*	20*	Light	Light	30	Yes	Yes
Much Wenlock - Longville	X	X	X	X	X	X	Yes	Yes

Notes: Figures indicate the maximum permitted speed. 20E - In emergency (diversions) only with maximum speed of 20mph. X - prohibited. The above excludes local restrictions in sidings, etc.

TRAIN LOADING : SEVERN JUNCTION (WELLINGTON - LONGVILLE) SECTION

DOWN SEVERN JUNCTION

64xx 0-6-0T
Section of line	Passenger	Minerals	Goods	Empties
Wellington - Horsehay	3	10	15	20
Horsehay - Lightmoor Jcn	3	25	30*	30*
Lightmoor Jcn - Buildwas	3	35	40*	40*
Buildwas - Much Wenlock	3	10	15	20
Much Wenlock - Longville	3	35	45*	45*

2251 0-6-0
Section of line	Passenger	Minerals	Goods	Empties
Wellington - Horsehay	3	11	17	22
Horsehay - Lightmoor Jcn	3	29	30*	30*
Lightmoor Jcn - Buildwas	3	40*	40*	40*
Buildwas - Much Wenlock	3	11	17	22
Much Wenlock - Longville	3	40	45*	45*

45xx 2-6-2T, 57xx 0-6-0T
Section of line	Passenger	Minerals	Goods	Empties
Wellington - Horsehay	4	12	18	24
Horsehay - Lightmoor Jcn	4	29	30*	30*
Lightmoor Jcn - Buildwas	4	40*	40*	40*
Buildwas - Much Wenlock	4	11	17	22
Much Wenlock - Longville	4	40	45*	45*

43xx 2-6-0, 51xx 2-6-2T, 56xx 0-6-2T,
Section of line	Passenger	Minerals	Goods	Empties
Wellington - Horsehay	4	16	24	30*
Horsehay - Lightmoor Jcn	4	30*	30*	30*
Lightmoor Jcn - Buildwas	4	40*	40*	40*
Buildwas - Much Wenlock	4	n/a	n/a	n/a
Much Wenlock - Longville	4	n/a	n/a	n/a

UP SEVERN JUNCTION

64xx 0-6-0T
Section of line	Passenger	Minerals	Goods	Empties
Longville - Much Wenlock	3	22	33	44
Much Wenlock - Buildwas	3	30	45	45*
Buildwas - Lightmoor Jcn	3	12	18	24
Lightmoor Jcn - Ketley	3	10	15	20
Ketley - Wellington	3	30	45	60

2251 0-6-0
Section of line	Passenger	Minerals	Goods	Empties
Longville - Much Wenlock	3	25	38	45*
Much Wenlock - Buildwas	3	33	45*	45*
Buildwas - Lightmoor Jcn	3	14	21	28
Lightmoor Jcn - Ketley	3	11	17	22
Ketley - Wellington	3	33	50	60*

45xx 2-6-2T, 57xx 0-6-0T
Section of line	Passenger	Minerals	Goods	Empties
Longville - Much Wenlock	4	25	38	45*
Much Wenlock - Buildwas	4	33	45*	45*
Buildwas - Lightmoor Jcn	4	15	23	30
Lightmoor Jcn - Ketley	4	12	18	24
Ketley - Wellington	4	33	50	60*

43xx 2-6-0, 51xx 2-6-2T, 56xx 0-6-2T,
Section of line	Passenger	Minerals	Goods	Empties
Longville - Much Wenlock	4	n/a	n/a	n/a
Much Wenlock - Buildwas	4	n/a	n/a	n/a
Buildwas - Lightmoor Jcn	4	20	30	30*
Lightmoor Jcn - Ketley	4	16	24	30*
Ketley - Wellington	4	40	60	60*

DOWN MADELEY BRANCH

64xx 0-6-0T
Section of line	Passenger	Minerals	Goods	Empties
Madeley Jcn - Lightmoor Jcn	n/a	20	30	30*
Oxley - Buildwas through trains.	n/a	20	30	40

2251 0-6-0
Section of line	Passenger	Minerals	Goods	Empties
Madeley Jcn - Lightmoor Jcn	n/a	23	30*	30*
Oxley - Buildwas through trains.	n/a	23	35	46

45xx 2-6-2T, 57xx 0-6-0T
Section of line	Passenger	Minerals	Goods	Empties
Madeley Jcn - Lightmoor Jcn	n/a	25	30*	30*
Oxley - Buildwas through trains.	n/a	27	38	50

43xx 2-6-0, 51xx 2-6-2T, 56xx 0-6-2T,
Section of line	Passenger	Minerals	Goods	Empties
Madeley Jcn - Lightmoor Jcn	n/a	30*	30*	30*
Oxley - Buildwas through trains.	n/a	36	50	60

28xx 2-8-0
Section of line	Passenger	Minerals	Goods	Empties
Madeley Jcn - Lightmoor Jcn	n/a	30*	30*	30*
Oxley - Buildwas through trains.	n/a	44	60	60

UP MADELEY BRANCH

64xx 0-6-0T
Section of line	Passenger	Minerals	Goods	Empties
Lightmoor - Madeley Jcn	n/a	20	30	30*
Buildwas - Oxley through trains	n/a	22	33	44

2251 0-6-0
Section of line	Passenger	Minerals	Goods	Empties
Lightmoor - Madeley Jcn	n/a	23	30*	30*
Buildwas - Oxley through trains	n/a	25	38	50

45xx 2-6-2T, 57xx 0-6-0T
Section of line	Passenger	Minerals	Goods	Empties
Lightmoor - Madeley Jcn	n/a	25	30*	30*
Buildwas - Oxley through trains	n/a	27	41	54

43xx 2-6-0, 51xx 2-6-2T, 56xx 0-6-2T,
Section of line	Passenger	Minerals	Goods	Empties
Lightmoor - Madeley Jcn	n/a	30*	30*	30*
Buildwas - Oxley through trains	n/a	36	54	60*

28xx 2-8-0
Section of line	Passenger	Minerals	Goods	Empties
Lightmoor - Madeley Jcn	n/a	24	36	48
Buildwas - Oxley through trains	n/a	24	36	48

*: load restricted by train length limit. Loadings given in units of coaches (passenger trains) and wagons (Goods and mineral trains)

TRAIN LOADING : SEVERN VALLEY SECTION & BRANCHES

DOWN SEVERN VALLEY

64xx 0-6-0T

Section of line	Passenger	Minerals	Goods	Empties
Kidderminster - Bewdley	11	45	45*	45*
Bewdley - Highley	9	34	45*	45*
Highley - Bridgnorth	9	22	33	44
Bridgnorth - Ironbridge	9	25	38	45*
Ironbridge - Buildwas	9	32	45*	45*
Buildwas - Berrington	9	26	39	45*
Berrington - Shrewsbury	9	29	44	45*

2251 0-6-0

Section of line	Passenger	Minerals	Goods	Empties
Kidderminster - Bewdley	11	45*	45*	45*
Bewdley - Highley	9	39	45*	45*
Highley - Bridgnorth	9	25	38	45*
Bridgnorth - Ironbridge	9	29	44	45*
Ironbridge - Buildwas	9	37	45*	45*
Buildwas - Berrington	9	30	45	45*
Berrington - Shrewsbury	9	33	45*	45*

45xx 2-6-2T, 57xx 0-6-0T

Section of line	Passenger	Minerals	Goods	Empties
Kidderminster - Bewdley	13	45*	45*	45*
Bewdley - Highley	10	42	45*	45*
Highley - Bridgnorth	10	27	41	45*
Bridgnorth - Ironbridge	10	31	45*	45*
Ironbridge - Buildwas	10	40	45*	45*
Buildwas - Berrington	10	32	45*	45*
Berrington - Shrewsbury	10	33	45*	45*

43xx 2-6-0, 51xx 2-6-2T, 56xx 0-6-2T,

Section of line	Passenger	Minerals	Goods	Empties
Kidderminster - Bewdley	13	36	45*	45*
Bewdley - Highley	13	45*	45*	45*
Highley - Bridgnorth	13	36	45*	45*
Bridgnorth - Ironbridge	13	41	45*	45*
Ironbridge - Buildwas	13	45*	45*	45*
Buildwas - Berrington	13	43	45*	45*
Berrington - Shrewsbury	13	45*	45*	45*

HARTLEBURY - WOOFFERTON

64xx 0-6-0T

Section of line	Passenger	Minerals	Goods	Empties
Hartlebury - Stourport	9	34	45*	45*
Stourport - Bewdley	9	29	44	45*
Bewdley - Cleobury M.	9	16	24	32
Cleobury M - Neen Sollars	9	20	30	40
Neen Sollars - Newnham Bge	9	40	45*	45*
Newnham Bge - Tenbury Wells	9	30	45	45*
Tenbury Wells - Woofferton	11	28	42	45*

HARTLEBURY - WOOFFERTON
2251 0-6-0

Section of line	Passenger	Minerals	Goods	Empties
Hartlebury - Stourport	9	39	45*	45*
Stourport - Bewdley	9	33	45*	45*
Bewdley - Cleobury M.	9	18	27	36
Cleobury M - Neen Sollars	9	23	35	45*
Neen Sollars - Newnham Bge	9	45*	45*	45*
Newnham Bge - Tenbury Wells	9	35	45*	45*
Tenbury Wells - Woofferton	11	32	45*	45*

HARTLEBURY - WOOFFERTON
45xx 2-6-2T, 57xx 0-6-0T

Section of line	Passenger	Minerals	Goods	Empties
Hartlebury - Stourport	10	42	45*	45*
Stourport - Bewdley	10	36	45*	45*
Bewdley - Cleobury M.	9	20	30	40
Cleobury M - Neen Sollars	9	25	38	45*
Neen Sollars - Newnham Bge	9	45*	45*	45*
Newnham Bge - Tenbury Wells	9	37	45*	45*
Tenbury Wells - Woofferton	10	35	45*	45*

HARTLEBURY - WOOFFERTON
43xx 2-6-0, 51xx 2-6-2T, 56xx 0-6-2T,

Section of line	Passenger	Minerals	Goods	Empties
Hartlebury - Stourport	13	45*	45*	45*
Stourport - Bewdley	13	45*	45*	45*
Bewdley - Cleobury M.	9	26	39	45*
Cleobury M - Neen Sollars	9	33	45*	45*
Neen Sollars - Newnham Bge	9	45*	45*	45*
Newnham Bge - Tenbury Wells	9	45*	45*	45*
Tenbury Wells - Woofferton	10	45*	45*	45*

UP SEVERN VALLEY

64xx 0-6-0T

Section of line	Passenger	Minerals	Goods	Empties
Shrewsbury - Berrington	9	25	38	45*
Berrington - Buildwas	9	26	39	45*
Buildwas - Linley	9	35	45*	45*
Linley - Bridgnorth	9	25	38	45*
Bridgnorth - Highley	9	22	33	44
Highley - Bewdley	9	38	45*	45*
Bewdley - Kidderminster	10	22	33	44

2251 0-6-0

Section of line	Passenger	Minerals	Goods	Empties
Shrewsbury - Berrington	9	29	44	45*
Berrington - Buildwas	9	30	45	45*
Buildwas - Linley	9	40	45*	45*
Linley - Bridgnorth	9	29	44	45*
Bridgnorth - Highley	9	25	38	45*
Highley - Bewdley	9	44	45*	45*
Bewdley - Kidderminster	10	25	38	45*

45xx 2-6-2T, 57xx 0-6-0T

Section of line	Passenger	Minerals	Goods	Empties
Shrewsbury - Berrington	10	31	45*	45*
Berrington - Buildwas	10	32	45*	45*
Buildwas - Linley	10	44	45*	45*
Linley - Bridgnorth	10	31	45*	45*
Bridgnorth - Highley	10	27	41	45*
Highley - Bewdley	10	45*	45*	45*
Bewdley - Kidderminster	10	27	41	45*

43xx 2-6-0, 51xx 2-6-2T, 56xx 0-6-2T,

Section of line	Passenger	Minerals	Goods	Empties
Shrewsbury - Berrington	13	41	45*	45*
Berrington - Buildwas	13	43	45*	45*
Buildwas - Linley	13	45*	45*	45*
Linley - Bridgnorth	13	41	45*	45*
Bridgnorth - Highley	13	36	45*	45*
Highley - Bewdley	13	45*	45*	45*
Bewdley - Kidderminster	10	36	45*	45*

WOOFFERTON - HARTLEBURY

64xx 0-6-0T

Section of line	Passenger	Minerals	Goods	Empties
Woofferton - Tenbury Wells	11	40	45*	45*
Tenbury Wells - Newnham Bge	9	40	45*	45*
Newnham Bge - Cleobury M.	9	18	27	36
Cleobury M - Bewdley	9	20	30	40
Bewdley - Hartlebury	9	22	33	44

WOOFFERTON - HARTLEBURY
2251 0-6-0

Section of line	Passenger	Minerals	Goods	Empties
Woofferton - Tenbury Wells	11	45*	45*	45*
Tenbury Wells - Newnham Bge	9	45*	45*	45*
Newnham Bge - Cleobury M.	9	20	30	40
Cleobury M - Bewdley	9	23	35	45*
Bewdley - Hartlebury	9	25	38	45*

WOOFFERTON - HARTLEBURY
45xx 2-6-2T, 57xx 0-6-0T

Section of line	Passenger	Minerals	Goods	Empties
Woofferton - Tenbury Wells	13	45*	45*	45*
Tenbury Wells - Newnham Bge	9	45*	45*	45*
Newnham Bge - Cleobury M.	9	22	33	44
Cleobury M - Bewdley	9	23	38	45*
Bewdley - Hartlebury	9	27	41	45*

WOOFFERTON - HARTLEBURY
43xx 2-6-0, 51xx 2-6-2T, 56xx 0-6-2T,

Section of line	Passenger	Minerals	Goods	Empties
Woofferton - Tenbury Wells	13	45*	45*	45*
Tenbury Wells - Newnham Bge	9	45*	45*	45*
Newnham Bge - Cleobury M.	9	30	45	45*
Cleobury M - Bewdley	9	33	45*	45*
Bewdley - Hartlebury	9	36	45*	45*

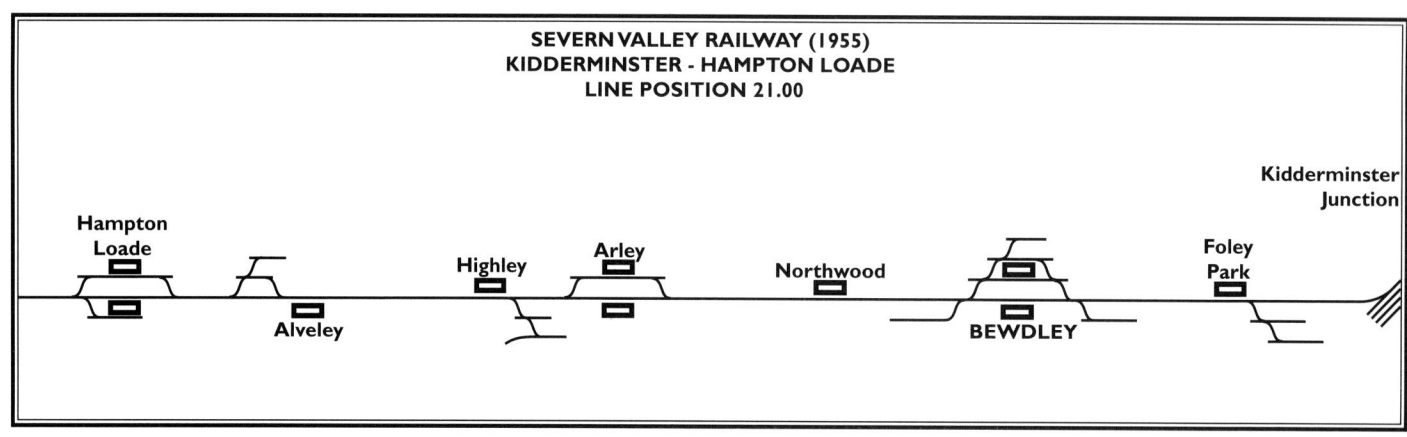

CONTROLLER'S LOG: For once it is the northern section of the line that has the preponderance of trains - not that the total is great - compared with only one service at work on the lower section.

The latter is the diesel railcar that has been flitting about the southern end of the route since arriving in Kidderminster with the 13.45 ex Shrewsbury. It has just arrived in Bridgnorth with the 20.26 from Bewdley; the Severn Valley connection out of the 16.45 express from Paddington.

Its next working will be the last in its daily diagram; the 20.05 from Bridgnorth to Kidderminster which is, although unadvertised as such, a through service to Worcester. The railcar will then stable for the night before re-entering traffic in the morning with the 04.50 (empty) to Kidderminster for the 05.48 Kidderminster to Alveley. Its two companion diesels are nowhere to be seen: one has just finished a stint on the Woofferton branch and is on the point of leaving Kidderminster for Worcester prior to finishing its day with a Great Malvern - Droitwich Spa service whilst the other - which only works on the Severn Valley in the mornings - is waiting to leave Worcester with a Honeybourne working.

Mention was made of a couple of surprise workings on the northern section and one of these concerns the 57xx 0-6-0PT which earlier worked the 19.55 Wellington to Much Wenlock.

In former times this working was based at Much Wenlock, the engine starting the day with the 06.50 to Wellington and finishing with the 19.55 but after the closure of Much Wenlock shed, the working was transferred to Wellington with the engine running out light each morning and returning light after stabling the stock of the 19.55.

However, since the boxes between Buildwas and Wellington close at 21.00 and none are equipped with block switches that would otherwise allow the line to remain open without signalmen, the engine cannot return to Wellington via the direct route. To matters worse, the level crossing gates at Ketley are left across the railway line between 21.00 and 05.05.

The alternative therefore is a long detour via Shrewsbury, the engine having to run twenty-three miles as opposed to the direct eleven. In addition to the extra mileage, Wellington shed has to take care to ensure that the driver on the working signs the road between Buildwas and Shrewsbury which is not a route worked by many drivers at Wellington shed.

The other unusual working is the up

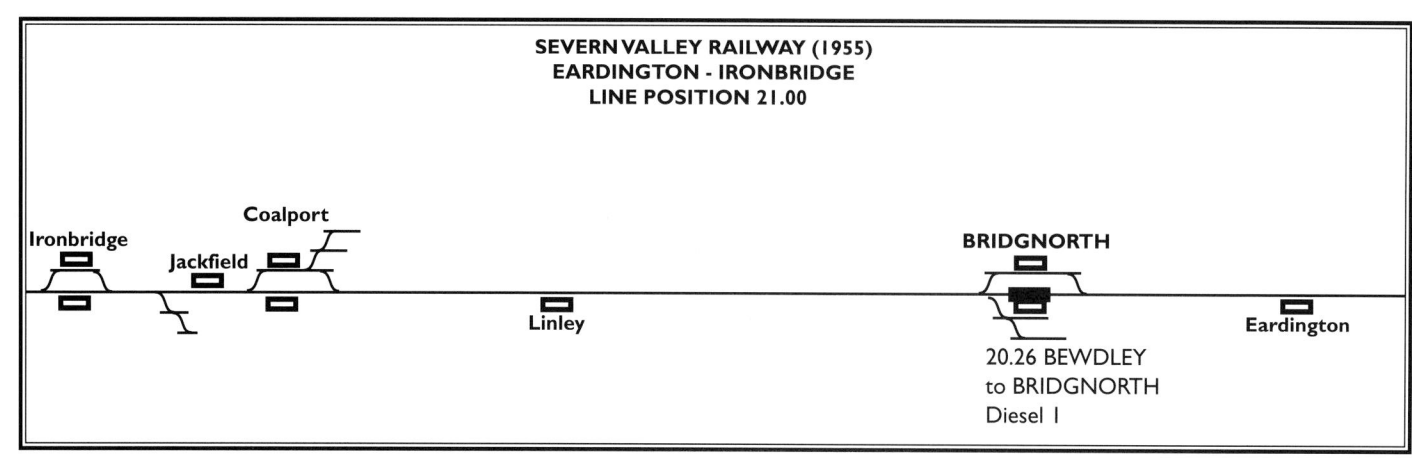

passenger train which has just crossed the down Salop goods at Berrington and is making its way towards Cound. Three and a half hours has passed since the previous Severn Valley train from Shrewsbury and it was felt that this was too early for the line to be closed. The closure of signalboxes on the southern section prevents a through train being run to Kidderminster and as a compromise the 20.45 operates to Ironbridge, returning to Shrewsbury at 21.35.

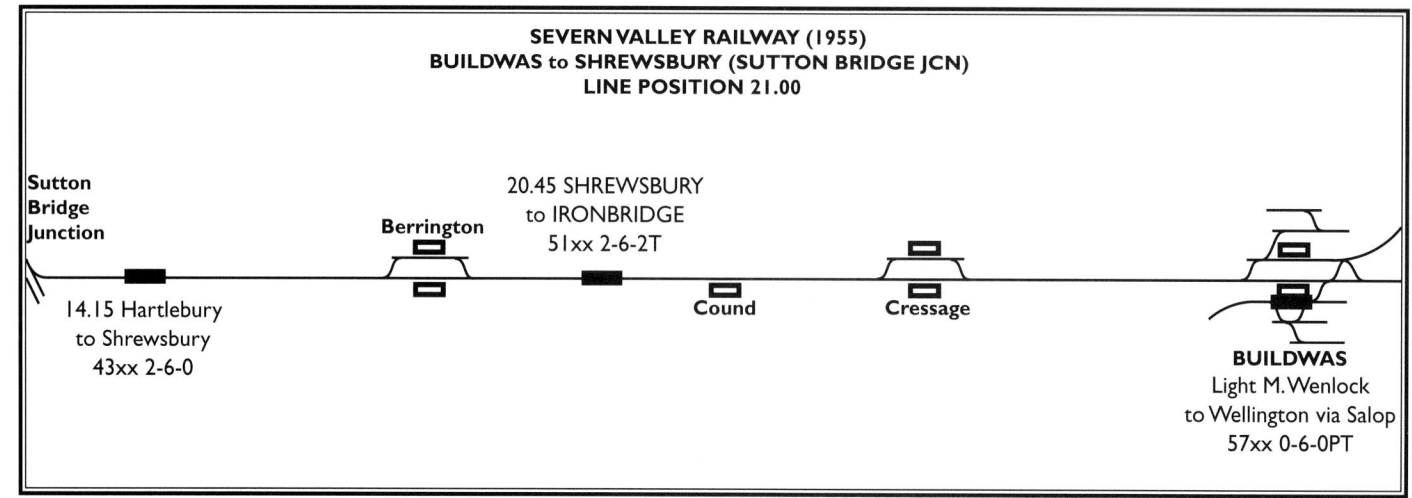

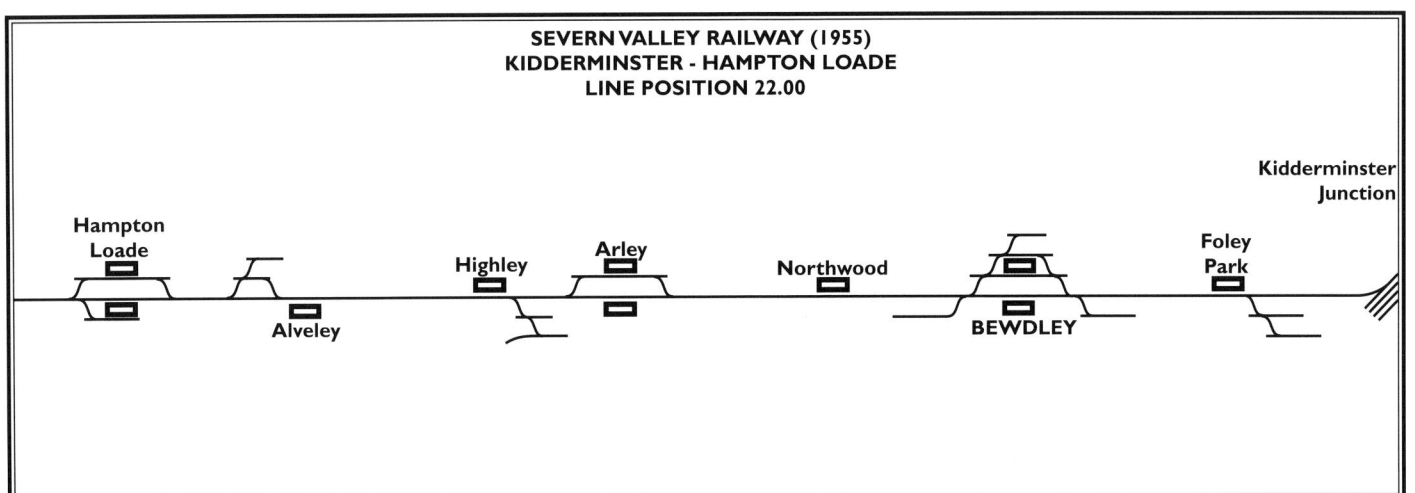

CONTROLLER'S LOG: The Severn Valley is now all but dormant; the boxes south of Ironbridge having switched out for the night with those to the north waiting for the 21.35 Ironbridge - Shrewsbury to clear their sections so that they too can close. The last train of the day being a Bridgnorth to Shrewsbury working makes an interesting contrast with pre-grouping arrangements when the last train of the day ran between Bridgnorth and Kidderminster.

There are, of course, no night trains on the - much to the chagrin of the signalmen since it is the one night when they would like an early finish - it is possible to leave Shrewsbury more than three hours later since the 20.26 Bewdley - Bridgnorth railcar is extended to Buildwas where it meets the 20.45 Shrewsbury - Buildwas. The arrangement works in both directions and northbound passengers arriving in Buildwas are able to continue forward to Shrewsbury in the return working of the 20.45.

Tonight, though, a weekday with only one morning trains. Needless to say, traffic flows are not so heavy as to make this an especially onerous task and the arrangements rarely take more than ten or fifteen minutes.

A particular drawback of the two-shift railway is that it is very difficult to operate excursion trains to distant points. A day excursion from, say, Ironbridge to Paddington leaving at seven in the morning and reaching London at about midday could hardly, if the passengers are to have their moneys worth,

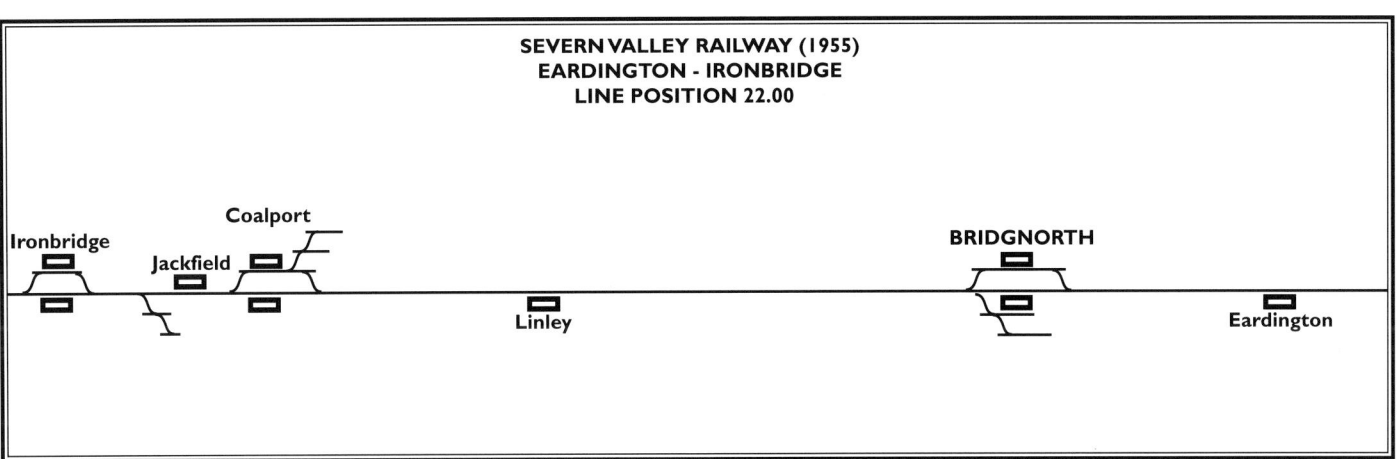

Severn Valley and the 21.35 ex Ironbridge is the closest the line gets to such a thing given that it connects at Shrewsbury with the 20.55 Birkenhead to Paddington express. In spite of the rather roundabout route, it is not a bad way of travelling to London since shortly after 23.00 one can be settling into a sleeping berth with a good eight hours sleep ahead.

On weekdays the last train from Shrewsbury to Kidderminster is the 17.33 but on Saturdays train on the system and a dwindling number of signalmen - south of Bridgnorth the boxes close as soon as they have received the out of section signal for the 21.05 Bridgnorth to Kidderminster - one's duties become largely contemplative. A summation is made of the empty wagons required in the morning by Alveley and each of the station yards and a check is made of the yards in the Kidderminster, Hartlebury and Worcester areas to ensure that they are accessible by the return from Paddington much before seven which would mean reaching Kidderminster long after the boxes on the Severn Valley had switched out. One cannot even arrange for a proportion of the boxes to be specially covered since not one of the signalboxes on the route is equipped with a block switch. It can therefore be seen that to keep the line open until midnight or later would be an expensive proposition and thus long-distance specials are a rarity.

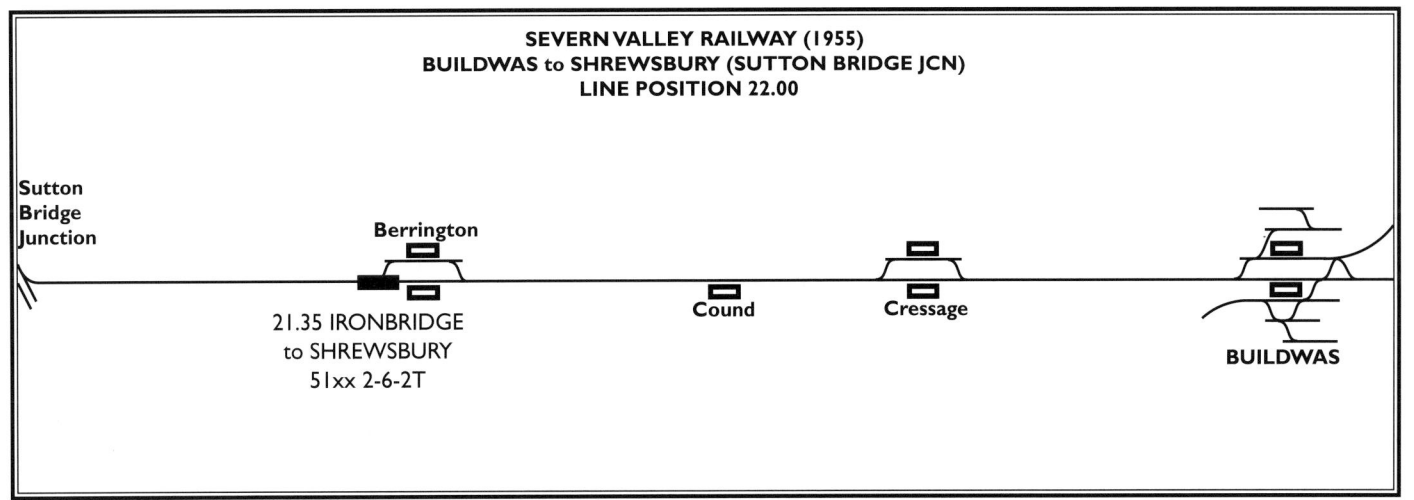

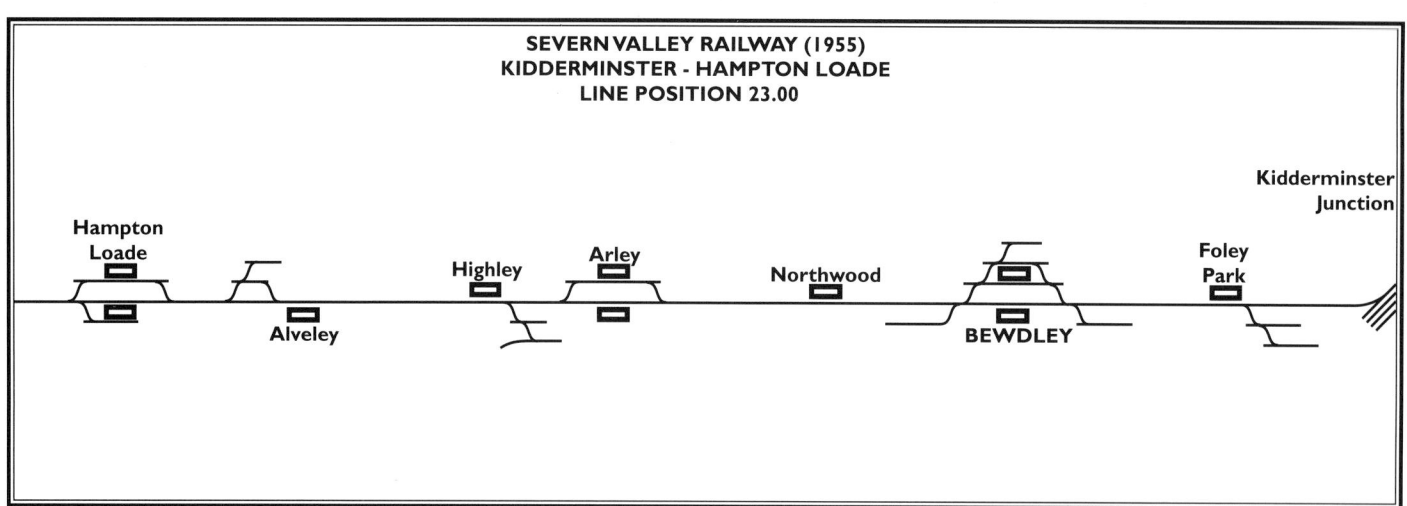

CONTROLLER'S LOG: The Severn Valley is now completely closed and will remain dormant until five in the morning and as the 21.35 Ironbridge to Shrewsbury disappears off the edge of the world at Sutton Bridge Junction, there is nothing is left to do - unless there are some special workings to be arranged between Kidderminster and Foley Park (q.v.) - except to put one's hat on and head for home.

There is, however, time to reflect on one or two features of the line; one of which if Bewdley and Ironbridge. During the autumn, however, when the sugar beet season is in full flow, the Alveley loadings are handsomely exceeded by trip workings of coal or beet between Kidderminster and the sugar beet factory at Foley Park.

During the hours of ordinary operation the trips are worked by a 57xx 0-6-0PT with up to 35 loaded wagons, the maximum that can be taken by any class of engine over the Kidderminster - Foley Park section. (Permitted when the line is otherwise closed.

A train of sixty wagons - almost twice the norm for the line - can be worked from Kidderminster to Foley Park *provided it is propelled* (ie the engine pushing from the rear) *with the brake van leading and a second brakevan located in the centre of the train.* Both brakevans must be manned in order to pass handsignals back to the driver.

To avoid the need for keeping Bewdley South signalbox open, the latter can allow

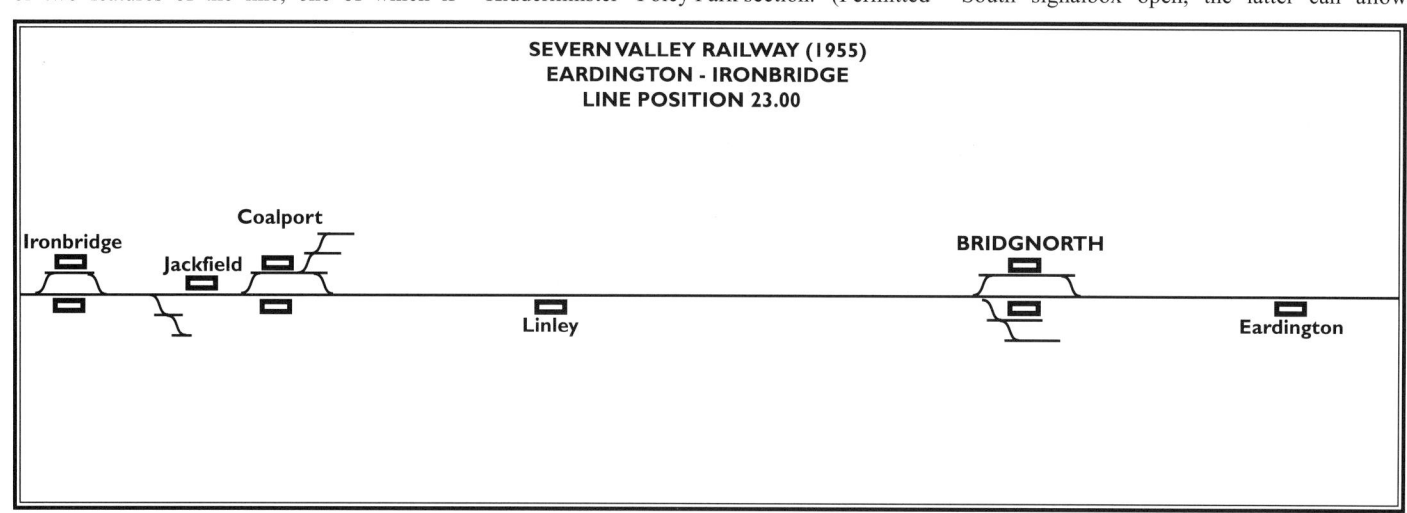

not unique on BR was certainly very singular. Generally the heaviest Severn Valley trains are the coal services worked by 43xx 2-6-0's from Aveley to Kidderminster or Hartlebury which load to 36 loaded mineral wagons. A 28xx 2-8-0 could take 44 wagons - one short of the line maximum - were it not for the fact that eight coupled locomotives are barred between engines over this section, incidentally, include all GWR engines except King 4-6-0's and 47xx 2-8-0's).

However when traffic is exceptionally busy - and the block loads of beet and coal arriving in Kidderminster for Foley Park have to be seen to be believed - then a special concession is given provided the working is confined to the hours Kidderminster Junction to release a token for the section to Foley Park thus reducing the cost of the operation.

Propelling from Kidderminster to Foley Park is not confined to the 60-wagon trains and the ordinary 35-wagon trips can also be propelled in which case only one brakevan - the leading vehicle - is required.

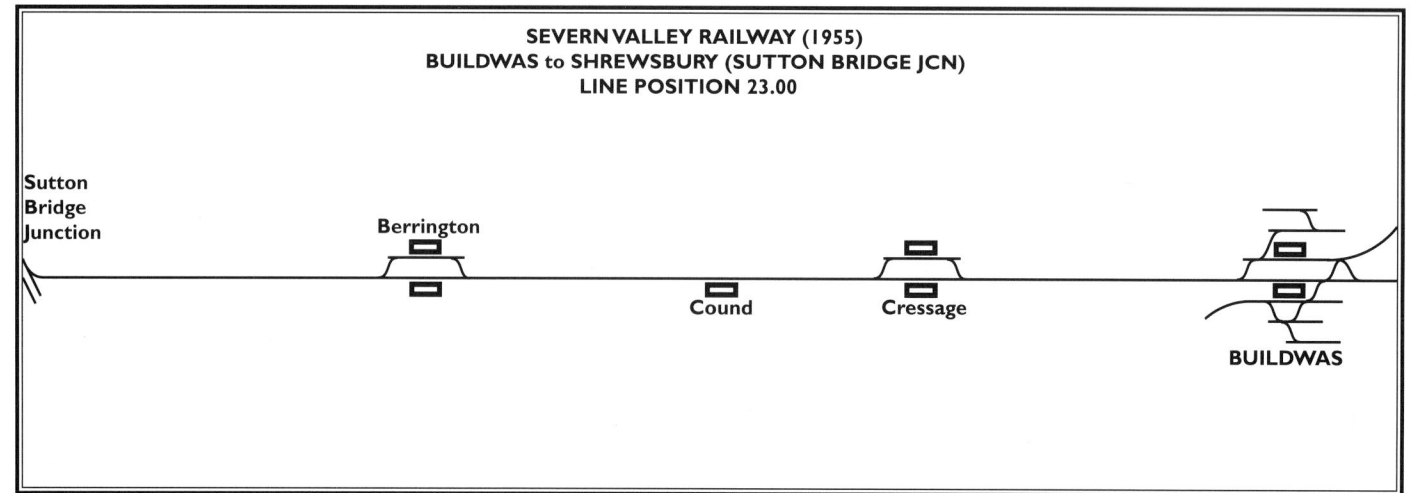

NEEN SOLLARS

The curiously named Neen Sollars was as typical a Great Western branch location as one was likely to find, made up of up and down - staggered - platforms, signalbox and a crossing loop although in the normal course of events trains were not booked to pass. The station was located on a 1 in 80 gradient rising to the east and because of this all goods trains from the Bewdley direction had to halt at a point just beyond Cleobury Mortimer to pin down wagon brakes, stopping again at Neen Sollars to release them. Because of this gradient, it was decreed that goods traffic could only be dealt with in the up direction and therefore any traffic for Birmingham and the West had to be collected by the 11.30 Kidderminster - Woofferton goods and taken to the end of the branch and back again. For all its rustic charm, Neen Sollars was not a haunt for the steam enthusiast since ten of the twelve daily passenger trains were worked by diesel railcars; only the afternoon Kidderminster - Leominster service being booked to steam. The views on this page show Railcar W19 (Worcester) approaching and calling at the station with a Woofferton - Kidderminster train on Saturday 15th May 1954. The Westbound (Down) loop - the line nearest the camera - was removed in late 1955.

EASTON COURT

14xx 0-4-2T 1445 calls with the 16.46 Tenbury Wells to Woofferton Auto.

The Tenbury Railway (as opposed to the Tenbury and Bewdley) had only one intermediate station and this was the tiny if somewhat overgrown Easton Court situated almost exactly halfway between Woofferton and Tenbury Wells. There was a standing joke in railway circles that the station had more names than platforms since it was also known as Easton Court for Little Hereford or Easton Court Halt. (Its official British Railways designation was 'Easton Court for Little Hereford' located on the Tenbury Joint. This in the late 1950's!). There was no passing loop or block post - lightweight goods had to be handled at the platform and the train service, shown in full below, was not designed to quicken the pulse of the enthusiast. The Leominster-based Auto made a number of appearances during the rush hour (sic) but for the rest of the day most trains were worked by Worcester-based diesel railcars. The only conventional train was the evening return service between Kidderminster and Leominster.

\multicolumn{5}{c}{EASTON COURT STATION WORKING : 1955}
Train	Arr	Engine	Dep	Destination
07.22 Ludlow	07.40	Leominster 1 : Auto	07.41	Tenbury Wells (07.45)
07.58 Tenbury Wells	08.02	Leominster 1 : Auto	08.03	Woofferton (08.08)
08.30 Woofferton	08.35	Leominster 1 : Auto	08.36	Tenbury Wells (08.40)
08.45 Tenbury Wells	08.49	Leominster 1 : Auto	08.50	Woofferton (08.55)
08.50 Kidderminster	09.44	Railcar: Worcester 2	09.45	Woofferton (09.50)
10.05 Woofferton	10.10	Railcar: Worcester 2	10.11	Kidderminster (11.12)
10.18 Kidderminster	11.13	Railcar: Worcester 3	11.14	Woofferton (11.19)
12.22 Woofferton	12.26	Railcar: Worcester 3	12.27	Kidderminster (13.13)
11.30 Kidderminster (Goods)		57xx: Kidderminster 109	*14/40**	*Woofferton (14.50)*
14.10 Kidderminster	15.14	Railcar: Worcester 3	15.15	Woofferton (15.20)
15.30 Woofferton (Goods)		57xx: Kidderminster 109	*15/30**	*Kidderminster (18.22)*
15.47 Woofferton	15.52	Railcar: Worcester 3	15.53	Kidderminster (16.47)
16.05 Craven Arms	16.35	Leominster 1 : Auto	16.36	Tenbury Wells (16.40)
16.46 Tenbury Wells	16.50	Leominster 1 : Auto	16.51	Woofferton (16.56)
16.48 Kidderminster	17.44	57xx: Kidderminster 110	17.45	Leominster (18.04)
18.20 Leominster	18.40	57xx: Kidderminster 110	18.41	Kidderminster (20.08)
18.25 Kidderminster	19.24	Railcar: Worcester 3	19.25	Woofferton (19.30)
19.50 Woofferton	19.55	Railcar: Worcester 3	19.56	Kidderminster (20.50)
		* Calls when required.		

MUCH WENLOCK

The arrival of a train was clearly an event in Much Wenlock and under the gaze of a party of admirers - including one who has talked his way onto the footplate - 57xx 0-6-0PT 3732 of Wellington runs round its train and takes water before working back to Wellington on 19th September 1959. (V. R. Webster: KRM)

The Severn Junction originally ran from Wellington to Marsh Farm Junction, near Craven Arms, and provided thus a connection between the London - Birkenhead, the Severn Valley and the Shrewsbury - Hereford lines. Quaint rather than prosperous, the passenger service was cut back to Much Wenlock in December 1951 although a daily goods working was retained over the seven mile section between Much Wenlock and Longville. The remaining service consisted of seven trains between Wellington and Much Wenlock together with a goods service to Longville and Buildwas. The gradients in the line were amongst the most severe in the country with trains from Buildwas to Much Wenlock having to climb continuous gradients of around 1 in 40 whilst much of the route between Buildwas and Wellington was only fractionally easier at 1 in 45. During the late 1930's an attempt was made to reduce the running costs of the line by replacing steam with diesel railcars but the gradients proved too fearsome and steam remained in charge until the end. After the cessation of services between Craven Arms and Much Wenlock, the small engine shed at the latter was closed with the work being transferred to Wellington whose 57xx engines thereafter covered all the lines' work. This resulted in the curious position in which the engine of the last train to arrive at Much Wenlock had to return to Wellington via Berrington and Shrewsbury due to the fact that the direct line between Buildwas and Wellington closed at nine in the evening.

The engine working was more complicated than might be supposed and far from there being a single 57xx 0-6-0 which spent the day shuttling between Wellington and Much Wenlock, no less than four engines were needed to maintain the service.

MUCH WENLOCK STATION WORKING : 1955				
Train	Arr	Engine	Dep	Destination
Light ex Wellington loco	06.05	57xx - Wellington 461		
		57xx - Wellington 461	06.50	Wellington (07.35)
06.48 Wellington (Mixed	07.57	57xx - Wellington 460		
		57xx - Wellington 460	08.35	Wellington (09.34)
08.16 Wellington	09.10	57xx - Wellington 461		
		57xx - Wellington 461	09.35	Longville (Goods)
10.40 Longville (Goods)	11.16	57xx - Wellington 461		
		57xx - Wellington 461	11.40	Wellington (12.28)
11.17 Wellington	12.10	57xx - Wellington 464		
		57xx - Wellington 464	13.00	Wellington (13.48)
14.30 Buildwas (Goods)	14.48	57xx - Wellington 467		
		57xx - Wellington 467	15.00	Buildwas Goods (15.17)
15.10 Wellington	16.00	57xx - Wellington 461		
16.10 Coalbrookdale	16.30	57xx - Wellington 460		
		57xx - Wellington 461	16.40	Wellington (17.32)
16.30 Wellington	17.20	57xx - Wellington 464		
		57xx - Wellington 460	17.30	Light to Buildwas
		57xx - Wellington 464	17.45	Wellington (18.37)
17.50 Wellington	18.34	57xx - Wellington 461		
		57xx - Wellington 461	19.05	Wellington (19.52)
19.55 Wellington	20.45	57xx - Wellington 464		
		57xx - Wellington 464	21.00	Light to Wellington via Salop

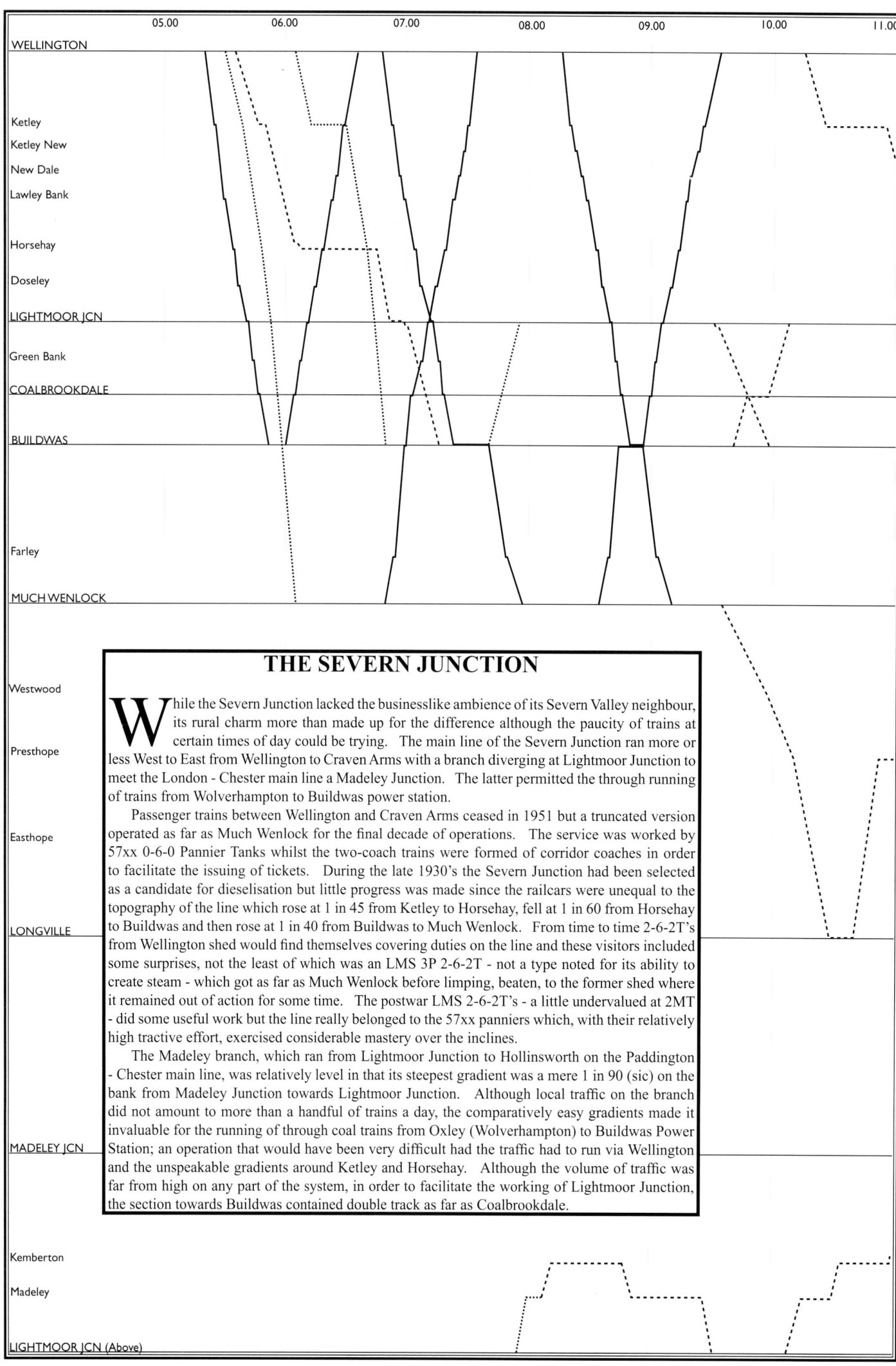

THE SEVERN JUNCTION

While the Severn Junction lacked the businesslike ambience of its Severn Valley neighbour, its rural charm more than made up for the difference although the paucity of trains at certain times of day could be trying. The main line of the Severn Junction ran more or less West to East from Wellington to Craven Arms with a branch diverging at Lightmoor Junction to meet the London - Chester main line a Madeley Junction. The latter permitted the through running of trains from Wolverhampton to Buildwas power station.

Passenger trains between Wellington and Craven Arms ceased in 1951 but a truncated version operated as far as Much Wenlock for the final decade of operations. The service was worked by 57xx 0-6-0 Pannier Tanks whilst the two-coach trains were formed of corridor coaches in order to facilitate the issuing of tickets. During the late 1930's the Severn Junction had been selected as a candidate for dieselisation but little progress was made since the railcars were unequal to the topography of the line which rose at 1 in 45 from Ketley to Horsehay, fell at 1 in 60 from Horsehay to Buildwas and then rose at 1 in 40 from Buildwas to Much Wenlock. From time to time 2-6-2T's from Wellington shed would find themselves covering duties on the line and these visitors included some surprises, not the least of which was an LMS 3P 2-6-2T - not a type noted for its ability to create steam - which got as far as Much Wenlock before limping, beaten, to the former shed where it remained out of action for some time. The postwar LMS 2-6-2T's - a little undervalued at 2MT - did some useful work but the line really belonged to the 57xx panniers which, with their relatively high tractive effort, exercised considerable mastery over the inclines.

The Madeley branch, which ran from Lightmoor Junction to Hollinsworth on the Paddington - Chester main line, was relatively level in that its steepest gradient was a mere 1 in 90 (sic) on the bank from Madeley Junction towards Lightmoor Junction. Although local traffic on the branch did not amount to more than a handful of trains a day, the comparatively easy gradients made it invaluable for the running of through coal trains from Oxley (Wolverhampton) to Buildwas Power Station; an operation that would have been very difficult had the traffic had to run via Wellington and the unspeakable gradients around Ketley and Horsehay. Although the volume of traffic was far from high on any part of the system, in order to facilitate the working of Lightmoor Junction, the section towards Buildwas contained double track as far as Coalbrookdale.

WORKING TIMETABLE - PASSENGER & GOODS

WELLINGTON - BUILDWAS - MUCH WENLOCK - LONGVILLE (CRAVEN ARMS) - 1955

Train					05.35	05.35			08.47				
From					Well	Well			Kemb'tn				
Class	Pass	Light	Goods	EBV	Goods	Goods	Pass	Mixed	Pass	Goods	Goods	Goods	Goods	Goods
Depot	Well460	Well461	Well462	Well463	Well462	Well462	Well460	Well460	Well461	Well463	Well460	Well461	Well461	Well461
Engine	57xx	57xx	57xx	57xx	57xx	57xx	57xx	57xx	57xx	57xx	57xx	57xx	57xx	57xx
WELLINGTON	05.20	05.30	05.35	06.05			06.48		08.16	10.15				
Ketley Jcn	05/23	05/35	05/41	06/10			06/51		08/19	10/21				
Ketley	05.24		05.46	06.12			06.52		08.20	10.25				
Ketley	05.25	05/38	05.49	06.30			06.53		08.21	10.55				
Ketley Town									08.23					
New Dale							06.57		08.26					
Lawley Bank	05.30						07.00		08.29					
Horsehay			06.04		(06.04)		07.04		08.33	11.14				
Horsehay	05.34	05/48	(06.45)	06/40	06.45		07.05		08.34					
Doseley	05.37						07.08		08.37					
Lightmoor Jcn	05/40	05/52		06/44	06.51	07.01	07/12		08/39	09/31				
Lightmoor	05.41						07.13		08.40	09.33				
Green Bank	05.44						07.16		08.43					
Coalbrookdale	05.47						07.19		08.46					
BUILDWAS	05.51			06.50		07.16	07.23		08.50	09.58				
BUILDWAS		05/58						07.40	08.56					
Bradley														
Farley								07.50	09.04					
MUCH WENLOCK		06.05						07.57	09.10					
MUCH WENLOCK											09.35			
Westwood														
Westwood Siding												09.47	09.57	
Preethope													10.01	10.10
Easthope														
LONGVILLE														10.21
Destination														

HOLLINSWOOD BRANCH

Train									08.47					
From									Kemb'tn					
Class								Goods	Goods					
Depot								Well463	Well463					
Engine								57xx	57xx					
HOLLINSWOOD														
Madeley Junction														
Kemberton									08.47					
Madeley								08.51	09.26					
Lightmoor Jcn (Above)									09/31					
Destination									B'was					

LONGVILLE (CRAVEN ARMS) - MUCH WENLOCK - BUILDWAS - WELLINGTON : 1955

Train							09.40		10.40					
From							B'was		L'ville					
Class	Pass	Pass	EBV	Pass	Pass	Goods	Goods	Goods	Goods	Pass	Pass	Goods	Pass	ECS
Depot	Well460	Well461	Well463	Well460	Well460	Well462	Well462	Well461	Well461	Well461	Well464	Well467	Well460	Well460
Engine	57xx	57xx	57xx	57xx	57xx	57xx	57xx	57xx	57xx	57xx	57xx	57xx	57xx	57xx
LONGVILLE							10.40							
Easthope														
Preethope							10.52	11.02						
Westwood Siding														
Westwood														
MUCH WENLOCK								11.16						
MUCH WENLOCK		06.50		08.35							11.40	13.00	15.00	
Farley														
Bradley		06.54		08.39							11.45	13.04		
BUILDWAS		06.59		08.44							11.50	13.09	15.17	
BUILDWAS	06.00	07.00	07.40		08.56	09.40					11.55	13.13		15.25
Coalbrookdale	06.05	07.05			09.00	09.47	09.57				12.00	13.18		15.30
Green Bank	06.08	07.08			09.03						12.03	13.21		15.33
Lightmoor	06.11	07.11			09.06						12.06	13.24		15.35	15.36
Lightmoor Jcn	06/12	07/12	07/55		09/09		10/08				12/07	13/25		15.37
Doseley	06.15	07.15			09.10						12.10	13.28		
Horsehay	06.18	07.18			09.13						12.13	13.31		
Horsehay	06.19	07.19			09.14						12.14	13.32		
Lawley Bank	06.23	07.23			09.18						12.18	13.36		
New Dale	06.25	07.25			09.20						12.20	13.38		
Ketley Town		07.28			09.23						12.22	13.41		
Ketley	06.28	07.29			09.24						12.23	13.42		
Ketley	06.29	07.30			09.25						12.24	13.43		
Ketley Jcn	06/31	07/32			09/27						12/26	13/45		
WELLINGTON	06.36	07.35			09.34						12.28	13.48		
Destination			Madeley				H'wood							

HOLLINSWOOD BRANCH

Train		07.40			09.40	09.40	09.40	09.40						
From		B'was			B'was	B'was	B'was	B'was						
Class		EBV	Goods		Goods	Goods	Goods	Goods						
Depot		Well463	Well463		Well462									
Engine		57xx	57xx		57xx									
Lightmoor Jcn (Above)		07/55			10/08									
Madeley		08.00	08.08		10.15	10.30								
Kemberton			08.12		10.34	10.59								
Madeley Junction					11.06	11.11								
HOLLINSWOOD					11.17									
Destination														

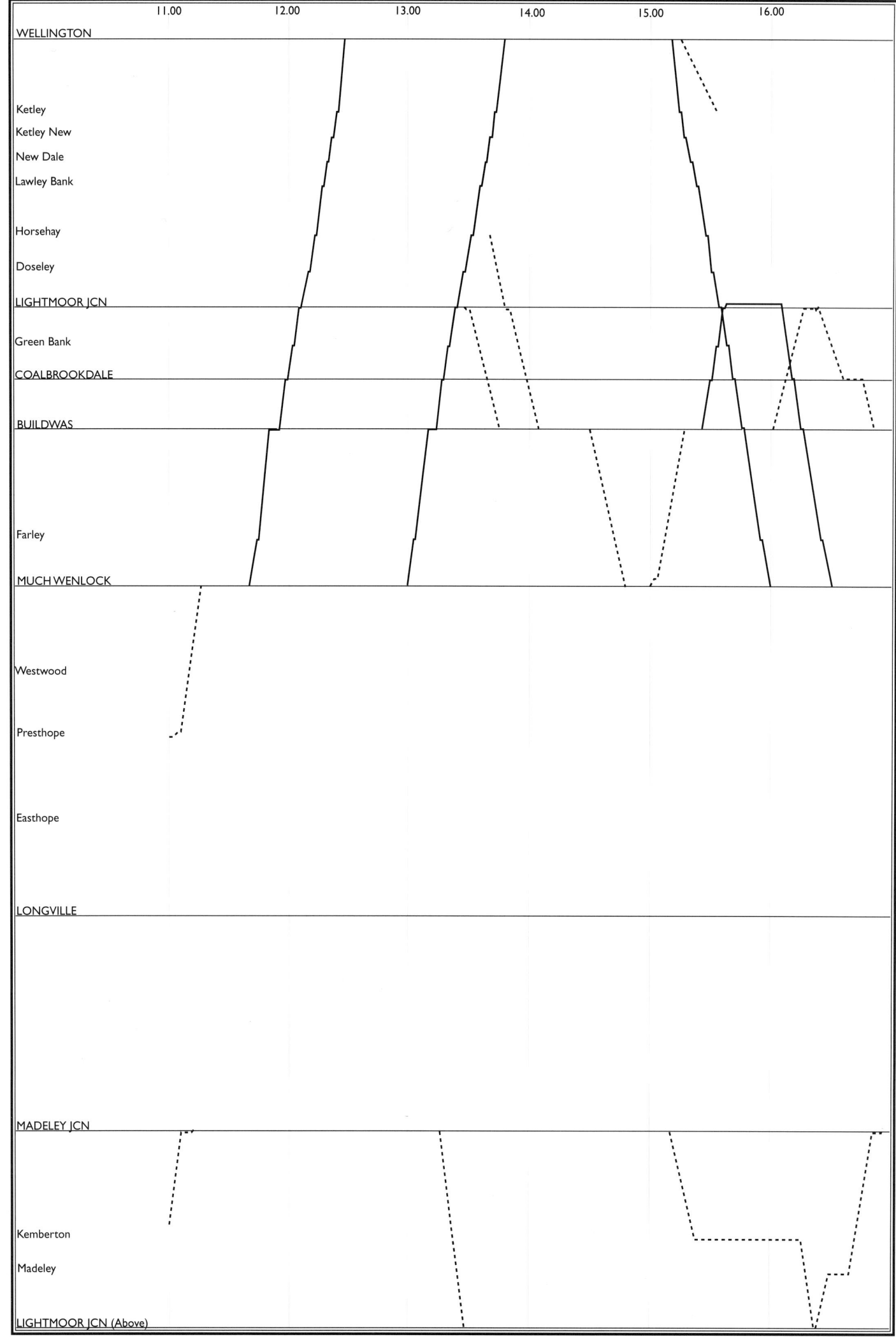

WORKING TIMETABLE - PASSENGER & GOODS

WELLINGTON - BUILDWAS - MUCH WENLOCK - LONGVILLE (CRAVEN ARMS) - 1955

Train		13.05							15.10	15.10			
From		H'wood							Madeley	Madeley			
Class	Pass	Goods	Goods	Goods	Pass	Goods	ECS	School	Goods	Goods	Pass	Pass	Pass
	Well464	Well467	Well460	Well467	Well461	Well462	Well460	Well460	Well 468	Well 468	Well464	Well461	Well464
Engine	57xx	57xx	57xx	57xx	57xx	57xx	57xx	57xx	57xx	57xx	57xx	57xx	57xx
WELLINGTON	11.17				15.10	15.15					16.30	17.50	19.55
Ketley Jcn	11/20				15/13	15/29					16/32	17/53	19/58
Ketley	11.22				15.15	15.33					16.34	17.54	19.59
Ketley	11.23				15.17						16.35	17.55	20.00
Ketley Town	11.24				15.20						16.37	17.56	20.02
New Dale	11.26				15.23						16.40	17.59	20.05
Lawley Bank	11.29										16.43	18.01	20.08
Horsehay	11.33				15.27						16.47	18.03	20.12
Horsehay	11.34		13.40		15.28						16.48	18.04	20.13
Doseley	11.37				15.31						16.51	18.07	20.16
Lightmoor Jcn	11/40	13/28	13/48		15/34		16.05		16/21		16/54	18/09	20/19
Lightmoor	11.41				15.35						16.55	18.11	20.20
Green Bank	11.44				15.38						16.58	18.12	20.23
Coalbrookdale	11.47				15.41		16.08	16.10	16.36	16.45	17.01	18.14	20.26
BUILDWAS	11.51	13.45	14.05		15.45			16.14		16.50	17.05	18.18	20.30
BUILDWAS	11.56			14.30	15.46			16.15			17.06	18.20	20.31
Bradley													
Farley	12.05				15.55			16.25			17.15	18.29	20.40
MUCH WENLOCK	12.10			14.48	16.00			16.30			17.20	18.34	20.45
MUCH WENLOCK													
Westwood													
Westwood Siding													
Preethope													
Easthope													
LONGVILLE													
Destination													

HOLLINSWOOD BRANCH

Train		13.05							15.10	
From		H'wood							Madeley	
Class	Goods	Goods						Goods	Goods	
Depot	Well467	Well467						Well 468	Well 468	
Engine	57xx	57xx						57xx	57xx	
HOLLINSWOOD	13.05									
Madeley Junction	13.10	13.16						15.10		
Kemberton								15/18		
Madeley								15.22	16.15	
Lightmoor Jcn (Above)		13/28							16/21	
Destination										

LONGVILLE (CRAVEN ARMS) - MUCH WENLOCK - BUILDWAS - WELLINGTON : 1955

Train								18.15		
From								B'was		
Class	Goods	Pass	Goods	Goods	Light	Pass	Goods	Goods	Pass	Light
	Well467	Well461	Well462	Well 468	Well460	Well464	Well460	Well460	Well461	Well464
Engine	57xx	57xx	57xx	57xx	57xx	57xx	57xx	57xx	57xx	57xx
LONGVILLE										
Easthope										
Preethope										
Westwood Siding										
Westwood										
MUCH WENLOCK										
MUCH WENLOCK		16.40			17.30	17.45			19.05	21.00
Farley										
Bradley		16.45				17.49			19.09	
BUILDWAS		16.50			17/39	17.54			19.14	21.10
BUILDWAS	16.01	16.55		17.06		18.02	18.15		19.15	
Coalbrookdale		16.50				18.07			19.20	
Green Bank		17.03				18.10			19.23	
Lightmoor		17.06				18.13			19.26	
Lightmoor Jcn	16/16	17/07		17/21		18/14	18.27	18.35	19/27	
Doseley		17.10				18.17			19.30	
Horsehay		17.13				18.20		18.50	19.33	
Horsehay		17.14		17/33		18.21		19.00	19.34	
Lawley Bank		17.18		17P35		18.25		19P04	19.38	
New Dale		17.20				18.27		19P04	19.40	
Ketley Town		17.23				18.30			19.43	
Ketley		17.24		17P47		18.31		19P16	19.44	
Ketley		17.25	17.30	19P49		18.32		19P18	19.45	
Ketley Jcn		17/29	17/37	17/51		18/34		19/31	19/49	
WELLINGTON		17.32	17.42	17.56		18.37		19.37	19.52	
Destination	H'wood								Salop	

HOLLINSWOOD BRANCH

Train	16.01	16.01	16.01							
From	B'was	B'was	B'was							
Class	Goods	Goods	Goods							
Depot	Well467	Well467	Well467							
Engine	57xx	57xx	57xx							
Lightmoor Jcn (Above)	16/16									
Madeley	16.29	16.39								
Kemberton										
Madeley Junction		16.50	16.55							
HOLLINSWOOD			17.01							
Destination										

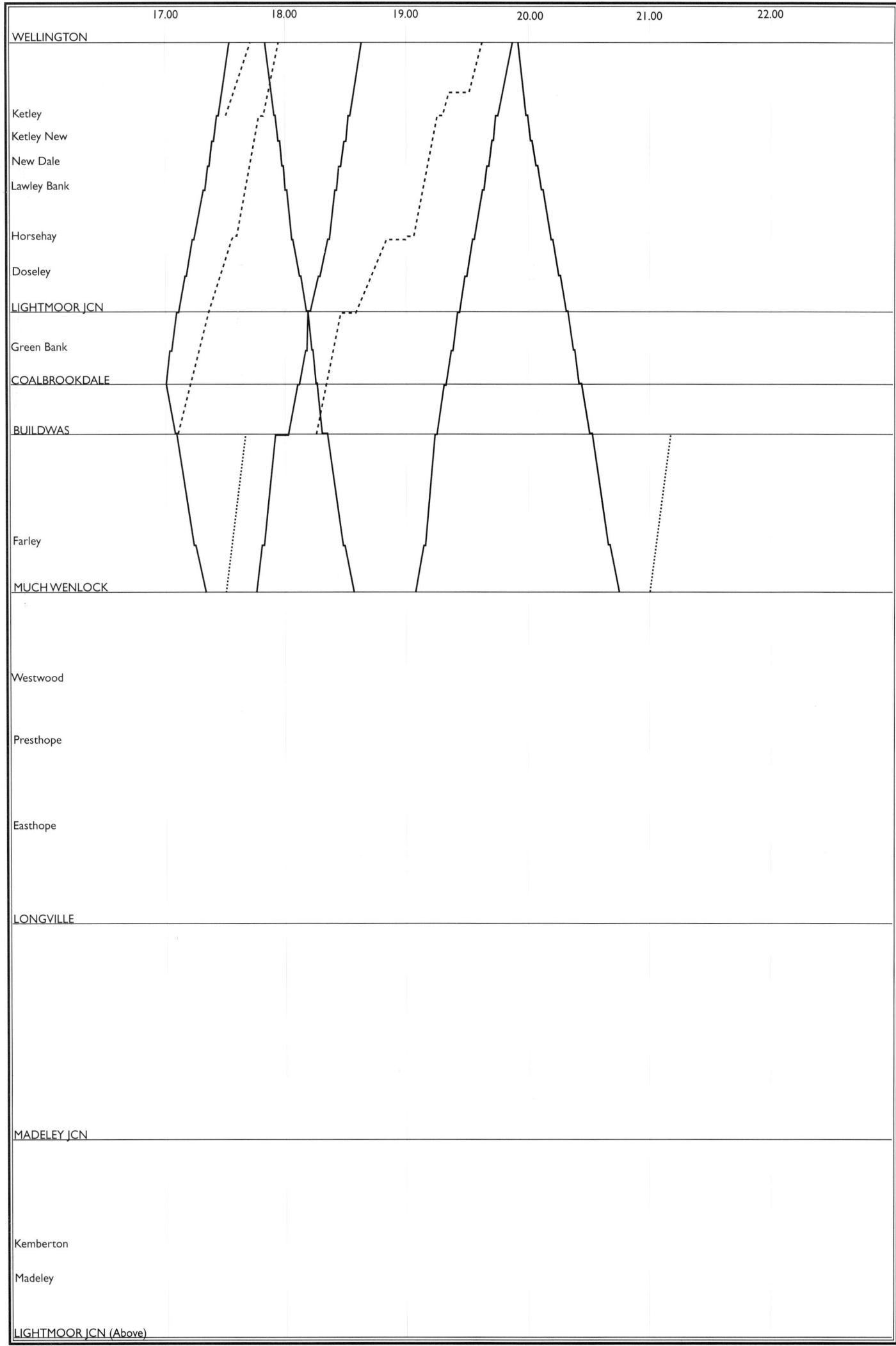

ALLOCATION & MOVEMENTS : WELLINGTON (84H)

Engine	Class	Aug-50	Sep-50	Oct-50	Nov-50	Dec-50	Jan-51	Feb-51	Mar-51	Apr-51	May-51	Jun-51	Jul-51
4154	4MT : 51xx 2-6-2T (1928)												
5109	4MT : 51xx 2-6-2T (1928)												
5125	4MT : 51xx 2-6-2T (1928)												
5137	4MT : 51xx 2-6-2T (1928)											To Banbury	X
5138	4MT : 51xx 2-6-2T (1928)												
5139	4MT : 51xx 2-6-2T (1928)												
5178	4MT : 51xx 2-6-2T (1928)												
4400	3MT : 44xx 2-6-2T (1904)										W/D	X	X	X
4401	3MT : 44xx 2-6-2T (1904)												
4403	3MT : 44xx 2-6-2T (1904)										To Laira	X	X
4406	3MT : 44xx 2-6-2T (1904)												
3613	3F : 57xx 0-6-0T (1933)												
3687	3F : 57xx 0-6-0T (1933)												
3732	3F : 57xx 0-6-0T (1933)												
3749	3F : 57xx 0-6-0T (1933)												
3760	3F : 57xx 0-6-0T (1933)												
3775	3F : 57xx 0-6-0T (1933)						To Worcs	X	X	X	X	X	X
4605	3F : 57xx 0-6-0T (1933)	X	X	X	X	X	X	X	X	X	X	Ex Wolves	
9624	3F : 57xx 0-6-0T (1933)												
9630	3F : 57xx 0-6-0T (1933)												
9639	3F : 57xx 0-6-0T (1933)												
9742	3F : 57xx 0-6-0T (1933)	X	X	X	X	X	X	X	X	Ex Oxley			
5758	3F : 57xx 0-6-0T (1929)												
7754	3F : 57xx 0-6-0T (1929)												
2030	2F : 2021 0-6-0T (1897)												
1619	2F : 16xx 0-6-0PT (1949)												

ALLOCATION & MOVEMENTS : WELLINGTON (84H)

Engine	Class	Aug-51	Sep-51	Oct-51	Nov-51	Dec-51	Jan-52	Feb-52	Mar-52	Apr-52	May-52	Jun-52	Jul-52
4154	4MT : 51xx 2-6-2T (1928)												
5109	4MT : 51xx 2-6-2T (1928)												
5125	4MT : 51xx 2-6-2T (1928)												W/D
5138	4MT : 51xx 2-6-2T (1928)												
5139	4MT : 51xx 2-6-2T (1928)												
5178	4MT : 51xx 2-6-2T (1928)												
4401	3MT : 44xx 2-6-2T (1904)						To Exeter	X	X	X	X	X	X
4406	3MT : 44xx 2-6-2T (1904)								To Tondu	X	X	X	
3613	3F : 57xx 0-6-0T (1933)												
3687	3F : 57xx 0-6-0T (1933)						To Llanelly	X	X	X	X	X	X
3732	3F : 57xx 0-6-0T (1933)												
3749	3F : 57xx 0-6-0T (1933)												
3760	3F : 57xx 0-6-0T (1933)												
3782	3F : 57xx 0-6-0T (1933)	X	X	X	X	X	Ex Salop	To Salop	X	X	X	X	X
4605	3F : 57xx 0-6-0T (1933)												
5758	3F : 57xx 0-6-0T (1933)												
7754	3F : 57xx 0-6-0T (1933)												
9624	3F : 57xx 0-6-0T (1933)												
9630	3F : 57xx 0-6-0T (1933)												
9639	3F : 57xx 0-6-0T (1933)												
9742	3F : 57xx 0-6-0T (1933)												
2030	2F : 2021 0-6-0T (1897)							W/D	X	X	X	X	X
1619	2F : 16xx 0-6-0PT (1949)												

ALLOCATION & MOVEMENTS : WELLINGTON (84H)

Engine	Class	Aug-52	Sep-52	Oct-52	Nov-52	Dec-52	Jan-53	Feb-53	Mar-53	Apr-53	May-53	Jun-53	Jul-53
4154	4MT : 51xx 2-6-2T (1928)												To Car'then
4158	4MT : 51xx 2-6-2T (1928)	X	X	X	X	Ex P. Road							
4178	4MT : 51xx 2-6-2T (1928)	X	X	X	X	X	X	Ex Car'then					
5109	4MT : 51xx 2-6-2T (1928)												
5138	4MT : 51xx 2-6-2T (1928)				W/D	X	X	X	X	X	X	X	X
5139	4MT : 51xx 2-6-2T (1928)				W/D	X	X	X	X	X	X	X	X
5178	4MT : 51xx 2-6-2T (1928)												
3613	3F : 57xx 0-6-0T (1933)												
3732	3F : 57xx 0-6-0T (1933)												
3749	3F : 57xx 0-6-0T (1933)												
3760	3F : 57xx 0-6-0T (1933)												
4605	3F : 57xx 0-6-0T (1933)												
5712	3F : 57xx 0-6-0T (1933)	X	X	X	X	X	X	Ex Tyseley					
5745	3F : 57xx 0-6-0T (1933)	X	X	X	X	X	X	X	Ex Tyseley				
5758	3F : 57xx 0-6-0T (1933)												
7754	3F : 57xx 0-6-0T (1933)												
9624	3F : 57xx 0-6-0T (1933)												
9630	3F : 57xx 0-6-0T (1933)												
9639	3F : 57xx 0-6-0T (1933)												
9741	3F : 57xx 0-6-0T (1933)	X	X	X	X	X	X	Ex Stourb'ge					
9742	3F : 57xx 0-6-0T (1933)												
9774	3F : 57xx 0-6-0T (1933)	X	X	X	X	X	X	X	Ex Chester				
2061	2F : 2021 0-6-0T (1897)	X	X	X	X	X	X	Ex Wolves					
1619	2F : 16xx 0-6-0PT (1949)							To Stourbge	X	X	X	X	X

ALLOCATION & MOVEMENTS : WELLINGTON (84H)

Engine	Class	Aug-53	Sep-53	Oct-53	Nov-53	Dec-53	Jan-54	Feb-54	Mar-54	Apr-54	May-54	Jun-54	Jul-54
4155	4MT : 51xx 2-6-2T (192	X	Ex Worcs										
4158	4MT : 51xx 2-6-2T (1928)												
4178	4MT : 51xx 2-6-2T (1928)												
5109	4MT : 51xx 2-6-2T (1928)												
5178	4MT : 51xx 2-6-2T (1928)												
9435	4F: 94XX 0-6-0T (1949)	X	X	Ex Wolves	To Wolves	X	X	X	X	X	X	X	X
3613	3F : 57xx 0-6-0T (1933)												
3732	3F : 57xx 0-6-0T (1933)												
3744	3F : 57xx 0-6-0T (1933)	X	X	X	X	X	X	X	Ex Oxley				
3749	3F : 57xx 0-6-0T (1933)												
3760	3F : 57xx 0-6-0T (1933)												
4605	3F : 57xx 0-6-0T (1933)												
5712	3F : 57xx 0-6-0T (1933)												
5745	3F : 57xx 0-6-0T (1933)												
5758	3F : 57xx 0-6-0T (1933)												
7754	3F : 57xx 0-6-0T (1933)												
9624	3F : 57xx 0-6-0T (1933)												
9630	3F : 57xx 0-6-0T (1933)												
9639	3F : 57xx 0-6-0T (1933)												
9741	3F : 57xx 0-6-0T (1933)												
9742	3F : 57xx 0-6-0T (1933)												
9774	3F : 57xx 0-6-0T (1933)												
2061	2F : 2021 0-6-0T (1897)												

ALLOCATION & MOVEMENTS : WELLINGTON (84H)

Engine	Class	Aug-54	Sep-54	Oct-54	Nov-54	Dec-54	Jan-55	Feb-55	Mar-55	Apr-55	May-55	Jun-55	Jul-55
4155	4MT : 51xx 2-6-2T (1928)										To Tyseley	X	X
4158	4MT : 51xx 2-6-2T (1928)												
4178	4MT : 51xx 2-6-2T (1928)					To Tyseley	X	Ex Tyseley					
5109	4MT : 51xx 2-6-2T (1928)										To Stour'bge	X	X
5164	4MT : 51xx 2-6-2T (192	X	X	X	X	X	X	X	X	X	Ex Tyseley		
5167	4MT : 51xx 2-6-2T (192	X	X	X	X	X	X	X	X	X	X	Ex Stour'bge	
5178	4MT : 51xx 2-6-2T (1928)												
3613	3F : 57xx 0-6-0T (1933)												To Duffryr
3732	3F : 57xx 0-6-0T (1933)												
3744	3F : 57xx 0-6-0T (1933)												
3749	3F : 57xx 0-6-0T (1933)												
3760	3F : 57xx 0-6-0T (1933)												
4605	3F : 57xx 0-6-0T (1933)												
5712	3F : 57xx 0-6-0T (1933)												
5745	3F : 57xx 0-6-0T (1933)												
5758	3F : 57xx 0-6-0T (1933)												
7754	3F : 57xx 0-6-0T (1933)												
9624	3F : 57xx 0-6-0T (1933)												
9630	3F : 57xx 0-6-0T (1933)												
9639	3F : 57xx 0-6-0T (1933)												
9741	3F : 57xx 0-6-0T (1933)												
9742	3F : 57xx 0-6-0T (1933)												
9774	3F : 57xx 0-6-0T (1933)												
1663	2F: 16xx 0-6-0PT (1949)	X	X	X	X	X	X	X	NEW				
2061	2F: 2021 0-6-0T (1897)										W/D	X	X	X

ALLOCATION & MOVEMENTS : WELLINGTON (84H)

Engine	Class	Aug-55	Sep-55	Oct-55	Nov-55	Dec-55	Jan-56	Feb-56	Mar-56	Apr-56	May-56	Jun-56	Jul-56
4142	4MT : 51xx 2-6-2T (192	X	Ex P. Road										
4158	4MT : 51xx 2-6-2T (1928)												
4178	4MT : 51xx 2-6-2T (1928)												
5164	4MT : 51xx 2-6-2T (1928)												
5167	4MT : 51xx 2-6-2T (1928)												
5178	4MT : 51xx 2-6-2T (1928)												
3732	3F : 57xx 0-6-0T (1933)												
3744	3F : 57xx 0-6-0T (1933)												
3749	3F : 57xx 0-6-0T (1933)												
3760	3F : 57xx 0-6-0T (1933)												
4605	3F : 57xx 0-6-0T (1933)												
5712	3F : 57xx 0-6-0T (1933)												
5745	3F : 57xx 0-6-0T (1933)												
5758	3F : 57xx 0-6-0T (1933)												
7754	3F : 57xx 0-6-0T (1933)												
9624	3F : 57xx 0-6-0T (1933)				To Stour'bge	X	X	X	X	X	X	X	X
9630	3F : 57xx 0-6-0T (1933)												
9639	3F : 57xx 0-6-0T (1933)												
9741	3F : 57xx 0-6-0T (1933)												
9742	3F : 57xx 0-6-0T (1933)												
9774	3F : 57xx 0-6-0T (1933)	To Banbury	Ex Banbury										
1663	2F: 16xx 0-6-0PT (1949)												

ALLOCATION & MOVEMENTS : WELLINGTON (84H)

Engine	Class	Aug-56	Sep-56	Oct-56	Nov-56	Dec-56	Jan-57	Feb-57	Mar-57	Apr-57	May-57	Jun-57	Jul-57
4110	4MT : 51xx 2-6-2T (1928)	X	X	X	X	Ex Tyseley							
4120	4MT : 51xx 2-6-2T (1928)	X	X	X	X	X	X	X	Ex B'head				
4142	4MT : 51xx 2-6-2T (1928)												
4158	4MT : 51xx 2-6-2T (1928)												
4178	4MT : 51xx 2-6-2T (1928)	To N. Abbot	X	X	X	X	X	X	X	X	X	X	X
5164	4MT : 51xx 2-6-2T (1928)	To N. Abbot	X	X	X	X	X	X	X	X	X	X	X
5167	4MT : 51xx 2-6-2T (1928)												
5178	4MT : 51xx 2-6-2T (1928)	To N. Abbot	X	X	X	X	X	X	X	X	X	X	X
82004	3MT 2-6-2T (1952)	Ex N. Abbot											
82006	3MT 2-6-2T (1952)	Ex N. Abbot											
82009	3MT 2-6-2T (1952)	Ex N. Abbot											
82034	3MT 2-6-2T (1952)	Ex N. Abbot	To Treherbert	X	X	X	X	X	X	X	X	X	X
3732	3F : 57xx 0-6-0T (1933)												
3744	3F : 57xx 0-6-0T (1933)												
3749	3F : 57xx 0-6-0T (1933)												
3760	3F : 57xx 0-6-0T (1933)												
4605	3F : 57xx 0-6-0T (1933)												
5712	3F : 57xx 0-6-0T (1933)												
5745	3F : 57xx 0-6-0T (1933)				To Tyseley	X	X	X	X	X	X	X	X
5758	3F : 57xx 0-6-0T (1933)												
7754	3F : 57xx 0-6-0T (1933)												
9630	3F : 57xx 0-6-0T (1933)												
9639	3F : 57xx 0-6-0T (1933)												
9741	3F : 57xx 0-6-0T (1933)								To Worcs	X	X	Ex Worcs	
9742	3F : 57xx 0-6-0T (1933)								To Duffryn	X	X	X	X
9774	3F : 57xx 0-6-0T (1933)												
1663	2F : 16xx 0-6-0PT (1949)												

ALLOCATION & MOVEMENTS : WELLINGTON (84H)

Engine	Class	Aug-57	Sep-57	Oct-57	Nov-57	Dec-57	Jan-58	Feb-58	Mar-58	Apr-58	May-58	Jun-58	Jul-58
4110	4MT : 51xx 2-6-2T (1928)												
4120	4MT : 51xx 2-6-2T (1928)												
4142	4MT : 51xx 2-6-2T (1928)								To Worcs	X	X	X	X
4158	4MT : 51xx 2-6-2T (1928)												
5167	4MT : 51xx 2-6-2T (1928)												
82004	3MT 2-6-2T (1952)												
82006	3MT 2-6-2T (1952)												
82007	3MT 2-6-2T (1952)	X	X	X	X	X	X	X	X	X	X	X	Ex L. Spa
82009	3MT 2-6-2T (1952)												
3732	3F : 57xx 0-6-0T (1933)												
3744	3F : 57xx 0-6-0T (1933)												
3749	3F : 57xx 0-6-0T (1933)												
3760	3F : 57xx 0-6-0T (1933)												
4605	3F : 57xx 0-6-0T (1933)												
5712	3F : 57xx 0-6-0T (1933)			W/D	X	X	X	X	X	X	X	X	X
5758	3F : 57xx 0-6-0T (1933)												
7754	3F : 57xx 0-6-0T (1933)												
9630	3F : 57xx 0-6-0T (1933)												
9639	3F : 57xx 0-6-0T (1933)												
9741	3F : 57xx 0-6-0T (1933)												
9774	3F : 57xx 0-6-0T (1933)												
1663	2F : 16xx 0-6-0PT (1949)												

ALLOCATION & MOVEMENTS : WELLINGTON (84H)

Engine	Class	Aug-58	Sep-58	Oct-58	Nov-58	Dec-58	Jan-59	Feb-59	Mar-59	Apr-59	May-59	Jun-59	Jul-59
4110	4MT : 51xx 2-6-2T (1928)												
4120	4MT : 51xx 2-6-2T (1928)												
4158	4MT : 51xx 2-6-2T (1928)												
5167	4MT : 51xx 2-6-2T (1928)												
82004	3MT 2-6-2T (1952)											To Salop	X
82006	3MT 2-6-2T (1952)												
82007	3MT 2-6-2T (1952)	To Wrexham	X	X	X	X	X	X	X	X	X	X	X
82009	3MT 2-6-2T (1952)											To Salop	X
3626	3F : 57xx 0-6-0T (1933)	X	X	X	X	X	X	Ex Wrexham (GC)					
3732	3F : 57xx 0-6-0T (1933)												
3744	3F : 57xx 0-6-0T (1933)												
3749	3F : 57xx 0-6-0T (1933)			To Wrexham (GC)	X	X	X	X	X	X	X	X	X
3760	3F : 57xx 0-6-0T (1933)				To Wrexham (GC)	X	X	X	X	X	X	X	X
4605	3F : 57xx 0-6-0T (1933)												
5758	3F : 57xx 0-6-0T (1933)		To Pill	X	X	X	X	X	X	X	X	X	X
7754	3F : 57xx 0-6-0T (1933)						W/D	X	X	X	X	X	X
9630	3F : 57xx 0-6-0T (1933)												
9639	3F : 57xx 0-6-0T (1933)												
9741	3F : 57xx 0-6-0T (1933)												
9774	3F : 57xx 0-6-0T (1933)												
1663	2F : 16xx 0-6-0PT (1949)			To Wrexham (GC)	X	X	X	X	X	X	X	X	X

ALLOCATION & MOVEMENTS : WELLINGTON (84H)

Engine	Class	Aug-59	Sep-59	Oct-59	Nov-59	Dec-59	Jan-60	Feb-60	Mar-60	Apr-60	May-60	Jun-60	Jul-60
4110	4MT : 51xx 2-6-2T (1928)		To Stour'bge	X	X	X	X	X	X	X	X	X	X
4120	4MT : 51xx 2-6-2T (1928)												To Tyseley
4158	4MT : 51xx 2-6-2T (1928)												
5167	4MT : 51xx 2-6-2T (1928)		To Salop	X	X	X	X	X	X	X	X	X	X
82004	3MT 2-6-2T (1952)	Ex Salop		To Bath	X	X	X	X	X	X	X	X	X
82006	3MT 2-6-2T (1952)						To Bristol (BR)	X	X	X	X	X	X
82009	3MT 2-6-2T (1952)	Ex Salop					To Bristol (BR)	X	X	X	X	X	X
82030	3MT 2-6-2T (1952)	X	X	X	Ex Worcs		To Bristol (BR)	X	X	X	X	X	X
82038	3MT 2-6-2T (1952)	X	Ex Worcs				To Bristol (BR)	X	X	X	X	X	X
3626	3F : 57xx 0-6-0T (1933)												
3732	3F : 57xx 0-6-0T (1933)												
3744	3F : 57xx 0-6-0T (1933)												
4605	3F : 57xx 0-6-0T (1933)												
9621	3F : 57xx 0-6-0T (1933)	X	X	X	X	X	Ex Croes N						
9630	3F : 57xx 0-6-0T (1933)												
9639	3F : 57xx 0-6-0T (1933)												
9741	3F : 57xx 0-6-0T (1933)												
9774	3F : 57xx 0-6-0T (1933)												
41201	2MT 2-6-2T (1946)	X	X	X	Ex A'gavenny								
41204	2MT 2-6-2T (1946)	X	X	X	X	X	Ex Oswestry						
41231	2MT 2-6-2T (1946)	X	X	X	X	X	X	X	Ex Wrexham				
41232	2MT 2-6-2T (1946)	X	X	X	X	X	X	Ex Wrexham					
41241	2MT 2-6-2T (1946)	X	X	X	Ex Bath								

63

KIDDERMINSTER RAILWAY MUSEUM

A very large collection of railway memorabilia, from pen nibs, finials and signs of all sorts to signalling equipment, numberplates and nameplates.

****

A comprehensive collection of photographs, both black and white and colour, readily available for private research or for publication.

****

An extensive paper archive with timetables, plans, maps, correspondence and books some dating back to the mid-1800s.

****

Regular popular events, such as photograph fairs, postcard fairs, signalling courses, film shows and art exhibitions - and of course an excellent tea room!

****

Open daily from May to end of September, weekends and school holidays for the rest of the year.
Admission free.

Website: www.krm.org.uk
Email: krm@krm.org.uk
Telephone: 01562 825316

Registered Charity: 518479

Station Approach, Comberton Hill, Kidderminster, Worcestershire DY10 1QX

The Severn Valley ended at Sutton Bridge Junction, three quarters of a mile South West of Shrewsbury, where it merged with the LNW/GWR Shrewsbury & Hereford Joint. Sutton Bridge was a busy location for in addition to the Severn Valley and the very heavy volume of traffic over the Joint line, the signalbox also dealt with services to and from the Cambrian via Welshpool. The Severn Valley line can be seen disappearing behind the signalbox.

SUTTON BRIDGE JUNCTION (SEVERN VALLEY SERVICES) : 1955			
Train	Pass	Engine	Destination
08.15 Shrewsbury	08/18	51xx 2-6-2T: Salop 100	Stourbridge Junction
06.55 Worcester	09/18	51xx 2-6-2T: Worcs 451	Shrewsbury (09.21)
10.15 Coton Hill	10/18	43xx 2-6-0: Salop 150	*Hartlebury Goods (19.15)*
Light ex Buildwas	10/41	57xx 0-6-0PT: Well 463	*Coton Hill (10.58)*
11.25 Shrewsbury	11/28	51xx 2-6-2T: Worcs 451	Hartlebury (13.12)
10.35 Kidderminster	12/29	Railcar: Worcs 1	Shrewsbury (12.32)
13.45 Shrewsbury	13/48	Railcar: Worcs 1	Kidderminster (15.45)
14.00 Hartlebury	15/53	51xx 2-6-2T: Worcs 451	Shrewsbury (15.58)
15.50 Shrewsbury	15/53	51xx 2-6-2T: Salop 101	Kidderminster (17.34)
17.33 Shrewsbury	17/38	51xx 2-6-2T: Worcs 451	Kidderminster (19.18)
16.23 Kidderminster	18/12	51xx 2-6-2T: Salop 100	Shrewsbury (18.15)
18.25 Hartlebury	20/12	51xx 2-6-2T: Salop 101	Shrewsbury (20.17)
20.45 Shrewsbury	20/48	51xx 2-6-2T: Salop 101	Ironbridge (21.19)
14.15 Hartlebury (Goods)	21/11	43xx 2-6-0: Salop 150A	*Coton Hill (21.14)*
Light ex Much Wenlock	21/35	57xx 0-6-0PT: Well 464	*Wellington loco*
21.35 Ironbridge	22/07	51xx 2-6-2T: Salop 101	Shrewsbury (22.17)

A visit to Kidderminster can kill two very interesting birds with one stone. In addition to the many attractions provided by the Severn Valley Railway (and an hour on Kidderminster SVR station can make the last fifty years seem like a bad dream), Kidderminster is also the home of the Kidderminster Railway Museum which lays before the visitor a feast of exhibits that defy description.